Bridging Worlds Through

General Semantics

Also edited by Mary Morain
Teaching General Semantics
Classroom Exercises in General Semantics

Bridging Worlds Through General Semantics
is the first of a two-volume collection of articles
from the first 40 years of *Et cetera*.

Bridging Worlds Through General Semantics

Selections from the first 40 years
of *Et cetera*
1943 - 1983

Edited by
Mary Morain

University of Charleston Library
Charleston, WV 25304

INTERNATIONAL SOCIETY FOR GENERAL SEMANTICS
San Francisco

BRIDGING WORLDS THROUGH GENERAL SEMANTICS
Copyright © 1984 by
The International Society for General Semantics

LCCCN: 84-082325
ISBN: 0-918970-34-2

Contents

Foreword	ix
For the Newcomer to General Semantics	xi

I. BACKGROUND

Seventeenth-Century Semanticists Ralph Renwick, Jr.	3
Science and Common Sense P.W. Bridgman	12
An American Indian Model of the Universe Benjamin Lee Whorf	30
The Symbol: The Origin and Basis of Human Behavior Leslie A. White	39
The Threat of Clarity Garrett Hardin	52

II. THE CONTRIBUTION OF GENERAL SEMANTICS

General Semantics *(abridged)* Charlotte S. Read	63
General Semantics$_{1952}$ *(abridged)* Irving J. Lee	73
Evaluation: With and Without Words *(abridged)* Irving J. Lee	78
Semantic Aspects of Language and Mathematics *(abridged)* Anatol Rapoport	82

Mathematical Biophysics, Cybernetics
and General Semantics *(abridged)*   98
    Anatol Rapoport and Alfonso Shimbel

Towards a Unification of Physics and Psychology   118
    Michael E. Gorman

III. APPLICATIONS IN DAILY LIVING

Sensory Awareness   131
    Charlotte Read

Music, the Discipline of Silence   133
    Stewart W. Holmes

Body Language: Nonverbal Behavior
as a Communicative Stimulus   140
    Phillip V. Lewis

Fashion: The Sartorial Communication Revolution   144
    Paul Lippert

Do You Know How to Listen? *(abridged)*   152
    Wendell Johnson

The Power of Words   158
    J. Samuel Bois

Searching for the Right Word: The Semantics
of Heterosexual Relationships   166
    Nicholas Johnson

The Making of a Nonsexist Dictionary   178
    Alma Graham

The Belief in Magic   187
    Wendell Johnson

IV. COMMUNICATION IN THE LARGER SOCIETY

The Task of the Listener   197
    S.I. Hayakawa

Propaganda Neil Postman	208
Language Clues for the Rhetorical Critic Dan F. Hahn	216
Why Politics Bore Us Dan F. Hahn	224
Metaphor and Social Belief Weller Embler	234
Whorf's Hypothesis: The Case of Dutch and English C. Weggelaar	249
Semantic Difficulties in International Communication *(abridged)* Edmund S. Glenn	264
Nemawashi: A Japanese Form of Interpersonal Communication Mitsuko Saito	278
Mexican Assumptions About Interpersonal Relations Rogelio Diaz-Guerrero, M.D.	289
On Communication Across Cultural Lines Edmund S. Glenn	293
Public and Instant Diplomacy Moshe Ben-Eliezer	299
Self-Interest and International Communication Robert E. Kingsley	309

V. RELIABLE RESEARCH

Popper's Fallibilism Henry Perkinson	315
Biasing Effects of Experimenters Robert Rosenthal	333

FOREWORD

FORTY-ONE YEARS HAVE passed since the International Society for General Semantics published the first issue of *Et cetera* (ETC.). To select from the richness provided by 160 issues—reaching from the fall of 1943 through the summer of 1983—has been an exhilarating but demanding task. Paradoxically perhaps, this has been made somewhat easier because Russell Joyner, the Society's Executive Director, and I early made a decision that our collection of articles could not only be a resource and a treasury but also an introduction to general semantics for serious new inquirers. Selections could be chosen and arranged to serve this dual purpose.

The collection fills two volumes. This first book begins with articles from early issues which give a background against which to see Korzybski's work. Charlotte Read's fine introductory summary to general semantics follows, together with passages from characteristically practical introductions to the field by the master teacher, Irving Lee, and papers which give views on its relationship to various fields of science. Applications and implications in aspects of modern living covering a wide range of experience follow. The book ends with two recent papers addressing a question central to general semantics: What is reliable research?

Most of these articles appear as originally published. A few have been shortened but left otherwise intact. Abridgements have been noted in the Table of Contents.

The articles to appear in a second book demonstrate how a general semantics orientation can be useful and illuminating in specific fields, including education, counselling, medicine and business.

I hope that many of the outstanding contributions to recent issues of *Et cetera* will soon be incorporated in a book devoted to Media Ecology. This new field, involving the study of communication and its effect on social processes, investigates the structure and effects of communication media. Reading through past issues of *Et cetera* has been a rewarding experience. I warmly recommend it. Hopefully, others will continue to make additional collections of articles from these rich sources. Such is the value of their extensional, open-ended approach that we can expect articles, even from the earliest years, to have relevance forty years from now and beyond. We owe a debt to those who have written for the magazine, and the three distinguished editors: S.I. Hayakawa 1943-1970, Thomas W. Weiss 1970-1976, and Neil Postman, our editor since 1977.

MARY MORAIN 1984

For the Newcomer to General Semantics

INFORMATION REVOLUTIONS ARE giving us new understanding of time and space, of the very small and the seemingly boundless. Even the substances and the capabilities of our bodies are being seen in new light. Personal and social interactions are being changed by radio, television and computers. Yet few people adequately grasp the inter-related and process character of our world. Most remain slaves of language, addicted to thinking in terms of ironclad categories, of good or bad, black and white, mind or body. Psychologically, we are short-circuited by our automatic associational responses.

The ongoing revolutions in biotechnology, in the physical and life sciences, need to be matched by a revolution in our general approach and understanding, in our basic thinking and perceiving.

There have been many definitions, many descriptions, of general semantics, but to me a particularly succinct and valid one is that with which Charlotte Read opens her paper, in Section II of this book. She refers to it as a "theory of evaluation based on modern scientific knowledge." Here the word "evaluation" carries the meaning of a wide range of human reactions — "thinking," "feeling" and "perceiving," including those reactions which appear to be chiefly physiological or "subconscious" such as blushing and dreaming. General semantics is concerned with the full range. "Evaluation" also centers attention on the human being as perceiver and reactor. Central to the system is recognition that whatever we discover and react to is conditioned by our individual human makeup, the result of transactions between our environment and ourselves.

Alfred Korzybski, formulator of the system, chose the term "general semantics" for it when he had almost completed work building his "science of man." Important in the system is the concept that a key to what is human is our ability to create and to react to symbols, our ability to symbolize and, particularly, to make use of language. This makes possible our cultures, our civilizations, and both the social adaptations and maladaptations of individuals.

Other scholars had studied humans as symbol and language users and the process behind the development of language. Linguists and logicians had specialized uses for the term "semantics." But until the publishing of Korzybski's *Science and Sanity* — 33 years into this century — few beside the learned thought systematically about the role of language or used the word "semantics."

The *general* in general semantics is crucial. What is new in *Science and Sanity: An Introduction to Non-Aristotelian Systems and General Semantics*, is its sweeping synthesis and its humane and practical purposefulness. The book recognizes and makes real those aspects of twentieth century science of great practical use to the nonscientist — those which lead to the realization that the human use of convenient symbols takes place in a dynamic, interconnected, nonverbal world. *Science and Sanity* demonstrates that we can change our perceptions and our uses of language so that they become more adequate tools for group survival and personal happiness and adjustment.

Korzybski was motivated by far more than intellectual creativity. He wanted to make a difference not only in academic and scientific communities but in the lives of *all* men, women and children. His work was meant to be *at one and the same time* an intellectual system and a teaching tool.

In 1938 the Institute of General Semantics was organized, and it was directed by Korzybski until his death in 1950. The Institute's program for linguistic, epistemologic, scientific research and education is now carried on at 3029 Eastern Ave., Baltimore, Md. 21224. The "General Semantics Bulletin," founded in 1950, is the Institute's annual publication for members and libraries.

Although there was appreciation of *Science and Sanity* by thoughtful individuals and scholars of many disciplines, the dramatic influence of the book was particularly strong among some English and language arts teachers, psychological counselors, management engineers, and writers. Eager to spread these fresh insights and this novel training, gifted communicators undertook popularizations of the basic principles. They simplified Korzybski's vocabulary while keeping words and phrases such as *evaluation, orientation,* and *levels of abstraction,* key terms for which it is difficult to find synonyms in the English language.

Two books in particular had wide impact: *The Tyranny of Words* by Stuart Chase and *Language in Action* by S.I. Hayakawa. In the world at large "general semantics" for many people became "semantics," a new realization of the influence of language in human affairs, a healthy knowledge that the same word or phrase can signify different things to different people and that one should be wary of disputes over the meanings of words. "Semantics" became a household word.

Enthusiastic interpreters came (and still come) to the task with their own field of interest in mind and with their own individual approach. As Irving Lee writes in Section III of this book, these interpretations have been provided with "a perspective, a means whereby some disconnected areas become related." Korzybski had "systematized what everyone knew piecemeal."

Et cetera, (ETC.), the chief publication of the International Society for General Semantics, appeared in August, 1943, under the editorship of S.I. Hayakawa. He was at its helm for 27 years. On its twentieth anniversary in 1963, Lloyd Morain expressed a common feeling when he wrote that Hayakawa, in disseminating general semantics, "had maintained the enthusiasm for new interpretations and empathy with wide areas of society." Succeeding editors have pursued this goal through the forty years which are represented here.

Contributors to the magazine have come chiefly from those in language arts, the social sciences, education, counselling, from management and, increasingly, from students of Media Ecology. Many write on communication as an interrelated process without particularly separating verbal and nonverbal elements. In some *Et cetera* articles, there are references to Korzybski's concepts and terminology, but even where they are not referred to, his work has been a unifying influence. He brought the sciences into a helpful and comfortable relationship with the language-centered fields. As Irving Lee noted, he made it all come together. He did it by creating a new field of general semantics. Many writers in *Et cetera* have had, before meeting up with general semantics, some notion of the complexity of language and a realization that one must think of the individual as a whole in an environment as a whole; but the new integration has been useful, even inspiring, and in the magazine they have been given a vehicle in which to make use of their new evaluations. General semantics encourages the study of processes behind the curtain of language. It investigates the relations between words, what words refer to and the human beings involved, the effects of language on evaluation and evaluation on language. It is this approach that helps tie together the varied *Et cetera* articles.

The newcomer is advised to read Section I first. These earlier papers set the stage. Charlotte Read's lead article for Section II gives essential aspects of Korzybski's system, how he draws from twentieth century knowledge of our dynamic, interconnected, complex world to produce tools for coping with life. Her article stresses that we adjust to life by abstracting from experience on different levels, and shows the need to make the structure of our language follow the structure of the nonverbal process-world. Selections from talks by Irving Lee list ways to use these general semantics insights.

The other articles of Section II will appeal especially to readers interested in the relationships of general semantics with mathematics, physics, psychiatry.

The first four papers of Section III emphasize the nonverbal, silent level of that continuous abstracting process which makes up life experience. Charlotte Read's note on "Sensory Awareness" describes one method of discovering "what it feels like" to concentrate on that level, and how this can be part of "consciousness of abstracting." Stewart Holmes describes a method involving music which he finds useful. A paper on "Body Language" points to the critical part the nonverbal plays in communication. A delightful discussion of fashion reveals another example.

For one who realizes that the meaning of words does not lie in words but in the person using them, listening can be really challenging, as Wendell Johnson points out. Because no words can completely represent the rich, nonverbal emotional world, old feelings can sometimes be transformed if new terms are used. A paper by J. Samuel Bois provides a moving example of this. Nicholas Johnson examines how, when we are caught up in a broad social change, it is hard to find appropriate levels from among those available. "The Making of a Nonsexist Dictionary," on the other hand, dramatically chronicles the power of dictionary editors to encourage new viewpoints. Section III ends with a classic lecture from Wendell Johnson's introductory course in general semantics. In Johnson's words, "As expectations become more realistic, the individual encounters less disappointment and discouragement and confusion." In this, Johnson shows how important it is that one tries to make the structure of one's "verbal maps" fit the structure of the nonverbal "territory."

Section IV holds articles more specifically dealing with life in the larger community. S.I. Hayakawa addresses the heavy problems presented to voters and customers—all who are at the receiving end of one-way communication. In dealing with the question, "How does one find the needle of legitimate meaning in the haystack of nonsense?" he presents distinctions in kinds of language. Neil Postman makes clear that classifying language in the field of public affairs is not easy, and Dan Hahn gives some practical tips.

Weller Embler's paper is a bridge to the role of language in intercultural differences. He demonstrates the enormous effect of popular metaphors in giving solidity to a people's current social beliefs. Over and above the powerful connotations which words carry for us, C. Weggelaar feels that, in its very structure, every language contains a number of assumptions about the nature of reality. Earlier, Edmund Glenn wrote of how different national philosophies are visible even in the configuration of subway systems. When different philosophies are embodied in similar words and phrases, mischief in international conferences often results. Final articles discuss aspects of communication within cultures, between cultures, and between governments.

In Section V are two important, recent papers, reminders that scientists are investigators, scouts, if you will, of nonverbal territory, much of which may be hidden from most of us. Insistence that the investigative attitudes of the scientist have relevance for the whole range of human affairs is a central tenet of general semantics.

Korzybski's general semantics and the various simplifications and developments have a wide variety of significance to different people. Some see it as primarily an intellectual system to be discussed and evaluated along with other systems in the academic universe of discourse. For many people it is first and last a set of practical tools of help in communication and adjustment. For others it is an orientation, giving added meaning to experience and establishing standards of behavior. For still others, of course, it clearly carries all three meanings.

Some of these varied interpretations can be found in the articles which make up this book.

It is also true that there now seem to have developed two primary differences of another kind in the use of the term general semantics. One limits the use to Korzybski's rich and comprehensive system together with what has clearly developed from it. The other extends the term to cover the long history of interest in language or to any study or comment on the dynamic role of symbols and methods of communication in human life.

Making for further confusions in discussion about the field is the fact that there are enormous differences among those who talk of it, in the amount of study they have given to it, and the extent to which this study has had a practical effect on their habits of thought and action.

Differences in interpretation may at first seen confusing, but one can apply a basic general semantic principle and remember that the meanings of words are those which individual human beings give to them. Before arid arguments over what general semantics *is* get under way, one might ask each individual with whom one is talking to spell out its particular significance to *him* or *her*; and then start from there. Probably a really interesting and productive exchange can then take place.

It is reassuring to realize that to whatever use and to whatever degree a general semantics approach is put, it can well lead to more careful observation, greater sensitivity in relation to others, and generally a more open and relaxed attitude toward life experience.

M.M.

I.
BACKGROUND

SEVENTEENTH-CENTURY SEMANTICISTS

Ralph Renwick, Jr.

IN 1663 A FRENCH SCHOLAR traveling in England attended a meeting of the newly established Royal Society and was impressed by its calm, concise deliberations. The tone of discussion was objective; disagreements did not lead to quarrels. The scientists whom Samuel Sorbière thus praised were not merely being polite. They were determined to communicate with maximum clarity; in fact, the following year they set up a committee for language reform. The group included John Dryden, John Evelyn, and Bishop Sprat, later the Society's official historian. They were to meet once or twice a month and occasionally report to the Society. Although the committee was permanently suspended because of fire and plague in 1666, its work reflected the feeling of many philosophers that efficient scientific communication demanded closer correspondence between symbol and thing symbolized.[1]

These men were following the promptings of Francis Bacon, who had spotted the roadblocks language placed before the scientist. In the *Advancement of Learning* (1605), he attacks the Ciceronians because, diverted from classical scholarship by philology, they had become persuaders, writing for ornateness, polish, balance, rather than for "weight of matter." Bacon also ridicules the disputations of the schoolmen, who study only a few classical writers, such as their "dictator," Aristotle, and "spin

---

Dr. Ralph Renwick, Jr. was a professor in the Department of Communication Skills at Michigan State University.

out unto us laborious webs of learning." He insists that knowledge is to be sought not for delight or reputation but "for the benefit and use of men"—man's physical comfort.[2]

In the first part of the *Novum Organum* (1620) Bacon discusses the relationship between language and scientific progress. He first notes the complexity of the physical entities which the scientists' words will symbolize: "the subtlety of nature is greater many times than the subtlety of the senses and understanding." He discards the syllogism, because of its frequent failure to correspond to material reality. The words in a syllogism symbolize "notions"; "if the notions themselves are confused and over-hastily abstracted from the facts," logic is worthless. The only valid method of investigation is therefore "a true induction."

Bacon analyzes language more closely in his famous discussion of the four idols. The most troublesome of all is that of the marketplace:

> Now words, being commonly framed and applied according to the capacity of the vulgar, follow those lines of division which are most obvious to vulgar understanding. And whenever an understanding of greater acuteness or a more diligent observation would alter those lines to suit the true divisions of nature, words stand in the way and resist the change. Whence it comes to pass that the high and formal discussions of learned men end oftentimes in disputes about words and names; with which . . . it would be more prudent to begin, and so by means of definitions reduce them to order. Yet even definitions cannot cure this evil in dealing with natural and material things; since the definitions themselves consist of words, and those words beget others: so that it is necessary to recur to individual instances, and those in due series and order . . . (p. 269)[3]

Essentially, the difficulty is mass communication, or rather participation by the masses in the communication process. Bacon's viewpoint was antique; he was not concerned with the survival of democracy in an age of electronic transmission; he had no inkling of the latter, and probably no interest in the former. "Vulgar" referred to the mob, who were not then any political problem—this was long before the Jacquerie. It was merely a matter of popular usage impeding the inquiries of a few scholars.

Bacon's criticisms of the language of controversy rang especially true for those of his followers who witnessed the civil war; it was in part due to their weariness of political and theological quarrels that they devoted themselves to science. The men who during the Commonwealth met to share scientific knowledge realized that language is behavior. In his *History of the Royal Society*, Thomas Sprat tells of their gatherings before 1660. They met to breathe "a freer air," and to converse without involvement in "the passions and madness of that dismal age." Sprat argues that men interested in science will not enter religious strife. "Spiritual frenzies" such as those of the last twenty years "can never stand long before a clear and deep skill in Nature." Science was one field in which clear communication would be possible.

> For such a candid and unpassionate company as that was, and for such a gloomy season, what could have been a fitter subject to pitch upon than natural philosophy? . . . It was Nature alone which could pleasantly entertain them, in that estate . . . while the consideration of men and human affairs may affect us with a thousand various disquiets, *that* never separates us into mortal factions; *that* gives us room to differ without animosity and permits us to raise contrary imaginations upon it without any danger of a civil war.[4]

When the Society was finally organized with royal approval, Sprat says, these men intended to avoid the tortuous style of theological and political pamphleteering.

> . . . they have endeavored to separate the knowledge of Nature from the colors of rhetoric, the devices of fancy, or the delightful deceit of fables . . . they have attempted to free it from the artifice, the humors, and passions of sects; to render it an instrument whereby mankind may obtain a dominion over things, and not only over one another's judgments. (pp. 61-62)

Sprat devotes a separate section to the need for accurate, unemotional language. Society members realized that abuse of language could ruin their program for scientific advancement. He notes how other professions, presumably public office and the ministry, have been "overwhelmed" by "superfluity of talking," and says he could almost claim that "eloquence ought to be banished out of civil societies, as a thing fatal to peace and good manners." The members of the Society therefore avoided "amplifications, digressions and swellings of style," and tried to revive a "primitive purity" of language in which men represented "so many *things* in almost an equal number of *words*." They were required to speak in a "natural, naked" manner, approaching as nearly as possible "mathematical plainness" (pp. 112-113).[5]

Expressions such as "things, not words," are typical of Baconians of this time. Some of them proposed not only stylistic simplification, but changes in the actual materials of language. In 1654, Seth Ward, professor of astronomy at Oxford, advocated a new language with a symbol for each thing and each idea. William Petty, one of the Society's founders, attempted to exclude abstractions; words should describe objects rather than theories. He proposed a "Dictionary of Sensible Words" to show what perceptible referent belonged to each word.[6]

Perhaps the outstanding linguistic innovator was John Wilkins, also a Society founder and mentor of Sprat's history. His *Essay Toward a Real Character* (1668) classifies objects by a combination of lines, curves, hooks, loops and dots; symbolization includes genus and species. There are no symbols for anything not proven to exist, such as fairies or ghosts; supposedly symbol fits referent exactly. Wilkins' assumption that a universal language will be practicable is based on optimistic rationalism. Since men agree "in the same principle of Reason,"[7] they will perceive objects similarly; if every object or idea had its own sign, a communication would greatly improve.

The scope of Wilkins' book is vast. It summarizes the origins and defects of language, and outlines all classifications which the new symbols must represent. Since syntax must also be shown, the book presents a complete grammar. It develops a new phonetic alphabet entirely separate from the line-hook-dot system, based on an analysis of the physiology of verbal sounds. After demonstrating the new system it ends with a glossary of line-and-curve symbols for many English words.

Of course, Wilkins' scheme is quixotic. These attempts to remove at once all defects in linguistic communication are mere curiosities and actually compare rather poorly with what is probably the greatest seventeenth-century treatise on language, the third book of Locke's *Essay Concerning Human Understanding*. Written because Locke's philosophical inquiries revealed the importance of communication, this discussion aims to minimize linguistic causes of disagreement. If the defects of language were taken into consideration, he says, "a great many of the controversies that make such a noise in the world would of themselves cease."

For Locke, of course, language originates in sense perception: if we could trace abstract terms to their sources, we would find "the names which stand for things that fall not under our sense to have had their first rise from sensible ideas." But Locke does not feel that word represents physical object. Words represent ideas, not by any connection between sound and idea, but by "a voluntary imposition, whereby such a word is made arbitrarily the mark of such an idea." Locke has no illusions about the accuracy of verbal communication. Frequently words are "secretly referred"; the speaker too quickly assumes that meaning is perfectly conveyed.[8]

Locke's chapter on "General Terms" shows how impossible and useless it would be for every particular thing to have a separate name. Abstraction is therefore necessary. Before showing its dangers, Locke analyzes the process.

> For, let any one reflect, and tell me wherein does his idea of "man" differ from that of "Peter" and "Paul," or his idea of "horse" from that of "Bucephalus," but in the leaving out something that is peculiar to each individual, and retaining so much of those particular complex ideas of several particular existences as they are found to agree in? (p. 329)

Complex abstractions differ according to the individual: "that is covetousness to one man, which is not so to another." Adding the time dimension, Locke warns of physical mutability:

> All things that exist, besides their Author, are all liable to change . . . Thus that which was grass today is tomorrow the flesh

of a sheep, and, within a few days after becomes part of a man . . . (p. 335)

Thus the idea of a horse or man is immutable only when it is a pure abstraction. Turning to the imperfections of language, Locke says that communication fails because it is difficult to know the sensory background of complex ideas or, as he puts it, to know the "standards" by which meaning is to be determined. There are various causes of confusion: the perceptible origins of the ideas are remote or forgotten; the learning process breeds different interpretations; there is even disagreement over the nature of physical entities because individuals draw on different sensory memories for concepts of the same substance. Later Locke isolates two language problems which are given much attention today. First, men often use words to signify the "real essence" of substances, which makes words troublesome because they now refer to something for which no name can stand. Men do this, Locke continues, because they assume that nature works "regularly." They believe that examples of a species can be similar.

> This supposition, however, that the same precise internal constitution goes always with the same specific name, makes men forward to take those names for the representatives of those real essences, though indeed they signify nothing but the complex ideas they have in their minds when they use them. (p. 406)

Locke also recognizes the dependence of meaning on context. Having habitually associated a meaning with a word, the speaker assumes that his use of the word will be understood. He feels that he has virtually produced the thing he is talking of, and takes others' words for what he has considered them to mean in the past, neither trying to explain his meaning or to understand theirs. The result is "noise and wrangling" without "improvement or information."

To remedy these abuses, Locke urges that abstractions be clearly defined, and that names of substances be "conformable to things as they exist." Where common usage lacks an adequate name, a new term, or old word with a new meaning can be used, if immediately clarified by synonyms or by "showing" — producing the referent (p. 417).[9]

The seventeenth-century attack on semantic confusion shows much insight into linguistic pitfalls which the persuasive capabilities of our age have forced us to analyze. As we look back on Bacon, Sprat, and Wilkins, we can perhaps say that we know the magnitude of the problem better than they did. They were sure that the senses were the road to truth, and we are not. Even though we admire the language of science for minimizing ambiguity and for enabling at least some minds to meet in a world of ideological combat, our anxiety about final goals is not removed by the assertion that the "relief of man's estate" is our chief task.

Again, we have long since abandoned the simple, hopeful psychology of the Age of Reason. We know that we cannot even trust our perceptions, to say nothing of relying on human rationality. Even if we accepted the determinism of Locke's associationist disciples, we know better than they did how difficult it is to change Man by changing his environment.

Furthermore, living in a time of mature scientific advance, we know that to say that a word should stand for a thing is asking far more than was dreamed of by a scientifically inclined gentleman-of-leisure in the 1660s. Finally, the problem is greatly magnified by what science has done for mass communication and for the art of war. We analyze the impact of the media because they touch the hearts of millions whose allegiance can be used for our destruction. We also know that communication can undermine civil liberty. If we lived in an era of flintlock guns and live audiences, what Khrushchev says to the Central Committee might make us tolerate larger military appropriations, and, spending a leisurely afternoon at the coffee house, we might get into arguments about whether or not he would bury us (would he say it?), but our composure would not really be disturbed.

Bacon, Sprat, and Locke spoke to a handful of intellectuals; they did not fear that the defects of communication might threaten the nation. They were interested merely in avoiding distracting quarrels, and in getting on with the main business of scientific investigation. Certainly, the seventeenth-century critics of language, confident that monarchy would keep order, would agree with Locke that popular usage was good enough for the mob:

> This exactness [of language] is absolutely necessary in inquiries after philosophical knowledge, and in controversies about truth. And though it would be well, too, if it extended itself to common conversation and the ordinary affairs of life; yet, I think, that is scarce to be expected. Vulgar notions suit vulgar discourse: and both, though confused enough, yet serve pretty well the market and the wake. Merchants and lovers, cooks and tailors, have words wherewithal to despatch their ordinary affairs; and so, I think, might philosophers and disputants too, if they had a mind to understand, and to be clearly understood. (pp. 415-416)

If they contract with the modern semanticist in failing to see language as powerful social control, Sprat and his contemporaries had some inkling of communication as behavior in that they realized that disagreement was often aggravated by faulty language. Intellectual historians have pointed out similarities between the seventeenth century and our times: the profound doubts occasioned by advancing knowledge, the ideological conflicts, the revolutions and wars. It is no accident that men of both periods traced social turmoil to language. Perhaps the basic difference between the semantic investigations of the two ages lies in their divergent social climates, the seventeenth century being dominated by the few, and our times by the many.

NOTES AND REFERENCES

1. Henry Lyons, *The Royal Society* (Cambridge, 1944), pp. 25, 55.
2. J.M. Robertson, ed., *The Philosophical Works of Francis Bacon* (London, 1905), pp. 53-55.
3. Thomas Hobbes' *Leviathan* (Ch. V) echoes Bacon's analysis.
4. Thomas Sprat, *The History of the Royal Society of London for the Improving of Natural Knowledge* (London, 1667), pp. 55-56.
5. The Royal Society's efforts in language reform were reflected in the increased clarity of Restoration prose.
6. Richard F. Jones, "Science and Language in England of the Mid-Seventeenth Century," *Journal of English and Germanic Philology*, XXXI (1932), 316-320. See also Otto Funke, *Zum Weltsprachen-problem in England im 17 Jahrhundert* (Heidelberg, 1929; *Anglis-tische Forschungen*, Heft 69). pp. 1-5.

7. John Wilkins, *An Essay Towards a Real Character and a Philosophical Language* (London, 1668), pp. 20-21.
8. John Locke, *An Essay Concerning Human Understanding* (London, n.d.), pp. 324-325.
9. Swift parodied various Royal Society projects in Gulliver's third voyage. In the Academy at Lagado (Ch.V) there is a language reformer who would abolish words entirely: "since words are only names for *things*, it would be more convenient for all men to carry about them such things as are necessary to express the particular business they are to discourse on." Advocates of this scheme travel about with a load of objects on their backs, for direct sensory communication.

From the Spring 1962 Et cetera.

SCIENCE AND COMMON SENSE

P.W. Bridgman

I SHALL HAVE TO BEGIN by recalling some matters that have been said so many times that I can expect only to bore you, but this is a risk that I can see no way to avoid if I am to make my main point. You all know that, since the turn of the century, discoveries have been made in physics, culminating in the unlocking of nuclear energy in the atomic bomb, which have entirely revolutionized our outlook, not only our outlook with regard to the construction of the world around us, but our philosophical ideas as well with regard to our relationship to the world. It is the latter to which I would like to direct your attention.

The new discoveries that have forced the revolution were in the realms of relativity and quantum phenomena. We shall see later that the quantum phenomena were more revolutionary in their implications than the relativity phenomena, but historically it is probable that the relativity phenomena played the more important role at first. The new relativity phenomena were highly paradoxical and included such effects as meter sticks whose length changed when they were set in motion, clocks that ran slow when moving, and weights that became heavier when moving. In fact, these effects were so paradoxical and contrary to common sense that some physicists and most men in the street refused to accept them and even sought to throw them out of court by ridicule.

Author of *The Logic of Modern Physics*, **Dr. P.W. Bridgman** was a professor of Physics at Harvard University. He was awarded the Nobel Prize in Physics in 1946.

But the facts refused to be thrown out of court, and the paradoxes were resolved by Einstein's theory of restricted relativity. This theory embraced, in the first place, the mathematical machinery by which all the experimental facts were correlated into a single mathematical structure. But no less notable as an intellectual achievement and equally essential to the removal of paradox was Einstein's handling of the physical concepts that entered the mathematical edifice. It is this latter that is our concern.

There are two aspects of Einstein's handling of the physical concepts. There is, in the first place, a realization that the paradoxes involved primarily questions of meaning and that the common-sense meanings of such terms as *length* and *time* were not sharp enough to serve in the situations presented by the new facts. In the second place, there was the method by which the necessary increased sharpness was imparted to the meanings. This method was to specify the operations that were involved in concrete instances in applying the term whose meaning was in question. For example, what do we mean when we say that two events are simultaneous? Einstein insisted that we do not know what we mean unless we can give some concrete procedure by which we may determine whether or not any two specific events are simultaneous. Analysis of the concrete procedures that we might use brings out the fact, not noticed before, that what we do to determine whether or not two events are simultaneous depends to a certain extent on the events themselves and is different and more complicated if the two events take place at different places than if they take place here. Furthermore, this analysis disclosed that what an observer does to determine whether two distant events are simultaneous is different from what another observer does who is in motion with respect to him. Simultaneity of two distant events is, therefore, not an absolute property of the events, the same for all observers, but is relative to the observers.

It is the same with length. What do we mean when we ask what the length of a moving object is? Applying the operational criterion of meaning, the meaning is to be sought in what we do when we measure the length of the moving object. When we analyze what we might do, we discover that there are several different possible procedures, equally acceptable to common sense. Thus, if we are asked to measure the length of a moving street-car, we might take an instantaneous photograph of it and measure the length of the photograph, or we might board the car, meter stick in hand, and proceed to measure it as we would any ordinary stationary object. If we get the same answer by the two procedures, we shall doubtless be satisfied and think that our catechizer was unnecessarily fussy in insisting that we tell exactly what we do to measure the length.

But here is where the new experimental facts come in that were not suspected before relativity theory. For it turns out that when we make our measurements with extreme precision, or when the streetcar is moving with very great velocity, the results of the two methods are not the same, so that the precise method must be specified if we want to talk exactly about the length of the moving car. In other words, it is ambiguous to talk about the "length" of a moving object until we have specified exactly how the length is to be measured; and when we have specified the exact procedure, the results we get are generally different, depending on what the exact procedure is. In particular, by one of the two procedures just indicated, the length of the moving car would be the same as when it is stationary; and, by the other, it would be less. We see at once that we cannot treat this situation by the methods of common sense and say that it is absurd that the length should change when the car moves, because it *must* change according to at least one of our possible definitions. Realization of this at once removes the atmosphere of paradox from the statement that the length changes when the object is set in motion.

The precise way that we define length when the body moves is a matter of choice, and we will make our choice in the way most convenient for us in the light of all the experimental facts. It would take us much too deeply into relativity theory to attempt to see why the method that Einstein chose for defining the length of a moving object is, all things considered, the most convenient for the physicist. Suffice it to say that the method chosen was not the method that leaves the length unchallenged by the motion, although such a method is possible and, for certain restricted purposes, might be considered more convenient.

Relativity theory has thus shown the importance of precision of meanings. It has disclosed that some of the apparently simple terms of common sense are actually complex when we attempt to apply them in situations beyond the bounds of ordinary experience. In these new situations, we are forced to make a choice between procedures that are equivalent in the ordinary range. The account we give of the new situation depends on the procedure that we choose — that is, on the meaning we give our terms. In discovering that in fact we do need to make distinctions of which we have never thought and which to a naive first impression appear a matter of indifference, we are discovering that in fact the world is not constructed according to the preconceptions of common sense.

The sort of phenomena with which quantum theory is concerned teach the same lesson as relativity theory, namely, that the world is not constructed according to the principles of common sense. However, the way in which common sense fails is somewhat different in the case of quantum phenomena. The unfamiliar world of relativity theory was the world of high velocities; the new world of quantum theory is the world of the very small.

Quantum theory began modestly enough with the discovery that some of the most familiar facts of daily life cannot be understood on the basis of the common-sense views of matter prevalent at the end of the last century. For example it was impossible to understand why we cannot see a kettle full of boiling water in the dark. Common sense, when translated into mathematics, said that we should see it, but every burned child knows that we cannot. The paradox has now been removed from this and other related effects, so that we now understand, in a way that would have been incredible 25 years ago, most of the phenomena displayed by ordinary matter. This understanding has been provided by quantum theory. The theory is highly mathematical and it is well-nigh impossible to give an adequate outline of it in nontechnical language, but the one simple crude idea back of it all is that when we deal with very small things, such as atoms or electrons, the ordinary common-sense conception of *things* is no longer valid. The renunciation of common sense thus demanded by quantum theory is more drastic than that demanded by relativity theory. For now we get ourselves into *logical inconsistencies* if we try to think of things in the microscopic domain in the same way that we think of the objects of ordinary experience.

Suppose, for example, that I have a box with a partition in the middle and one electron on each side of the partition. I remove the partition for a moment, so that the electrons have an opportunity to exchange positions. I now find when I replace the partition that I again have one electron on each side of the partition. It now involves me in logical contradiction to ask whether the electron that is on the right side of the partition is the same electron that in the beginning was on the right side, or vice versa. Neither can I ask exactly how fast is the right-hand electron moving. Knowing that the electron is on the right of the partition makes it logically contradictory to know how fast it is moving. These are indeed revolutionary restrictions. Not to be able to ask which electron is which means that the electron does not have identity, and not being able to ask how fast it is moving means that the common-sense categories of space and time do not completely apply to it.

Consider another example. It is possible to make a so-called electron gun with which a stream of electrons may be fired at a target. If we start with a comparatively crude gun firing a coarse stream of electrons, we find the stream of electrons behaves much like a stream of water from a hose, so that we cannot hit with it a single sharp point of the target, but there is more or less scattering. Now common sense might lead us to expect that our marksmanship would become better as we refined the apparatus by making it more and more delicate and capable of dealing with a finer and finer stream of electrons. Experiment shows, however, that our common-sense expectations are entirely wrong, and that matters get worse instead of better as we refine the apparatus. In the end, when we have, at great pains, constructed a gun capable of firing single electrons, we find that we have almost completely lost control of the situation. No two shots ever come alike despite the best we can do, and we might as well spin a roulette wheel to find what part of the target any electron will hit.

The electron gun illustrates the general principle that, in the microscopic domain, events cannot be made to repeat. The situation thus disclosed is bad enough from the practical point of view, but I believe that it is even more upsetting from the conceptual point of view. For the one intellectual lesson that science has perhaps most insistently underlined is that our mental machinery is capable of making mistakes and that we continually have to verify and check what we are doing. The fundamental method of verification is repetition; the repeatable experiment has come to occupy such a position that the very definition of truth is often framed in terms of verification by repetition. It looks as though it does not mean anything in the quantum domain to ask for the truth about any specific event, yet how can I get along without the concept of truth? You may try to extricate yourself from the dilemma by saying that, although *I* may not verify the occurrence of some event by repeating the experiment, I *can* verify it by getting confirmation from some other observer who has also witnessed it. But this, unfortunately, is not a way out, because here we encounter another of those baffling properties of the microscopic world, namely, that an elementary event may be observed by only one observer. Confirmation by public report thus becomes impossible. To many, it might seem that thereby science is made impossible, science sometimes being defined in terms of publicity. However, if you are willing to grant that quantum theory is part of science, you see that matters are at least not quite as bad as this. Whatever the method by which eventually we get intellectual order into this situation, I think you can see that the observer must play a quite different role in the quantum domain than in the world of everyday life.

All these considerations mean that the conventional forms of thought are no longer applicable in the realm of the very small. I think you will agree that my foregoing statement is justified, namely, that the failure of common sense disclosed by quantum theory is more drastic than that disclosed by relativity theory. For, when in relativity theory we go to very high velocities, we merely encounter properties of matter that are strange to common experience, whereas when we go far enough in the direction of the very small, quantum theory says that our forms of thought fail, so that it is questionable whether we can properly think at all. One can imagine the consternation of our old philosophical friend Immanuel Kant who declared that space and time are *necessary* forms of thought.

What is the answer to the dilemma with which quantum theory confronts us, and where do the roots of the difficulty lie? Are we faced with the necessity of devising new ways of thinking? It does seem to me that eventually we shall have to find better ways of thinking, but I suspect that any improved method of thinking that we are capable of devising will eventually come up against essential limitations of some sort that will prevent its unlimited application. In the meantime, no agreement can be discerned at present among the experts with regard to the details of any way in which we might reform our thinking. As an example, there is the irreconcilable schism between the views of Einstein and Bohr on quantum phenomena. Whatever the eventual solution, I think we can at least be sure that it will be outside the realm of common sense. Furthermore, I believe the experts would at present agree that whatever new way we devise to think about the microscopic universe, the meaning of our new concepts will have to be found back at the level of the large-scale events of daily life, because this is the scale on which we live our lives, and it is we who are formulating the new concepts. This recognition and agreement entails, I believe, a consequence that is not commonly appreciated, namely, that the seeds and sources of the ineptness of our thinking in the microscopic range are already contained in our present thinking in the large-scale region and should have been capable of discovery by sufficiently acute analysis of our ordinary common-sense thinking.

I would now like to direct your attention to some qualities of our ordinary everyday thinking that are commonly overlooked but seem to be beginning to attract more attention and, I believe, may eventually give us truer understanding of the nature of our thinking process and its limitations. What I shall now say must be taken as strictly my own opinions. I have no professional philosophical competence to speak on these matters, and it is even probable that many of my fellow-physicists would not agree with me, if indeed they have any opinion on these matters at all.

You have doubtless had some acquaintance with cybernetics, a subject named and largely created by Professor Norbert Wiener at Massachusetts Institute of Technology and you know how much attention this subject is attracting and how many people are working at it. Apart from any specific results that may come out of all this activity, such for example as discovering how to make bigger and better robots that will continually usurp more and more of the functions of human intelligence, it seems to me that the mere fact that so many people are concerning themselves with this subject is going to have important repercussions. For when so many people try so hard to make a machine that functions like the human brain, the point of view will gradually spread that the human brain is itself a machine of sorts. It will also be recognized that this machine must have limitations inherent in its structure, and that the things which the machine can do, including in particular thinking, is in consequence also subject to limitations. Thinking is done by the brain, and the presumption is that thought has characteristics imposed by the character of the brain. At any rate, we will come to see that we may not expect to understand the nature of thought at least until we understand the nature of the brain. If you ask why we should be concerned with the nature of thought, I would reply: the realization that the nature of thought is something which cannot be merely taken for granted is a realization that seems to be gradually dawning on us as we ponder the significance of our failures in the fields of relativity and quantum theory.

You will not, I think, ponder for long what limitations are imposed on thought by the structure of the brain until it will suddenly strike you that what is really happening here is that the brain is trying to understand itself. But is not this a brash thing for the brain to try to do, for how can the brain analyze its own action, when any conclusions at which it arrives are themselves activities of the very brain that was the original problem to understand? At the very best, the situation would seem to be somewhat strained and artificial, and you may perhaps anticipate that any conclusions at which we may arrive cannot have as simple and straightforward a significance as we had perhaps hoped. This does indeed seem to be the case. What we are encountering here is a special case of a system trying to deal with itself. Such situations occur not infrequently, and it seems to be the general rule that such situations present special difficulties and infelicities.

Many of the well-known paradoxes of logic arise when a system tries to deal with itself. A stock example is the ostensibly complete map of the city in which the map itself is located. If the map is complete, it must contain a map of itself; that is, the map must have a map of the map, and this in turn demands a map of the map of the map, and you are off on a chase that has no end. Within the last few years, a theorem with regard to such a system has been proved, a theorem that has been hailed among logicians as a truly epoch-making discovery in logic. This theorem was enunciated by Gödel, now in the Institute for Advanced Study at Princeton. In very crude language, the theorem states that no logical system can ever prove that it itself is a perfect system in the sense that it may not contain concealed self-contradictions. This theorem, at one stroke, stultified the endeavors of some of the ablest mathematicians, just as earlier the discovery of new mathematical theorems had stultified the efforts of the circle-squarers and the angle-trisectors. Mathematicians had long been trying to prove by the principles of mathematics that mathematics contains no hidden inconsistencies, inconsistencies that some day might be discovered and bring down the whole imposing mathematical edifice in ruins. But Gödel's theorem showed that this is an impossible sort of thing to prove. The conclusion is that, if one wants to prove that mathematics is free from concealed self-contradictions, one has to use principles outside mathematics to prove it. If one then wants to prove that the new principles are free from contradiction, one must use other principles beyond and over those in question. We here encounter a regress that has no logical end and, humanly, ends in human weariness and the finite length of human life. This means that the human intelligence can never be sure of itself; it is not a tool capable of unlimited perfectibility, as is so often fondly imagined. All we can ever say is that, up to the present, we have found no inconsistencies where we have looked.

There is one other recent development that tends to make us more self-conscious of our intellectual limitations. In Hanover, New Hampshire, Adelbert Ames, Jr., with a number of collaborators, especially A. Hadley Cantril, of the department of psychology of Princeton University, has been studying in recent years how the perceptions of different people adapt themselves to situations that have been purposely devised to differ from the situations ordinarily encountered in daily life. For example, one can play tricks with perception by making lines converge or diverge which ordinary experience leads one to expect must be parallel. By combining various kinds of motion with curiosities of perspective, one can produce sensations completely foreign to ordinary experience, which the unaccustomed brain fits into its perceptual scheme in forced and unnatural ways. A striking example is the so-called trapezoidal window. A wooden frame like an ordinary window frame, except that the top and bottom sashes are not parallel, is rotated uniformly about a vertical axis. When the narrower end of the frame approaches the observer, the converging lines, associated ordinarily with greater distance, present the observer with an unaccustomed dilemma. Most observers resolve the dilemma by seeing the window frame in oscillating motion, back and forth, rather than in uniform rotation. In general, the way in which the observer perceives this and other strange situations varies with different persons and even varies with the same person, depending on what has been happening to him in the immediate past. This means that what a person sees in a given situation may, to a certain extent, be manipulated and controlled by another person.

Of course, there is nothing new in illusions. At Hanover, however, the study of such effects is being elaborated into a systematic technique for finding out about the nature of our perceptual processes. I think that most people, once they have seen the demonstrations, would be convinced that such studies cannot help being of great value in revealing details of the ways in which our perceptual machinery works.

Personally, however, I find these studies tremendously suggestive and stimulating from a point of view of greater generality, namely, in emphasizing the significance of the mere fact that we perceive at all. This is one of those things that are so universal we never think of them unless our attention is forced by some dramatic situation. Perception we have always had with us and we take it completely for granted. We *see things* out there in space moving about, and that is all there is to it. We accept these perceptions at their face value and, on them as a foundation, we build the pattern of our "reality." To this reality, we ascribe an absolute existence transcending its origin and ask ourselves how it is that the human brain can be capable of apprehending the absolute. By asking this question, we disclose our hazy feeling that what a brain can do is probably limited in some way. But except for this hazy feeling, it seems to me that the question is improperly put, and the fact that we ask it discloses an improper attitude on our part. Instead of asking how human brains can apprehend "reality," we should ask what sort of thing it is that the human brain can fashion to call reality. It was, I believe, Suzanne Langer who remarked that philosophy advances, not by finding the answers to the questions of preceding generations, but by finding that those questions were improperly put. Here it seems to me is obviously a question that has been improperly put. The perceptions of time and space have been furnished to us by the machinery of our nervous systems. This machinery is a terribly complicated thing, which in spite of its complication does not give rise to perception until it has received a long course of preparation and education. Anyone who has watched a small infant trying to coordinate its visual and tactual sensations recognizes that we acquire our perceptual abilities only by arduous practice. Yet we take our space and time with a deadly seriousness. Even so great a scientist as Sir Isaac Newton could say that space is the sensorium of God, and nearly every philosopher treats thought as in some way transcending the machine that thinks. It will doubtless be disturbing to many to give up our transcendentally fundamental time and space, but I think there is perhaps something to be gained also. Perhaps when we learn to take them less seriously we will not be so bedeviled by the logical contradictions in which they sometimes now involve us, as when we ask questions about the beginning or end of time or the boundaries of space.

There is another respect in which I have found the experiments of Ames most stimulating, namely, in disclosing details of our mental processes of which we are ordinarily completely unaware. For example, as one watches the rotating trapezoidal window, one's perceptions are in a continual state of flux, melting and forming and metamorphosing into one another in a way quite unfamiliar. How can one find words to describe such unfamiliar happenings, or how can one catch and hold such things? How can one even store in memory what he has experienced so that he may be sure that the manner of fusion of two perceptions which he has just experienced is the same as the manner of fusion which he experienced yesterday?

Of course, ever since psychoanalysis started, we have known that there are processes occurring in the brain that never get to the level of consciousnes, but here it seems to me that we have something different, because here we are encountering new sorts of conscious experience. Among these, there are *transient* mental phenomena, accessible to sufficiently acute introspection. For example, as we listen to our fellow, the meaning that he is trying to convey grows before it is complete. Meanings do not spring full grown into our minds but pass through a stage of development that is seldom, if ever, the subject of analysis. It seems to be a general characteristic of our mental processes that we like to operate with static and complete things — we want our words to have fixed meanings and we analyze space into points and time into instants. But to sufficiently acute analysis, the fixed and static does not occur — it is something that we have constructed, and in so doing we have constructed away a whole world of mental phenomena.

It would seem not impossible that this world of transient

phenomena and fine structure could be recovered and opened to us by deliberate cultivation and invention. What is needed is the invention of an introspectional microscope. Not until we have amassed a considerable experience of this world will we be able to talk about it or even remember our experiences. Gaining mastery of the microscopic world of introspection will involve much the same sort of thing that happens to a baby or to a kitten when its eyes are opened. Study of the process of gaining mastery of the new introspectional world may help us to reconstruct imaginatively what happened to us in our own babyhood.

It does not yet appear what the final method will be for dealing with all these considerations. I believe that the final solution will have to carry further the consequences of the insight that quantum theory has partially glimpsed, namely, that the observer must somehow be included in the system. The point of view of classical physics, and I believe also of all orthodox human thinking up to the present, was that the observer is a passive spectator, expressed sometimes by saying that what he observes would be the same whether he were watching or not. Quantum theory points out that this is only an approximation valid in the realm of large objects. The very act of observing a small object involves a reaction between the object and the observer, a reaction that must be allowed for in reconstructing the system from observation. To which we now add the insight that the relationship between the observed and the observer is a much more intimate relationship than these quantum considerations would suggest, and that it is in fact meaningless to try to separate observer and observed, or to speak of an object independent of an observer or, for that matter, of an observer in the absence of objects of observation.

It seems to me that our eyes are gradually opening. We are coming to recognize that it is a simple matter of observation that the observer is part of what he observes and that the thinker is part of what he thinks. We do not passively observe the universe from the outside, but we are all in it up to our necks, and there is no escape. It would be difficult to imagine anything more contrary to the tenets of common sense or to the attitude of the human race since it has begun to think. The commonsense way of handling our minds has, without doubt, been of decisive importance, and the discovery of the common-sense way of thinking was, doubtless, in the beginning a bit of an invention, perhaps the most important invention ever made. One of the things that we are in fact doing in accepting the common-sense way of thinking is to declare that, for our purposes, we do not need to complicate our thinking by continually holding ourselves to an awareness that the thinker cannot be divorced from what he thinks. We have thus brought about a tremendous simplification in our intellectual processes, and in the history of the human race the common-sense attitude has been more than justified. It seems to me, however, that we are approaching a position where we can recognize the limit of usefulness of this way of thinking. Common sense evolved in the comparatively simple situations of the primitive experiences of the human race, and although it may have been an invention, we may be sure that it was an unconscious invention, adopted with no due consideration of its limitations or possible alternatives.

The world with which common sense was evolved to cope was simple with respect to the range of physical phenomena that it embraced, and simple also with respect to the social organization of the communities in which common sense was practiced. In the last 50 years, we have drastically extended our physical range toward high velocities and toward the microscopic and have been able to retain our command of the situation only by discarding those common-sense methods of thinking about physical things which had served the human race from the beginning. We may well ask ourselves whether something analogous may not be expected to occur, or is not in fact already occurring, when we pass from the simple to the complex in phenomena other than those of the physical world, using *physical* in its narrower sense. There are at least two other classes of nonphysical situations. These are social situations and the situations presented by the creation of abstractions or by abstract thinking. Consider first the social situations.

There will be, I suppose, no disagreement with contention

that, in the last few generations, the complexity of our social environment has tremendously increased. With modern methods of communication with the speed of light and of transportation with more than the speed of sound, the social environment of each person is becoming effectively the whole world. Plain analogy with what has happened in physics suggests the question of whether we are not here encountering an extension of range in our social experience that will demand an analogous abandonment of common-sense methods of social thinking. By common-sense methods of social thinking, I mean those methods that developed in small communities and are fitted to deal with nothing more complex than the social situations presented by small communities. From this point of view, most of our social thinking would seem to be of the common-sense variety. One characteristic social attitude springing from such an origin is the conviction that there is one and only one "correct" or "right" social philosophy or world-view, or one line of conduct that one "ought" to follow. Such a point of view could be pretty well maintained in a community small enough to offer a background of uniform social experience to all its members and able to enforce conformity on all dissenters. But the impossibility of any such view has become amply apparent when the community has become the whole world, and we are forced to revise the very meanings that we attach to *truth* or *right* or *ought*. It would appear that there is a moral perception analogous to our physical perception of objects in space and time and, like our physical perceptions, dependent on our past experience. We may suppose that the savage, who has never seen a civilized window frame, when confronted for the first time with the rotating trapezoidal window, will see it, not in oscillating motion as we do, but in uniform rotation. Analogously, the Hindu, brought up in the religious traditions of his group, perceives as a moral imperative that he must not kill the mosquito that annoys him. The realization of this is not new; the anthropologist has been dinning it into our ears for some time. The anthropologist, however, could point his moral only in somewhat academic terms and mostly from the record of the past by presenting us with the divergent practices of different peoples in different epochs. The lesson is now pointed with incomparably more dramatic force in our endeavors to find a basis for the harmonious living together of the entire world, a problem that demands the simultaneous reconciliation of so many divergent outlooks. At the very least, we shall have to evolve a new social philosophy and discover some method of getting rid of the provincialism that seems so right to common sense.

In addition to the social situations, a second nonphysical factor in our lives is afforded by our abstract thinking. How long the human race has been thinking and talking abstractly I suppose even the anthropologist cannot tell us, but it appeals to me as a good guess that we developed our common-sense method of handling the situations of daily life before we began abstracting. It is known that there are primitive peoples that have not yet formed as simple abstractions as "tree." The extension of thinking from concrete objects to abstractions constituted an extension of range sufficiently great to suggest the question, inspired by our experience with relativity and quantum theory, of whether the methods adequate to deal with the world of concrete objects continue to be adequate to deal with abstractions. To put the question is to suggest the answer. In the answer, I believe we can glimpse the solution to a riddle that has long baffled us. There is a class of people whose profession is to deal with abstractions — that is, the philosophers. By long tradition, philosophical thinking has come to be regarded by most people as the most exalted of all thinking, and the philosopher is often regarded with an approach to veneration. But along with this veneration most people are disillusioned and feel the futility of the whole philosophical enterprise, because after 2000 years of argument philosophy has settled no questions and no two philosophers agree. This situation can be understood in a measure when we recognize that the philosopher essentially is applying to abstractions the same common-sense methods that are applicable in the realm of concrete objects. I think simple observation of any conventional philosophical system will justify this statement, or, if one wishes, one can find a formal argument by Philipp Frank to show that the theses of philosophy are essentially the theses of common sense extended into the realm of abstractions. For example, Plato ascribes to ideas a reality like the reality of the objects of common sense. But ideas are not like things, and to treat them like things is only a kind of poetry. The cure for the common-sense attitude toward abstractions is to seek the meaning of our abstract terms by an analysis at least as searching as the analysis that we have been forced to apply to such simple physical terms as *length* or *time*. Such an analysis is seldom applied to abstractions, but the common-sense implications in our verbal habits are uncritically accepted. For example, one of the great abstractions is truth. In talking about truth, one uses such expressions as *the* truth, or thinks of truth as eternal in the heavens, which all may know and on which all can agree. But just as in physics we have been forced to recognize that there is not the one length of common sense but different kinds of length, such as optical length or tactual length, depending on our choice of method of measurement, so analysis will disclose that there is not just the one truth of common sense but different kinds of truth, depending on the method used for establishing "truth." For example, scientific truth is not the same as theological truth, and we must not talk about them as if they were and as common sense wants us to. Since truth is such a frequent topic for discussion in philosophy, this one example will suggest the modifications in conventional philosophical thought that might follow the abandonment of the common-sense attitude toward truth. Perhaps the philosophers might even agree. Even if the philosophers prove unregenerate, outside the realm of philosophy abandonment of the common-sense attitude toward truth will go far toward eliminating bigotry and intolerance.

In conclusion, the problem of devising successful substitutes for common sense has not yet been solved, and we are standing only on the threshold of a new era in human thought. Although the final solution is not in sight, there are certain lessons that we can take to heart at present in the expectation that we shall not have to retreat. It seems to me that, as a minimum, we henceforth cannot regard a man as well educated who does not intuitively recognize that common sense is not to be taken for granted, or who does not handle his thinking as a tool in the awareness that every tool has limitations built into it. Such a man, looking to the past, can only be amazed that the human brain has, by cut-and-try methods, evolved procedures as effective as it has for dealing with the world around us; looking to the present, sees perhaps the most important reason for the present internal social difficulties of the human race in its uncritical use of traditional habits of thought; and looking to the future, can feel only optimism for the time when we shall have learned how to substitute consciously directed control of our thinking for the blind procedures of common sense.

From the Summer 1955 Et cetera.

AN AMERICAN INDIAN MODEL OF THE UNIVERSE

Benjamin Lee Whorf

I FIND IT GRATUITOUS to assume that a Hopi who knows only the Hopi language and the cultural ideas of his own society has the same notions, often supposed to be intuitions, of time and space that we have, and that are generally assumed to be universal. In particular, he has no general notion or intuition of *time* as a smooth flowing continuum in which everything in the universe proceeds at an equal rate, out of a future, through a present, into a past; or, in which, to reverse the picture, the observer is being carried in the stream of duration continuously away from a past and into a future.

After long and careful study and analysis the Hopi language is seen to contain no words, grammatical forms, constructions or expressions that refer directly to what we call *time*, or to past, present, or future, or to enduring or lasting, or to motion as kinematic rather than dynamic (*i.e.* as a continuous translation in space and time rather than as an exhibition of dynamic effort in a certain process) or that even refer to space in such a way as to exclude that element of extension or existence that we call *time*, and so by implication leave a residue that could be referred to as *time*. Hence, the Hopi language contains no reference to *time*, either explicit or implicit.

At the same time, the Hopi language is capable of account-

Benjamin Lee Whorf, a pioneer American linguist, studied how the structure of a language influences the manner in which its users see the world. His most important papers are collected in *Language, Thought, and Reality* (MIT Press).

ing for and describing correctly, in a pragmatic or operational sense, all observable phenomena of the universe. Hence, I find it gratuitous to assume that Hopi thinking contains any such notion as the supposed intuitively felt flowing of *time*, or that the intuition of a Hopi gives him this as one of its data. Just as it is possible to have any number of geometries other than the Euclidean which give an equally perfect account of space configurations, so it is possible to have descriptions of the universe, all equally valid, that do not contain our familiar contrasts of time and space. The relativity viewpoint of modern physics is one such view, conceived in mathematical terms, and the Hopi Weltanschauung is another and quite different one, nonmathematical and linguistic.

Thus, the Hopi language and culture conceals a *metaphysics*, such as our so-called naive view of space and time does, or the relativity theory does, yet a different metaphysics than either. In order to describe the structure of the universe according to the Hopi, it is necessary to attempt — insofar as it is possible — to make explicit this metaphysics, properly describable only in the Hopi language, by means of an approximation expressed in our own language, somewhat inadequately it is true, yet by availing ourselves of such concepts as we have worked up into relative consonance with the system underlying the Hopi view of the universe.

In this Hopi view, time disappears and space is altered, so that it is no longer the homogenous and instantaneous timeless space of our supposed intuition or of classical Newtonian mechanics. At the same time new concepts and abstractions flow into the picture, taking up the task of describing the universe without reference to such time or space — abstractions for which our language lacks adequate terms. These abstractions, by approximations of which we attempt to reconstruct for ourselves the metaphysics of the Hopi, will undoubtedly appear to us as psychological or even mystical in character. They are ideas which we are accustomed to consider as part and parcel either of so-called animistic or vitalistic beliefs, or of those transcendental unifications of experience and intuitions of things unseen that are felt by the consciousness of the mystic, or which are given out in mystical and (or) so-called occult systems of thought. These abstractions are definitely given either explicitly in words—psychological or metaphysical terms—in the Hopi language, or, even more, are implicit in the very structure and grammar of that language, as well as being observable in Hopi culture and behavior. They are not, so far as I can consciously avoid it, projections of other systems upon the Hopi language and culture made by me in my attempt at an objective analysis. Yet, if *mystical* be perchance a term of abuse in the eyes of a modern Western scientist, it must be emphasized that these underlying abstractions and postulates of the Hopian metaphysics are from a detached viewpoint equally (or to the Hopi, more) justified pragmatically and experientially as compared to the flowing time and static space of our own metaphysics, which are *au fond* equally mystical. The Hopi postulates equally account for all phenomena and their interrelations, and lend themselves even better to the integration of Hopi culture in all its phases.

The metaphysics underlying our own language, thinking, and modern culture (I speak not of the recent and quite different relativity metaphysics of modern science) imposes upon the universe two grand COSMIC FORMS, space and time; static, three-dimensional, infinite space, and kinetic, one-dimensional, uniformly and perpetually flowing time; two utterly separate and unconnected aspects of reality (according to this familiar way of thinking). The flowing realm of time is, in turn, the subject of a threefold division; past, present, and future.

The Hopi metaphysics also has its cosmic forms comparable to these in scale and scope. What are they? It imposes upon the universe two grand cosmic forms, which as a first approximation in terminology we may call *manifested* and *manifesting* (or, *unmanifest*) or again, OBJECTIVE and SUBJECTIVE. The objective or manifested comprises all that is or has been accessible to the senses, the historical physical universe, in fact, with no attempt to distinguish between present and past, but excluding everything that we call future. The subjective or manifesting comprises all that we call future, *but not merely this*; it includes equally and indistinguishably all that we call mental—

everything that appears or exists in the mind, or as the Hopi would prefer to say, in the *heart*, not only the heart of man, but in the heart of animals, plants, and things, and behind and within all the forms and appearances of nature in the heart of nature, and by an implication and extension which has been felt by more than one anthropologist, yet would hardly ever be spoken of by a Hopi himself, so charged is the idea with religious and magical awesomeness, in the very heart of the Cosmos, itself.[1] The subjective realm (subjective from our viewpoint, but intensely real and quivering with life, power, and potency to the Hopi) embraces not only our *future*, much of which the Hopi regards as more or less predestined in essence if not in exact form, but also all mentality, intellection, and emotion, the essence and typical form of which is the striving of purposeful desire, intelligent in character, toward manifestation — a manifestation which is much resisted and delayed, but in some form or other is inevitable. It is the realm of expectancy, of desire and purpose, of vitalizing life, of efficient causes, of thought thinking itself out from an inner realm (the Hopian *heart*) into manifestation. It is in a dynamic state, yet not a state of motion — it is not advancing towards us out of the future, but *already with us* in vital and mental form, and its dynamism is at work in the field of eventuating or manifesting, i.e. evolving without motion from the subjective by degrees to a result which is the objective. In translating into English the Hopi will say that these entities in process of causation *will come* or that they — the Hopi — *will come* to them, but in their own language there are no verbs corresponding to our *come* and *go* that mean simple and abstract motion, our purely kinematic concept. The words in this case translated *come* refer to the process of eventuating without calling it motion — they are *eventuates to here* (pew'i) or *eventuates from it* (angqö) or *arrived* (pitu, pl. öki) which refers only to the terminal manifestation, the actual arrival at a given point, not to any motion preceding it.

This realm of the subjective or of the process of manifestation, as distinguished from the objective, the result of this universal process, includes also — on its border but still pertaining to its own realm — aspect of existence that we include in our present time. It is that which is beginning to emerge into manifestation; that is, something which is beginning to be done, like going to sleep or starting to write, but is not yet in full operation. This can be and usually is referred to by the same verb form (the *expective* form in my terminology of Hopi grammar) that refers to our future, or to wishing, wanting, intending, etc. Thus, this nearer edge of the subjective cuts across and includes a part of our present time, viz. the moment of inception, but most of our present belongs in the Hopi scheme to the objective realm and so is indistinguishable from our past. There is also a verb form, the *inceptive* which refers to this *edge* of emergent manifestation in the reverse way — as belonging to the objective, as the edge at which objectivity is attained; this is used to indicate beginning or starting, and in most cases there is no difference apparent in the translation from the similar use of the expective. But at certain crucial points significant and fundamental differences appear. The inceptive, referring to the objective and result side and not like the expective to the subjective and causal side, implies the ending of the work causation in the same breath that it states the beginning of manifestation. If the verb has a suffix which answers somewhat to our passive, but really means that causation impinges upon a subject to effect a certain result — i.e. *the food is being eaten*, then addition of the *inceptive* suffix in such a way as to refer to the basic action produces a meaning of causal cessation. The basic action is in the inceptive state, hence whatever causation is behind it is ceasing, the causation explicitly referred to by the causal suffix is hence such as we would call past time, and the verb includes this and the incepting and the de-causating of the final state (a state of partial or total eatenness) in one statement. The translation is *it stops getting eaten*. Without knowing the underlying Hopian metaphysics it would be impossible to understand how the same suffix may denote starting or stopping.

If we were to approximate our metaphysical terminology more closely to Hopian terms, we should probably speak of the subjective realm as the realm of *hope* or *hoping*. Every language contains terms that have come to attain cosmic scope of reference, that crystallize in themselves the basic postulates of an unformulated philosophy, in which is couched the thought of a people, a culture, a civilization, even of an era. Such are our words reality, substance, matter, cause, and as we have seen space, time, past, present, future. Such a term in Hopi is the word most often translated *hope* — tunátya — *it is in the action of hoping, it hopes, it is hoped for, it thinks or is thought of with hope*, etc. Most metaphysical words in Hopi are verbs, not nouns as in European languages. The verb tunátya contains in its idea of hope something of our words thought, desire, and cause which sometimes must be used to translate it. The word is really a term which crystallizes the Hopi philosophy of the universe in respect to its grand dualism of objective and subjective; it is the Hopi term for *subjective*. *It refers to the state of the subjective, unmanifest, vital and causal aspect of the cosmos, and the fermenting activity toward fruition and manifestation with which it seethes* — *an action of hoping*, i.e. mental-causal activity, which is forever pressing upon and into the manifested realm. As anyone acquainted with Hopi society knows, the Hopi see this burgeoning activity in the growing of plants, the forming of clouds and their condensation in rain, the careful planning-out of the communal activities of agriculture and architecture, and in all human hoping, wishing, striving, and taking thought; and as most especially concentrated in prayer, the constant hopeful praying of the Hopi community, assisted by their exoteric communal ceremonies and their secret, esoteric rituals in the underground kivas — prayer which conducts the pressure of the collective Hopi thought and will out of the subjective into the objective. The inceptive form of tunátya, which is tunátyava, does not mean *begins to hope*, but rather *comes true, being hoped for*. Why it must logically have this meaning will be clear from what has already been said. The inceptive denotes the first appearance of the objective, but the basic meaning of tunátya is subjective activity or force; the inceptive is then the terminus of such activity. It might then be said that tunátya *coming true* is the Hopi term for objective, as contrasted with subjective, the two terms being simply two different inflectional nuances of the same verbal root, as the two cosmic forms are the two aspects of one reality.

As far as space is concerned, the subjective is a mental realm, a realm of no space in the objective sense, but it seems to be symbolically related to the vertical dimension and its poles the zenith and the underground, as well as to the *heart* of things, which corresponds to our word *inner* in the metaphorical sense. Corresponding to each point in the objective world is such a vertical and vitally *inner* axis which is what we call the wellspring of the future. But to the Hopi there is no temporal future; there is nothing in the subjective state corresponding to the sequences and successions conjoined with distances and changing physical configurations that we find in the objective state. From each subjective axis, which may be thought of as more or less vertical and like the growth-axis of a plant, extends the objective realm in every physical direction, though these directions are typified more especially by the horizontal plane and its four cardinal points. The objective is the great cosmic form of extension; it takes in all the strictly extensional aspects of existence, and it includes all intervals and distances, all seriations and number. Its *distance* includes what we call time in the sense of the temporal relation between events which have already happened. The Hopi conceive time and motion in the objective realm in a purely operational sense — a matter of the complexity and magnitude of operations connecting events — so that the element of time is not separated from whatever element of space enters into the operations. Two events in the past occurred a long *time* apart (the Hopi language has no word quite equivalent to our *time*) when many periodic physical motions have occurred between them in such a way as to traverse much distance or accumulate magnitude of physical display in other ways. The Hopi metaphysics does not raise the question of whether the things in a distant village exist at the same present moment as those in one's own village, for it is frankly pragmatic on this score and says that any *events* in the distant village can be compared to any events in one's own village only by an interval of magnitude that has both time and space forms in it. Events at a distance from the observer can only be known objectively when they are *past* (i.e. posited in the objective) and the more distant, the more *past* (the more worked upon from the subjective side. Hopi, with its preference for verbs, as compared to our own liking for nouns, perpetually turns out propositions about things into propositions about events. What happens at a distant village, if actual (objective) and not a conjecture (subjective) can be known *here* only later. If it does not happen *at this place* it does not happen *at this time*; it happens at *that* place and at *that* time. Both the *here* happening and the *there* happening are in the objective, corresponding in general to our past, but the *there* happening is the more objectively distant, meaning, from our standpoint, that it is further away in the past just as it is further away from us in space than the *here* happening.

As the objective realm displaying its characteristic attribute of extension stretches away from the observer toward that unfathomable remoteness which is both far away in space and long past in time, there comes a point where extension in detail ceases to be knowable and is lost in the vast distance, and where the subjective, creeping behind the scenes as it were, merges into the objective, so that at this inconceivable distance from the observer—from all observers—there is an all-encircling end and beginning of things where it might be said that existence, itself, swallows up the objective and the subjective. The border land of this realm is as much subjective as objective. It is the abysm of antiquity, the time and place told about in the myths, which is known only subjectively or mentally—the Hopi realize and even express in their grammar that the things told in myths or stories do not have the same kind of reality or validity as things of the present day, the things of practical concern. As for the far distances of the sky and stars, what is known and said about them is suppositious, inferential—hence, in a way subjective—reached more through the inner vertical axis and the pole of the zenith than through the objective distances and the objective processes of vision and locomotion. So the dim past of myths is that corresponding distance on earth (rather than in the heavens) which is reached subjectively as myth through the vertical axis of reality via the pole of the nadir—hence it is placed *below* the present surface of the earth, though this does not mean that the nadir — land of the origin myths is a hole or cavern as we should understand it. It is Palátkwapi *At the Red Mountains*, a land like our present earth, but to which our earth bears the relation of a distant sky — and similarly the sky of our earth is penetrated by the heroes of tales, who find another earthlike realm above it.

It may now be seen how the Hopi do not need to use terms that refer to space or time as such. Such terms in our language are recast into expressions of extension, operation, and cyclic process provided they refer to the solid objective realm. They are recast into expressions of subjectivity if they refer to the subjective realm — the future, the psychic-mental, the mythical period, and the invisibly distant and conjectural generally. Thus, the Hopi language gets along perfectly without tenses for its verbs.

NOTES AND REFERENCES

1. This idea is sometimes alluded to as the spirit of the Breath (hikswu) and as the Mighty Something ('a'ne himu) although these terms may have lower and less cosmic, though always awesome connotations.

Previous publications of Whorf's relevant to this article are: 'Gestalt Technique of Stem Composition in Shawnee,' Appendix to Part IV of C.F. Voegelin, *Shawnee Stems and the Jacob P. Dunn Miami Dictionary*, Prehistory Research Series No. 9, pp. 390-406 (Indiana Historical Society, 1940); 'The Hopi Language, Toreva Dialect,' in *Linguistic Structures in Native America*, pp. 158-183 (Viking Fund Publications in Anthropology, No. 6, 1946); 'The Punctual and Segmentative Aspects of Verbs and Hopi,' *Language*, 12.127-131 (1936); 'Some Verbal Categories of Hopi,' *Language*, 14.275-286 (1938); 'Science and Linguistics,' reprinted in Hayakawa, *Language in Action*, pp. 302-321 (1941); 'Linguistics as an Exact Science,' *Technology Review*, Vol. 43, No. 2 (1940); 'Language and Logic,' *Technology Review*, Vol. 43, No. 6 (1941); 'The Relation of Habitual Thought and Behavior to Language,' *Et cetera*, 1.197-215 (Summer 1944). The four articles immediately preceding have been reprinted by the Foreign Service Institute, Department of State: *Four Articles on Metalinguistics* (1949).

From the Autumn 1950 Et cetera.

THE SYMBOL: The Origin and Basis of Human Behavior

Leslie A. White

I

IN JULY, 1939, A CELEBRATION was held at Leland Stanford University to commemorate the hundredth anniversary of the discovery that the cell is the basic unit of all living tissue. Today we are beginning to realize and to appreciate the fact that the symbol is the basic unit of all human behavior and civilization. All human behavior originates in the use of symbols. It was the symbol which transformed our anthropoid ancestors into men and made them human. All civilizations have been generated, and are perpetuated, only by the use of symbols. It is the symbol which transforms an infant of homo sapiens into a human being; deaf mutes who grow up without the use of symbols are not human beings. All human behavior consists of, or is dependent upon, the use of symbols. Human behavior is symbolic behavior; symbolic behavior is human behavior. The symbol is the universe of humanity.

II

The great Darwin declared that 'there is no fundamental difference between man and the higher mammals in their mental faculties,' that the difference between them consists 'solely in his [man's] almost infinitely larger power of associating together the most diversified sounds and ideas,' (Ch. III, *The Descent*

Leslie A. White was a Professor of Anthropology, University of Michigan.

of Man). Thus the difference between the mind of man and that of other animals is merely one of degree, and it is not 'fundamental.'

Essentially the same views are held by many present day students of human behavior. Professor Ralph Linton, an anthropologist, writes in *The Study of Man*:[1] 'The differences between men and animals in all these [behavior] respects are enormous, but they seem to be differences in quantity rather than in quality,' (p. 79; the same idea is also expressed on p. 68). 'Human and animal behavior can be shown to have so much in common,' Professor Linton observes, 'that the gap [between them] ceases to be of great importance,' (p. 60). Dr. Alexander Goldenweiser, likewise an anthropologist, believes that 'In point of sheer psychology, mind as such, man is after all no more than a talented animal' and 'that the difference between mentality here displayed [by a horse and a chimpanzee] and that of a man is merely one of degree.'[2]

That there are numerous and impressive similarities between the behavior of man and that of ape is fairly obvious; it is quite possible that even chimpanzees in zoos have noted and appreciated them. Fairly apparent, too, are man's behavioral similarities to many other kinds of animals. Almost as obvious, but not easy to define, is a difference in behavior which distinguishes man from all other living creatures. I say 'obvious' because it is quite apparent to the common man that the non-human animals with which he is familiar do not and cannot enter, and participate in, the world in which he, as a human being, lives. It is impossible for a dog, horse, bird, or even an ape, ever to have *any* understanding of the meaning of the sign of the cross to a Christian, or of the fact that black (white among the Chinese) is the color of mourning. But when the scholar attempts to *define* the mental difference between animal and man he sometimes encounters difficulties which he cannot surmount and, therefore, ends up by saying that the difference is merely one of degree: man has a bigger mind, 'larger power of association,' wider range of activities, etc.[3]

There is a *fundamental* difference between the mind of man and the mind of non-man. This difference is one of kind, not one of degree. And the gap between the two types is of the greatest importance — at least to the science of comparative behavior. Man uses symbols; no other creature does. A creature either uses symbols or he does not; there are no intermediate stages.

III

A symbol is a thing the value or meaning of which is bestowed upon it by those who use it. I say 'thing' because a symbol may have any kind of physical form; it may have the form of a material object, a color, a sound, an odor, a motion of an object, a taste.

The meaning, or value, of a symbol is in no instance derived from or determined by properties intrinsic in its physical form: the color appropriate to mourning may be yellow, green, or any other color; purple need not be the color of royalty; among the Manchu rulers of China it was yellow. The meaning of the word 'see' is not intrinsic in its phonetic (or pictorial) properties. 'Biting one's thumb at'[4] someone might mean anything. The meanings of symbols are derived from and determined by the organisms who use them; meaning is bestowed by human organisms upon physical forms which thereupon become symbols.[5]

All symbols must have a physical form otherwise they could not enter our experience.[6] But the meaning of a symbol cannot be perceived by the senses. One cannot tell by looking at an x in an algebraic equation what it stands for; one cannot ascertain with the ears alone the symbolic value of the phonetic compound si; one cannot tell merely by weighing a pig how much gold he will exchange for; one cannot tell from the wave length of a color whether it stands for courage or cowardice, 'stop' or 'go'; nor can one discover the spirit in a fetish by any amount of physical or chemical examination. The meaning of a symbol can be communicated only by symbolic means, usually by articulate speech.

But a thing which in one context is a symbol is, in another context, not a symbol but a sign. Thus, a word is a symbol only when one is concerned with the distinction between its meaning and its physical form. This distinction *must* be made when one bestows value upon a sound-combination or when a previously bestowed value is discovered for the first time; it *may* be made at other times for certain purposes. But after value has been bestowed upon, or discovered in, a word, its meaning becomes identified, in use, with its physical form. The word then functions as a sign,[7] rather than as a symbol. Its meaning is then perceived with the senses. This fact that a thing may be both symbol (in one context) and non-symbol (in another context) has led to some confusion and misunderstanding.

Thus Darwin says: 'That which distinguishes man from the lower animals is not the understanding of articulate sounds, for as everyone knows, dogs understand many words and sentences,' (Ch. III, *The Descent of Man*).

It is perfectly true, of course, that dogs, apes,[8] horses, birds, and perhaps creatures even lower in the evolutionary scale, can be taught to respond in a specific way to a vocal command. But it does not follow that no difference exists between the meaning of 'words and sentences' to a man and to a dog. Words are both signs and symbols to man; they are merely signs to a dog. Let us analyze the situation of vocal stimulus and response.

A dog may be taught to roll over at the command 'Roll over!' A man may be taught to stop at the command 'Halt!' The fact that a dog can be taught to roll over in Chinese, or that he can be taught to 'go fetch' at the command 'roll over' (and, of course, the same is true for a man) shows that there is no necessary and invariable relationship between a particular sound combination and a specific reaction to it. The dog or the man can be taught to respond in a certain manner to *any* arbitrarily selected combination of sounds, for example, a group of nonsense syllables, coined for the occasion. On the other hand, any one of a great number and variety of responses may become evocable by a given stimulus. Thus, so far as the *origin* of the relationship between vocal stimulus and response is concerned, the nature of the relationship, i.e., the meaning of the stimulus, is not determined by properties intrinsic in the stimulus.

But, once the relationship has been established between vocal stimulus and response, the meaning of the stimulus becomes *identified with the sounds;* it is then *as if* the meaning were intrinsic in the sounds themselves. Thus, 'halt' does not have the same meaning as 'hilt' or 'malt.' A dog may be conditioned to respond in a certain way to a sound of a given wave length. Sufficiently alter the pitch of the sound and the response will cease to be forthcoming. The meaning of the stimulus has become identified with its physical form; its value is perceived with the senses.

Thus we see that in establishing a relationship between a stimulus and a response the properties intrinsic in the stimulus do not determine the nature of the response. But, *after the relationship has been established* the meaning of the stimulus is *as if* it were *inherent* in its physical form. It does not make any difference what phonetic combination we select to evoke the response of terminating self-locomotion. We may teach a dog, horse, or man to stop at any vocal command we care to choose or devise. But once the relationship has been established between sound and response, the meaning of the stimulus becomes identified with its physical form and is, therefore, perceivable with the senses.

So far we have discovered no difference between the dog and the man; they appear to be exactly alike. And so they are as far as we have gone. But we have not told the whole story yet. No difference between dog and man is discoverable so far as learning to respond appropriately to a vocal stimulus is concerned. But we must not let an impressive similarity conceal an important difference. A porpoise is not yet a fish.

The man differs from the dog—and all other creatures—in that *he can and does play an active role in determining what value the vocal stimulus is to have, and the dog cannot.* As John Locke has aptly put it, 'All sounds [i.e., in language] . . . have their signification from the arbitrary imposition of men.' The dog does not and cannot play an active part in determining the value of the vocal stimulus. Whether he is to roll over or go fetch at a given stimulus, or whether the stimulus for roll over be one combination of sounds or another is a matter in which the dog has nothing whatever to 'say.' He plays a purely passive role and can do nothing else. He learns the meaning of a vocal command just as his salivary glands may learn to respond to the sound of a bell. But man plays an active role and thus becomes a creator: Let x equal three pounds of coal and it does equal three pounds of coal; let removal of the hat in a house of worship indicate respect and it becomes so. This creative faculty, that of freely, actively, and arbitrarily bestowing value upon things, is one of the most commonplace as well as *the* most important characteristic of man. Children employ it freely in their play: 'Let's pretend that this rock is a wolf.'

The difference between the behavior of man and other animals then, is that the lower animals may receive new values, may acquire new meanings, but they cannot create and bestow them. Only man can do this. To use a crude analogy, lower animals are like a person who has only the receiving apparatus for wireless messages: He can receive messages but cannot send them. Man can do both. And this difference is one of kind, not of degree: a creature can either 'arbitrarily impose signification,' to use Locke's phrase, can either create and bestow values, or he cannot. There are no intermediate stages.[9] This difference may appear slight, but, as a carpenter once told William James in discussing differences between men, 'it's very important.' All *human* existence depends upon it and it alone.

The confusion regarding the nature of words and their significance to men and the lower animals is not hard to understand. It arises, first of all, from a failure to distinguish between the two quite different contexts in which words function. The statements, 'The meaning of a word[10] cannot be perceived with the senses,' and 'The meaning of a word can be perceived with the senses,' though contradictory, are nevertheless equally true. In the *symbol* context the meaning cannot be perceived with the senses; in the *sign* context it can. This is confusing enough. But the situation has been made worse by using the words 'symbol' and 'sign' to label, not the *different contexts*, but *one and the same thing:* the word. Thus a word is a symbol *and* a sign, two different things. It is like saying that a vase is a *doli* and a *kana* — two different things — because it may function in two contexts, esthetic and commercial.[11]

That which is a *symbol* in the context of origination becomes a *sign* in use thereafter. Things may be either signs or symbols to man; they can be only signs to other creatures.

IV

Very little indeed is known of the organic basis of the symbolic faculty: we know next to nothing of the neurology of symbolizing.[12] And very few scientists—anatomists, neurologists, physical anthropologists—appear to be interested in the problem. Some, in fact, seem to be unaware of the existence of such a problem. The duty and task of giving an account of the organic basis of symbolizing does not fall within the province of the sociologist or the cultural anthropologist. On the contrary, he should scrupulously exclude it as irrelevant to his problems and interests; to introduce it would bring only confusion. It is enough for the sociologist or cultural anthropologist to take the ability to use symbols, possessed by man alone, as given. The use to which he puts this fact is in no way affected by his, or even the anatomist's, inability to describe the symbolic process in neurological terms. However, it is well for the social scientist to be acquainted with the little that neurologists and anatomists do know about the structural basis of 'symboling.' We, therefore, review briefly the chief relevant facts here.

The anatomist has not been able to discover why men can use symbols and apes cannot. So far as is known the only difference between the brain of man and the brain of an ape is a quantitative one: '. . . man has no new kinds of brain cells or brain cell connections,' (A.J. Carlson, *op. cit.*). Nor does man, as distinguished from other animals, possess a specialized 'symbol-mechanism.' The so-called speech areas of the brain should not be identified with symbolizing. These areas are associated with the muscles of the tongue, larynx, etc. But symbolizing is not dependent upon these organs. One may symbolize with the fingers, the feet, or with any part of the body that can be moved at will.[13]

To be sure, the symbolic faculty was brought into existence by the natural processes of organic evolution. And we may reasonably believe that the focal point, if not the locus, of this faculty is in the brain, especially the forebrain. Man's brain is much larger than that of an ape, both absolutely and relatively.[14] And the forebrain especially is large in man as compared with ape. Now in many situations we know that quantitative changes give rise to qualitative differences. Water is transformed into steam by additional quantities of heat. Additional power and speed lift the taxi-ing airplane from the ground and transform terrestrial locomotion into flight. The difference between wood alcohol and grain alcohol is a qualitative expression of a quantitative difference in the proportions of carbon and hydrogen. Thus a marked growth in size of the brain in man may have brought forth a *new kind* of function.

V

All culture (civilization) depends upon the symbol. It was the exercise of the symbolic faculty that brought culture into existence and it is the use of symbols that makes the perpetuation of culture possible. Without the symbol there would be no culture, and man would be merely an animal, not a human being.

Articulate speech is the most important form of symbolic expression. Remove speech from culture and what would remain? Let us see.

Without articulate speech we would have no *human* social organization. Families we might have, but this form of organization is not peculiar to man; it is not *per se, human*. But we would have no prohibitions of incest, no rules prescribing exogamy and endogamy, polygamy or monogamy. How could marriage with a cross cousin be prescribed, marriage with a parallel cousin proscribed, without articulate speech? How could rules which prohibit plural mates possessed simultaneously but permit them if possessed one at a time, exist without speech?

Without speech we would have no political, economic, ecclesiastic, or military organization; no codes of etiquette or ethics; no laws; no science, theology, or literature; no games or music, except on an ape level. Rituals and ceremonial paraphernalia would be meaningless without articulate speech. Indeed, without articulate speech we would be all but toolless: we would have only the occasional and insignificant use of the tool such as we find today among the higher apes, for it was articulate speech that transformed the nonprogressive tool-using of the ape into the progressive, cumulative tool-using of man, the human being.

In short, without symbolic communication in some form, we would have no culture. 'In the Word was the beginning' of culture—and its perpetuation also.[15]

To be sure, with all his culture man is still an animal and strives for the same ends that all other living creatures strive for: the preservation of the individual and the perpetuation of the race. In concrete terms these ends are food, shelter from the elements, defense from enemies, health, and offspring. The fact that man strives for these ends just as all other animals do has, no doubt, led many to declare that there is 'no fundamental difference between the behavior of man and of other creatures.' But man does differ, not in *ends* but in *means*. Man's means are cultural means: culture is simply the human animal's way of living. And, since these means, culture, are dependent upon a faculty possessed by man alone, the ability to use symbols, the difference between the behavior of man and of all other creatures is not merely great, but basic and fundamental.

VI

The behavior of man is of two distinct kinds: symbolic and nonsymbolic. Man yawns, stretches, coughs, scratches himself, cries out in pain, shrinks with fear, 'bristles' with anger, and so on. Non-symbolic behavior of this sort is not peculiar to man; he shares it not only with other primates but with many other animal species as well. But man communicates with his fellows with articulate speech, uses amulets, confesses sins, makes laws, observes codes of etiquette, explains his dreams, classifies his relatives in designated categories, and so on. This kind of behavior is unique; only man is capable of it; it is peculiar to man because it consists of, or is dependent upon, the use of symbols. The nonsymbolic behavior of man is the behavior of man the animal; the symbolic behavior is that of man the human being.[16] It is the symbol which has transformed man from a mere animal to a human animal.

As it was the symbol that made mankind human, so it is with each member of the race. A baby is not a human being so far as his behavior is concerned. Until the infant acquires speech there is nothing to distinguish his behavior qualitatively from that of a young ape.[17] The baby becomes a human being when and as he learns to use symbols. Only by means of speech can the baby enter and take part in the human affairs of mankind. The questions we asked previously may be repeated now. How is the growing child to know of such things as families, etiquette, morals, law, science, philosophy, religion, commerce, and so on, without speech? The rare cases of children who grew up without symbols because of deafness and blindness, such as those of Laura Bridgman, Helen Keller and Marie Heurtin, are instructive.[18] Until they 'got the idea' of symbolic communication they were not human beings, but animals, they did not participate in behavior which is peculiar to human beings. They were 'in' human society as dogs are, but they were not *of* human society. And, although the present writer is exceedingly skeptical of the reports of the so-called 'wolf-children,' 'feral men,' etc., we may note that they are described, almost without exception, as without speech, 'beastly,' and 'inhuman.'

VII

Summary. The natural processes of organic evolution brought into existence in man, and man alone, a new and distinctive ability: the ability to use symbols. The most important form of symbolic expression is articulate speech. Articulate speech means communication of ideas; communication means preservation — tradition — and preservation means accumulation and progress. The emergence of the organic faculty of symbol-using has resulted in the genesis of a new order of phenomena: a superorganic, or cultural, order. All civilizations are born of, and are perpetuated by, the use of symbols. A culture, or civilization, is but a particular kind of form (symbolic) which the biologic, life-perpetuating activities of a particular animal, man, assume.

Human behavior is symbolic behavior; if it is not symbolic, it is not human. The infant of the genus homo becomes a human being only as he is introduced into and participates in that supraorganic order of phenomena which is culture. And the key to this world and the means of participation in it is — the symbol.

NOTES AND REFERENCES

1. New York, 1936.
2. *Anthropology*, p. 39; New York, 1937.
3. We have a good example of this in the distinguished physiologist, Anton J. Carlson. After taking note of 'man's present achievements in science, in the arts (including oratory), in political and social institutions,' and noting 'at the same time the apparent paucity of such behavior in other animals,' he, as a common man 'is tempted to conclude that in these capacities, at least, man has a qualitative superiority over other mammals,' ('The Dynamics of Living Processes, in *The Nature of the World and Man*, H.H. Newman, ed., p. 477; Chicago, 1926). But, since, as a scientist, Professor Carlson cannot *define* this qualitative difference between man and other animals, since as a physiologist he cannot explain it, he refuses to admit it, — '. . . the physiologist does not accept the great development of articulate speech in man as something qualitatively new; . . .' (p. 478) — and suggests helplessly that some day we may find some new 'building stone,' an 'additional lipoid, phosphatid, or potassium ion,' in the human brain which will explain it, and concludes by saying that the difference between the mind of man and that of non-man is 'probably only one of degree,' (*op. cit.*, pp. 478-79).
4. 'Do you bite your thumb at us, sir?' — *Romeo and Juliet*, Act I, Sc. 1.
5. 'Now since sounds have no natural connection with our ideas, but have all their signification from the arbitrary imposition of men . . .,' John Locke, *Essay Concerning the Human Understanding*, Bk. III, ch. 9.
   'When *I* use . . . [a] word, it means just what I choose it to mean,' said Humpty Dumpty to Alice (*Through the Looking Glass*).
6. This statement is valid regardless of our theory of experiencing. Even the exponents of 'Extra-Sensory Perception,' who have challenged Locke's dictum that 'the knowledge of the existence of any other thing [besides ourselves and God] we can have only by sensation,' (Bk. 4, ch. 11, *Essay Concerning the Human Understanding*,) have been obliged to work with physical rather than ethereal forms.
7. A *sign* is a physical form whose function is to indicate some other thing — object, quality, or event. The meaning of a sign may be intrinsic, inseparable from its physical form and nature, as in the case of the height of a column of mercury as an indication of temperature; or, it may be merely identified with its physical form, as in the case of a hurricane signal displayed by a weather bureau. But in either case, the meaning of the sign is perceived with the senses.
8. 'Surprising as it may seem, it was very clear during the first few months that the ape was considerably superior to the child in responding to

human words,' W.N. and L.A. Kellogg, *The Ape and the Child*, (New York, 1933).
9. Professor Linton speaks of 'the faintest foreshadowings of language . . . at the animal level,' (*op. cit.*, p. 74). But precisely what these 'faintest foreshadowings' are he does not say.
10. What we have to say here would of course, apply equally well to gestures (e.g., the 'sign of the cross,' a salute), a color, a material object, etc.
11. Like a word, the value of a vase may be perceived by the senses or imperceptible to them depending upon the context in which it is regarded. In an esthetic context its value is perceived with the senses. In the commercial context this is impossible; we must be *told* its value—in terms of price.
12. Cf. 'A Neurologist Makes Up His Mind,' by C. Judson Herrick, *Scientific Monthly*, August, 1939. Professor Herrick is a distinguished one of a not too large number of scientists who are interested in the structural basis of symbol using.
13. The misconception that speech is dependent upon the so-called (but miscalled) organs of speech, and, furthermore, that man alone has organs suitable for speech, is not uncommon even today. Thus Professor L.L. Bernard lists 'The fourth great organic asset of man is his vocal apparatus, also characteristic of him alone,' (*Introduction to Sociology*, J. Davis and H.E. Barnes, eds., p. 399; New York, 1927).

The great apes have the mechanism necessary for the production of articulate sounds: 'It seemingly is well established that the motor mechanism of voice in this ape [chimpanzee] is adequate not only to the production of a considerable variety of sounds, but also to definite articulations similar to those of man,' R.M. and A.W. Yerkes, *The Great Apes*, p. 301 (New Haven, 1929). Also: 'All of the anthropoid apes are vocally and muscularly equipped so that they could have an articulate language if they possessed the requisite intelligence,' E.A. Hooton, *Up From the Ape*, p. 167 (New York, 1931).

Furthermore, the mere production of articulate sounds would not be symbolizing any more than the mere 'understanding of words and sentences' (Darwin) is. John Locke made this clear two and a half centuries ago: 'Man, therefore had by nature his organs so fashioned, as to be *fit to frame articulate sounds*, which we call words. But this was not enough to produce language; for parrots, and several other birds, will be taught to make articulate sounds distinct enough, which yet, by no means, are capable of language. Besides articulate sounds, therefore, it was further necessary, that he should be *able to use these sounds as signs of internal conceptions;* and to make them stand as marks for the ideas within his own mind, whereby they might be made known to others . . . ,' Book III, Ch. 1, Secs. 2, 3, *Essay Concerning the Human Understanding*.

And J.F. Blumenbach, *a century later, declared in his On the Natural Variety of Mankind*, 'That speech is the work of reason alone, appears from this, that other animals, although they have nearly the same organs of voice as man, are entirely destitute of it,' (quoted by R.M. and A.W. Yerkes, *op. cit.*, p. 23).

14. Man's brain is about two and one-half times as large as that of a gorilla. 'The human brain is about 1/50 of the entire body weight, while that of a gorilla varies from 1/150 to 1/200 part of that weight,' (Hooton, *op. cit.*, p. 153).
15. 'On the whole, however, it would seem that language and culture rest, in a way which is not fully understood, on the same set of faculties . . .,' A.L. Kroeber, *Anthropology*, p. 108, (New York, 1923).
    It is hoped that this essay will make this matter more 'fully understood.'
16. It is for this reason that observations and experiments with apes, rats, etc., can tell us nothing about human behavior. They can tell us how ape-like or rat-like man is, but they throw no light upon human behavior because the behavior of apes, rats, etc., is nonsymbolic.
    The title of the late George A. Dorsey's best seller, *Why We Behave Like Human Beings*, was misleading for the same reason. This interesting book told us much about vertebrate, mammalian, primate, and even man-animal behavior, but virtually nothing about symbolic, i.e., human, behavior. But we are glad to add, in justice to Dorsey, that his chapter on the function of speech in culture, (Ch. II) in *Man's Own Show: Civilization* (New York, 1931), is probably the best discussion of this subject that we know of in anthropological literature.
17. In their fascinating account of their experiment with a baby chimpanzee, kept for nine months in their home and treated as their infant son was treated, Professor and Mrs. Kellogg speak of the 'humanization' of the little ape: 'She may thus be said to have become "more humanized" than the human subject . . .' (p. 315).
    This is misleading. What the experiment showed so strikingly was *how like an ape* a child of homo sapiens is *before he learns to talk*. The boy even employed the ape's 'food bark'! The experiment also demonstrated the ape's utter inability to learn to talk, which means an inability to become humanized at all.
18. The reader will find a resume of the more significant facts of these cases in W.I. Thomas, *Primitive Behavior*, pp. 50-54, 776-777 (New York, 1937).

From the Summer 1944 Et cetera.

THE THREAT OF CLARITY
Garrett Hardin

HE WHO SPEAKS IN favor of unclarity raises a justifiable suspicion that he merely seeks to attract attention; or worse, that he is promoting a subtle form of anti-intellectualism. To be accused of either is a serious matter, but every now and then, I think, someone must run the risk in hope of sensitizing us once more to the ever-present dangers of language. Language should periodically be put on trial, and when it is, even its accepted virtues, *e.g.*, clarity, must be doubted. Those who judge must listen to a devil's advocate. This is the role I play here in pointing out the dangers of clarity—or, if you wish, of "clarity."

Language subserves two functions: communication and thinking. As regards the first, it is perhaps not possible usefully to doubt the desirability of clarity. Of course, there is the superficial unclarity of tact, of poetry and parable, and of the replies of a skilled psychiatrist—but all these art forms can, from a more profound standpoint, be defended as real (though subtle) kinds of clarity in communication.

It is only when we come to consider language in its role *in thinking* that we begin to see a sense in which it is doubtful if clarity is always desirable. Ours is a language-limited world. We not only speak our language: we think in it, as a fish lives in water. For the most part we see the world as our language tells us to. Each of the many languages has its peculiar limitations which shut out certain aspects or views of reality to those who speak but one language. He who "masters" but one

---

Garrett Hardin teaches in the Department of Biological Sciences, University of California, Santa Barbara. This article originally appeared in *The American Journal of Psychiatry* (November, 1957) and is reprinted by permission. Dr. Hardin is the author of *Nature and Man's Fate* (1959) and has previously contributed to *Et cetera*.

language may thereby be mastered by it. To be completely "at home" in a language is to be structured to fit one particular and limited world of thought.

A few examples of the coupling of words to perception may be useful. Eskimos have separate words for falling snow, snow-on-the-ground, wind-driven-snow, snow-packed-into-ice, etc.; we make do with one word—*snow*.[1] Half a world away, Argentine gauchos have names to distinguish some 200 different color-patterns in horses.[2] The reason for diversity is obvious in both cases: interest dictated by culture. But distinctions, once made, "feed back" into the mind and cause it to perceive as much or as little variety in the world as language has words for. The gaucho who distinguishes 200 colors of horses lumps the vegetable world into four "species": *pasto* or fodder, *paja* or bedding straw, *cardo* or woody material; and *yuyos* for all other plants, including lilies, roses and cabbages. (The class of *yuyos* reminds us of the grab-bag group *Chaos*, which Linnaeus, the father of taxonomy, resorted to when he despaired of completing his analysis of the living world.) It would be going too far to say that the gauchos can see only four kinds of plants, but undoubtedly their perceptual world is impoverished by their linguistic one. Experimental evidence for this principle has been obtained by Lenneberg, who has found that an English-speaking person can, in a non-verbal test, more easily identify those colors that have recognized names in English than he can the distinguishable hues that have no names.[3]

Cautiously interpreted, the language of another people is a clue to their psychology. Rabbi Blau has remarked how curious it is:

> that the Hebrew language, though impoverished in many respects has preserved [in Leviticus XXI and in both *Tochechoth*] so many words that describe unsightly malformations and loathsome diseases. We lack classic Hebrew terms for many of the beautiful sights and sounds of this world — for colors, flowers, trees, birds — but we do not seem to be wanting in terms that bring before us the seamy side of life, that echo the groans of the sufferers, that reflect the gloom of darkened lives. One is reminded of those old-fashioned books on theology that contained nine chapters on hell and only one chapter on heaven.[4]

There are many chances for error, of course, in deducing a people's psychology from their language, as is suggested by the following puzzle. The two Greek words *chloros* and *achros* both have dictionary translations of "yellow." But usage indicates that the former sometimes means yellowish green, sometimes grayish brown; and the latter sometimes means greenish yellow, and at other times red (of all things).[5] What's going on here? It is hard to believe that the words refer only to color, but attempts to include intensity or luster in their meanings have only made the snarl worse. In desperation, one linguist has suggested that all the old Greeks must have been color-blind!

Does perception produce language, or language produce perception? This question is clearly in a class with, "Which came first, the chicken or the egg?" and there is no need to take sides. Whatever the origin of linguistic distinctions, once made they are part of a cybernetic system of mutual support of language and perception.[6] Call it a vicious circle, if you will. But it is not unbreakable: new cultural demands may force a finer analysis. Thus, in our own part of the world, we observe ski enthusiasts enlarging the language about snow to make it as finely discriminating as the Eskimos'. Regarding objective things like snow and horses and trees we need not concern ourselves overmuch with the limitations of a particular vocabulary, for it will enlarge when there is a cultural need for it to do so.

It is words of another sort that give us trouble — the words that stand for large classes of things, or for abstractions or difficult concepts. Here the couplings of words and reality is often excruciatingly *loose*. "What is intelligence?" "What is the cause of insanity?" "How can we control the unconscious?" Who has not winced at such questions? How can one possibly answer them? Yet, grammatically speaking, they look so simple, so clear! What is wrong?

The simplest objection to them is that each key word covers a confused multitude of concepts or things. Intelligence, for example, is a grab-bag term including at least four — and possibly nine or more — different abilities.[7] "The unconscious" is capable of at least sixteen different interpretations.[8] And "insanity" — who is so mad as to attempt to catalog its complexity? But the real problem posed by such words is far deeper than appears at first.

It must not be supposed that an attempt to find out what is behind such "big" words as "intelligence" and the "unconscious" will be warmly welcomed. These words, besides having the support of a long tradition, play an important role in the sociology of knowledge: they stop inquiry where it is most painful and difficult (and, it must be admitted, most likely to fail). When we say that "Intelligence solves our problems," or "The mind resists change," we think we have explained something. But an honest examination convinces us that we have "explained" only by resort to words whose meaning is so vague that they can "explain" almost anything. A word which acts as an explain-all has been called a *panchestron*, a word coined on the analogy of panacea, and a cure-all.[9] The history of human thought is littered with discarded panchresta: the many personal and omnipotent gods, the soul, and the "humours" of medieval medicine, for example. Bergson created an *élan vital* to explain the properties of living things; Driesch conceived an *entelechy* to explain the mysteries of embryology. "Mind," "instinct," and "love," though they may have defensible denotations, are certainly often used panchrestically. The literature of psychoanalysis is riddled with explain-alls: a single (and by no means exceptional) quotation should suffice: "The ego becomes suspicious: it proceeds to invade the territory of the id."[10]

If the psychology of language is to promote communication and thinking, the inhibition of these functions may be regarded as part of language's pathology. Always, of course, in a deep sense, pathology is as "normal" as the normal physiology in which it has its roots. "Every language," said the linguist Benjamin Lee Whorf, "incorporates certain points of view and certain patterned resistances to widely divergent points of view,"[11] and it is these points of view that determine both the strengths and the weaknesses of each language. As in so much of biology, discovery is greatly aided by comparative study. Experience has shown that the comparison of Indo-European languages among themselves has yielded only modest increments of knowledge: the greatest gain has been made when our languages have been compared with strikingly different tongues, for example with the many Indian dialects of North America, a program of study in which Sapir[12] and Whorf have been leaders.

The comparative study of two languages should throw as much light on the strengths and weaknesses of one as on the other — if carried out by a really neutral observer. In fact, however, the very few observers who have been equipped for this difficult work have been Indo-Europeans, and the most they have been able to do is lay bare the structure of *our* kind of language, using the exotic language as a probe. The reciprocal knowledge, desirable as it would be to have, is scarcely available. It is for this reason that only the characteristic weaknesses of Indo-European will be pointed out in the paragraphs to follow. The one-sided presentation does not stem from a Rousseau-like belief in the "noble savage." The savage has his troubles, too, but we should consider ourselves lucky enough if we come to understand our own.

We can begin with a very simple example, the analysis of which shows that our language is more mysterious than we ordinarily realize. Consider the declarative sentence, "*It rains.*" What is the *it* that rains? Well, *rain* rains . . . but that is an odd sentence, isn't it? "Rain" must be the implied antecedent of "it," but we never, in ordinary conversation, say "Rain rains"; always we assert the predicate of some vague and unspecified subject "it." We also say "It thunders," and we may say "It lightnings." Why? As Whorf has pointed out, we are compelled to make such sentences because of an over-riding metaphysical assumption of the Indo-European languages that everything in the world has two poles — an actor pole and an action pole, and that one cannot exist without the other, any more than a magnet can have a north pole only. The actor we represent by the subject of the sentence; the action by the verb. Always there must be both, so when we have trouble finding the actor for such processes as raining, thundering, and flashing (of lightning) we invent a subject called "it" to stand as actor. We would feel uneasy just saying "Rains!" or "Thunders!" or "Flashes!"

Other peoples feel otherwise. Hopi Indians, confronted with the same objective realities, use only the verbs without subjects, and feel quite secure. The metaphysics of their language is different and permits — even insists — that they use verbs-without-subjects to represent the events we denote by the nouns *lightning*, *wave*, *flame*, *meteor*, *puff of smoke*, and *pulsation*. The decision to invoke the noun category or the verb category in giving name to fact is as unconscious in the one language as in the other. As Emile Meyerson has said, *"L'homme fait de la métaphysique comme il respire, sans le vouloir et surtout sans s'en douter la plupart du temps."*[13] Comparative linguistic study makes it immensely easier for us to discover the unconscious metaphysic of our language and to make allowance for it.

Failure to appreciate the role of the structure of the Indo-European languages in affecting perception has repeatedly led western science into error. The "luminiferous ether" of classical physics was created for the express purpose of standing as a subject of the verb "to wave." When the Michelson-Morley experiment and Einstein's analysis finally showed the substantive ether had to be abandoned, the decision was a traumatic one. Similarly, in biology, the substantive "protoplasm" was created to stand as the subject of such verbs as "to metabolize." Led by F.G. Hopkins, biologists are now abandoning the substantive as a scientific concept.[14]

The structure of our language has probably played an important role in determining the order in which we have uncovered natural phenomena. Compare, for example, the ease with which we discovered and accepted the germ theory of disease with the difficulty encountered by the vitamin theory of nutrition. The former advance was made in a few decades in the latter half of the 19th century. Vitamins, by contrast, had to be discovered and rediscovered repeatedly, by Hawkins (1593), Lancaster (1601), Woodall (1639), Lind (1753), and Captain Hook (1772), among others, and yet at no time was the knowledge stabilized until Hopkins clearly defined the phenomenon (1906) and Funk named it (1912). Why was a vitamin so hard to accept and a disease germ so easy? Was the reason not, at least in part, because the latter fitted in with the metaphysic of Indo-European so much more easily than the former? We already had sentences of this sort, "A spirit makes him sick," in which we had only to substitute a new actor, *e.g.*, *Eberthella typhosa*, to create a new doctrine. In contrast, the sentence "What he doesn't eat makes him sick," failed to make sense to men who spoke, and thought, Indo-European. Biochemists had to find a substance to name, and had to create the substantive "vitamin" to stand as actor in a new sort of sentence, before the new idea could carry conviction. Even today, we still backslide frequently and say, "He has an avitaminosis," though how one can *have* a lack of something is most mysterious. Such sentences are just part of the pathology of our language.

The comparative historical study of the germ theory and the vitamin theory leads us to realize that there are at least two different kinds of analysis involved in scientific advance. The first kind we may speak of as the analysis by simple subdivision. The type question may be given in symbolic form: "Is all fruit, fruit — or are there apples and oranges?" Once the question is asked, success in finding an answer is almost assured. When one suspects diversity, he usually finds it. Thus the skier discovers many kinds of snow and the physician many kinds of fever. The "typhus" fever of two hundred years ago was found to be differentiable into two diseases — typhus and typhoid. Malaria gave way to malarias, and unitary hemophilia to many different hemophilias. Similarly, such classical psychiatric entities as schizophrenia must yield to *subdivisive analysis*. The work is not easy, but we always know what it is that we are trying to do.

The second type of analysis is far more difficult, for it involves changes in the categories of thought. We may call it *categorical analysis*. The type question takes this symbolic form: "Is it an apple or an orange that I'm dealing with — or is it perhaps the singing of a bird?" So stated, it sounds ridiculous; but inability to ask such an odd-sounding question has repeatedly delayed the progress of science. Consider "heat," for example. From the time of the ancient Greeks down to, and including, the work of Robert Boyle, the facts connected with heat were terribly confused because "heat" was assigned to the wrong category—that of the substantives. Being a substance, it should have weight, of course; convinced of this, a British physician, George Fordyce, found that heat did indeed have weight.[15] The first experiments of Count Rumford seemed to confirm this belief. But Rumford was convinced that the wrong category of thought was being employed in calorimetric studies, and so he went to a great deal of trouble to look for experimental errors, which he found and corrected, thus arriving at the correct conclusion that heat, like the singing of a bird, is an activity, a process—and not a substance or object, like apples or oranges. Its category has rather more to do with verbs than with nouns.

Subdivisive analysis is (comparatively) easy. Categorical analysis is always difficult. There are no rules for it. It requires insight and courage (or insanity) to slash away the unconscious strictures of language. Such action may generate an almost unbearable load of insecurity in the analyzer. Traditional language always *seems* clear. There seems to be great clarity in such sentences as these: *Heat flows. Life left him. He is possessed of a devil. He has a disease. He has a neurosis.* But, for all their apparent clarity, they are surely all wrong. Their categories are wrong. All of them assert false substantives, when the discussion should be couched in terms of processes.

It is not easy to abandon false language, nor need it always be completely abandoned when it is traditional. There may be no words, or only awkward language, for correct ideas that are new, and we cannot as human beings cut ourselves off from the support of our fellow men while we grope for new speech. As Thomas Mann said, "The word, even the most contradictory word, preserves contact—it is silence that isolates."[16] We cannot let linguistic perfectionism isolate us while we indulge in analysis. In the meantime, we must speak, even though we recognize that our idiom is, in some sense, false. So we say, "The sun sets" and "Heat flows," though we know these are false statements. So also may we continue to say, "He has an avitaminosis," or "She has a neurosis," though we know these statements are also false. For the sake of the present we must continue to speak; but for the sake of the future we must continue to analyze our language. And analysis, as Wittgenstein has said, is "the battle against the bewitchment of our intelligence by means of language."[17] This battle is not part of a push-button war waged from afar. We are in the midst of this battle as we are in the midst of life itself, using as a weapon against language, language itself. There is no other.

NOTES AND REFERENCES

1. Benjamin Lee Whorf, *Language, Thought and Reality* (New York: Wiley, 1956), p. 216.
2. Karl Vossler, *Volksprachen und Weltersprachen; Welt und Wort* (1946). Taken from Basilius. (See n. 5.)
3. Eric H. Lenneberg, *Language*, XXIX (1953), 46.
4. Rabbi Joel Blau, "The Defective in Jewish Law and Literature," *Jewish Eugenics and Other Essays* by Rabbi Max Reichler (New York: Bloch, 1916).
5. H Basilius, *Word*, VIII (1952), 95.
6. L. von Bertalanffy, *Philosophy of Science*, XXII (1955), 243.
7. Ward C. Halstead, *Brain and Intelligence* (Chicago: University of Chicago Press, 1947).
8. James C. Miller, *Unconsciousness* (New York: Wiley, 1942).
9. Garrett Hardin, *Science Monthly*, LXXXII (1956), 112.
10. This sentence is shortened, but not altered in sense, from Anna Freud, *The Ego and the Mechanisms of Defence* (New York: International Universities Press, 1946), p. 8.
11. Benjamin Lee Whorf, *op. cit.*, p. 247.
12. Edward Sapir, *Selected Writings of Edward Sapir in Language, Culture and Personality*, ed. D.C. Mandelbaum (Berkeley: University of California Press, 1949).
13. "Man makes metaphysics just as he breathes, without willing it and above all without doubting it most of the time." Quoted in J.H. Woodger, *Biological Principles* (London: Routledge and Kegan Paul, 1929), p. 47.
14. J. Needham (ed.), *Hopkins and Biochemistry* (Cambridge, England: W. Heffler, 1949).
15. Duane Roller, *The Early Development of the Concepts of Temperature and Heat* (Cambridge, Mass.: Harvard University Press, 1950), p. 49.
16. Thomas Mann, *The Magic Mountain* (New York: Knopf, 1927), Ch. VI.
17. Ludwig Wittgenstein, *Philosophical Investigations* (Oxford: Blackwell, 1953), p. 47.

From the Fall 1960 Et cetera.

II.
THE CONTRIBUTION OF GENERAL SEMANTICS

GENERAL SEMANTICS

Charlotte S. Read

GENERAL SEMANTICS IS A general theory of evaluation based on modern scientific knowledge and postulates. It was formulated by Alfred Korzybski (1879-1950) in his book, *Science and Sanity: An Introduction to Non-aristotelian Systems and General Semantics*, in 1933.[1]

The system, of which general semantics is the *modus operandi*, was called "non-aristotelian," as it includes and goes beyond the traditional "aristotelian." It does not fall within linguistics, but is an overarching system to which linguistics and other scientific, mathematical, etc., fields contribute. It represents a methodological synthesis of intellectual trends in the Western world that evolved during the first quarter of the twentieth century and earlier. It has both theoretical and practical aspects. As a methodology, general semantics offers means whereby the new outlooks may be learned, applied, and taught. In its concern with evaluation and behavior, it aims to bring achievements and growth in social areas into accord with those in scientific fields, and to unify the exact sciences and general human orientations methodologically. The name is often confused with "semantics," from which it differs in many respects.

Origins of General Semantics

The theory which was developed into "general semantics" originated in Korzybski's new definition of *man* as a *time-*

Charlotte S. Read is the Literary Executor of the Alfred Korzybski Estate and Director Emeritus, Institute of General Semantics. This article was reprinted from *The Encyclopedia of Library and Information Science*, Vol. 9, 1973, Marcel Dekker, Inc., New York.

binding class of life, as set forth in 1921 in his *Manhood of Humanity: The Science and Art of Human Engineering*.[2] In considering the forms of life, and differentiating men, animals, and plants, he made the following classifications on the basis of function: plants are called "chemistry-binding" or "energy-binding"; they have the ability to transform energy from the sun into organic chemical energy. Animals are called "space-binding"; they are able to move about from one place to another. Humans are called "time-binding." Together with the abilities of plants and animals, they also have the capacity to use the accumulated achievements inherited from past generations, to build upon them, and pass them on to the next generation. This unique time-binding capacity gives to man a different living dimension.

According to this theory, there are two widely different laws of progress; they represent different rates of growth. Knowledge in scientific and technological fields has advanced in a rapidly increasing geometrical progression, while developments in social areas have lagged behind, hampered by traditions and habits of bygone days. The great gap in rates of change has created imbalances which result periodically in social cataclysms.

In following through to the practical consequences of the time-binding theory, it became apparent that the chief means through which men have been able to transmit to each other, and from one generation to another, has been through the use of language and other symbolic forms of representation. Scientists, engineers, etc., who have been able to achieve remarkably predictable results, have used a special, rigorous language called *mathematics*, which is similar in structure to the processes they deal with. Our ordinary language, inherited from past generations, was found on investigation not to be similar in structure to the facts of science and life as known today.

Korzybski was particularly influenced by Cassius Jackson Keyser and his work in mathematical philosophy. Among Keyser's formulations was the principle of "fate and freedom": we have the freedom (in accord with the laws of thought) to choose our assumptions, but once chosen, the consequences follow with a "logical fate." Since we are usually not aware of our silent assumptions hidden in the structure and undefined terms of our language, and underlying our actions, we must investigate our assumptions. We must question whether they are based on facts as we understand them.

Among others whose work especially influenced Korzybski's early formulations were Alfred North Whitehead, Bertrand Russell, Henri Poincaré, and Albert Einstein. He sought to show what the import of their revolutionary theories was for our everyday lives. All our doctrines, and our education, would have to be revised, he concluded, in accordance with the new outlooks.

Besides the developments in mathematics, mathematical logic and foundations, physics, etc., the ground-breaking work of the early twentieth century in biology, neurology, psychology, psychiatry, colloidal chemistry, anthropology, etc., was also drawn upon. The underlying structural assumptions of these changing outlooks were seen to be aspects of one larger system embracing the new trends. This more inclusive system was formulated as a methodological integration, and was called "non-aristotelian" (not "anti-aristotelian").

The preceding euclidean, newtonian, and aristotelian systems which have influenced Western civilizations for centuries had a structurally interrelated world view. The non-euclidean and non-newtonian (einsteinian) systems already formulated were expressions of the altered perspectives that were emerging. The three new systems were found also to have an interdependent underlying structure and metaphysics. This new trilogy — non-euclidean, non-newtonian, and non-aristotelian — was *more general* than the old, and included the former ones as special cases.

A rough formulation of what was later to be called "general semantics" was published in 1924 under the title *Time-Binding: The General Theory*, with a further elaboration in 1926. In *Science and Sanity*, published in 1933, the general theory was presented in detail. For the second edition (1941) a 50-page new introduction was written including new material.

History of the Term "General Semantics"

Korzybski had decided in 1931 to call his work "general semantics." His reasons for selecting this name were given in the "Author's Note" in *Selections From Science and Sanity*, 1948,[3] as follows:

> The term "General Semantics" seemed most appropriate to me because of the derivation from the Greek *semainein*, "to mean," "to signify." A theory of evaluation seemed to follow naturally in an evolutionary sense from 1) "meaning" to 2) "signification" to 3) *evaluation, if we take into account the individual*, not divorcing him from his reactions, nor from his *neuro*-linguistic and *neuro*-semantic environments. Thus we allocate him in a *plenum* of some values, no matter what, and a *plenum* of language, which may be used to inform, or misinform by *commission* and/or *omission*, deceiving the individual himself and/or others. With such problems, without exception, the individual has to cope to be human at all. That's what I learned from the theory of time-binding and what I tried to convey to others through General Semantics and psycho-biological non-aristotelian considerations.

Premises and Principles of the Theory

The following assumptions are basic to general semantics: the dynamic, changing, nonadditive, nonlinear, process-character of the universe. Its orientations are holistic, infinite-valued, rational functional, flexible, etc. These may be contrasted with static, additive, linear, two-valued orientations, with predominantly subject-predicate verbal structures.

For example, the addition of one child in a family is not a simple "additive" event, but affects the entire family life and relationships. Two-valued polarizations in terms of "either-or" tend to freeze attitudes rigidly, rather than leave them flexible with many-valued possibilities.

"Abstracting" as a Key Term

The relational orientations mentioned were a part of the new world-view evolving in Western civilization. A distinguishing characteristic of general semantics is its construction in terms of orders of abstractions. The term "abstracting" refers to a general activity of all living protoplasm. On neurological levels, the nervous system *abstracts* (selects, omits, separates, summarizes, the summarizing and integrating being special aspects), etc.

From the multiplicity of ongoing processes, we abstract what we perceive through our "senses" (not to be separated from "mind"). These may be called "abstractions of lower orders." On another, higher, level we may *name* or *describe* what we see, hear, feel, etc. We may have indefinitely many higher orders of abstractions on verbal levels in the form of generalization, inferences, hypothesis, etc.

These higher orders are projected onto the submicroscopic processes going on around us, maintaining the "circularity of human knowledge" and giving the possibility of continuous feedback. It is necessary to check our beliefs, assumptions, or opinions in the light of the "facts," different experiences, or new knowledge, so that our evaluations will not be impaired or out-of-date. For example, if we rigidly cling to a stereotype learned years ago, it will be imposed on changing conditions and lead to misevaluations, conflicts, etc.

Consciousness of abstracting is central to general semantics theory, and involves the continuing awareness that at different neurological levels of our functioning we omit some factors, select others, that we summarize and generalize in a new form on higher orders. Korzybski's model, called the "Structural Differential," shows this stratification into different orders. It is used as a training model to incorporate this awareness into one's everyday reactions and for the analysis of any problem.

Humans, unlike animals, are not only able to abstract on indefinitely many higher orders in their generalizing, inferring, etc., but can know that they do so, can build theories and test them in practice, write books, can "think about thinking," etc. Generalizations of higher orders are acknowledged to have important benefits for economy and simplicity in building theories, and for the transmission of knowledge. They may also be dangerous if not checked with "facts" or related to consequences. Inferential knowledge, when consciously accepted as inferential, forms the hypothetical knowledge of modern science and ceases to be a dogma. The "as if" character of our knowledge can be applied to our ordinary living. Consciousness of our processes of abstracting and projecting is connected with the basic premises of general semantics.

General Semantics Premises

Using an analogy of relations between a map and the territory, the premises may be stated as:
> First. A map *is not* the territory.
> Second. A map does *not* represent *all* of a territory.
> Third. A map is *self-reflexive* in the sense that an "ideal" map would include a map of the map, etc., indefinitely, and the map would include the map-maker.

Applied to daily life and language:
> First. A word *is not* what it represents.
> Second. A word (or a statement) does *not* represent *all* of the "facts," etc.
> Third. Language is *self-reflexive* in the sense that in language we can speak *about* language.

The third premise turned out to be an application to everyday life of Bertrand Russell's theory of mathematical types. In developing his system Korzybski could not accept the mathematical theory by which Russell attempted to solve self-contradictions in the foundations of mathematics. But he found later that the principles of different orders of abstractions, multiordinality of terms, second-order reactions, etc., in effect generalized Russell's theory of mathematical types.

The link between the map and territory, the verbal and nonverbal, is seen on the basis of structural relationships. The dynamic process-world inferred by modern science is ever-changing, continuously in flux. Language and other symbolic forms are static in effect. How can the nonverbal and verbal forms become "similar in structure"? Here Korzybski used techniques derived from physico-mathematical methods, where change, motion, space-time, etc., are dealt with. By the use of a few simple devices, called *extensional devices*, the structure of language could be modified in such a way as to take into account process, duration of time, uniqueness, specificity, generality, environmental factors, holistic principles, etc.

Extensional Devices

Indexes. The use of a numerical subscript, showing the uniqueness of every person or event, indicating differences as well as similarities, as in: car_1, car_2, car_3, etc., $child_1$, $child_2$, $child_3$, etc., communication $medium_{1,2,3}$ n . . . (radio, television, movie, . . .).

Chain-indexes. The use of two or more subscripts to indicate multiple cause-effects, different conditions, or environmental factors. Thus $Smith_{1_1}$ [$Smith_{1-1}$] feeling ill as different from $Smith_{1_2}$ [or $Smith_{1-2}$] *feeling well; $book_{1_2}$ in a dry attic as different from $book_{1_2}$ in a damp cellar.*

Dates. Specifying a date, as a reminder of changes over a period of time. For example, $Communism^{1918}$ as different from $Communism^{1971}$.

The indexes and dates are not necessarily written or spoken, but rather are usually used silently, as a part of one's orientation in each situation.

Et cetera (etc.) to indicate that any statement can *not* cover *all* the characteristics of a situation, reminding one of the second premise. This aims to eliminate dogmatic "period-and-stop" attitudes and to develop flexibility and openness.

Hyphens. The use of hyphens brings to awareness the interconnectedness of the complexities in this world and indicates their inseparability. For example, "space-time," "psychosomatic," "organism-as-a-whole-in-an-environment."

Quotes. These serve as reminders that a term is not to be trusted, as it may violate scientific postulates or lead to metaphysical speculations, and that the reader may do well to take this into account in his interpretation. For example, "reality," "truth," etc.

Although the use of these devices appears simple and obvious, in practice it has not been found easy for adults, as it requires a change of orientation to a more "extensional" one.

The principle of *nonidentity* is at the basis of the system, and is connected with consciousness of abstracting, extensional devices, awareness of differences as well as similarities, etc. This states the denial of any existing identities whatsoever and posits the uniqueness of each individual and each event. "Identity" is used in this context as "absolute sameness in all aspects." Examples of false-to-facts identifications would be: acting on an inferential statement as if it were a factual one, responding to a person as if he were another person he somewhat resembles (father, mother, teacher), disregarding differences. Some identifications may be harmless, some disastrous in their consequences.

The involvement of the nervous system in all our reactions, including linguistic, was stressed by terms such as "neurolinguistic," and "neurosemantic." Korzybski brought out the deep psychological significance of mathematics as a form of human behavior (e.g., notions of "infinity," "invariance," "the semantics of the Einstein theory," "the psychological importance of the theory of aggregates and the theory of groups," etc.), and sought to bring neurologists and mathematicians closer together in understanding.

Applications and Teaching

Because of the generality of the theory, applications have ranged widely throughout almost every field, in professional or personal life. Far from regarding it as a panacea, those who work in general semantics are aware, as Korzybski was, that results can be expected only to the extent that it is acted upon, not only talked about. Usually, when it has been applied, the consequences have been found to be beneficial. The old dichotomies such as "intellect" and "emotion," "thinking" and "feeling," "body" and "mind" have given way in the new orientations, and the interrelationships of formerly separated categories are becoming more recognized.

Application of extensional methods to medicine has shown the old division of "organic" and "functional" diseases, as well as other dichotomies, to be no longer tenable. The methods have been found helpful as an aid to psychotherapy and in the alleviation of combat exhaustion on the battlefields. They have been applied to the practice of law, in business and industrial problems of management and efficiency, and in the handling of communication barriers; in hospitals, in prisons, and in home life, etc., to mention a few of the areas. Chiefly, however, the educational aspect has been emphasized.

It has been demonstrated that general semantics can be effectively taught to young children, and that it can result in significant changes in thinking quality which do not ordinarily accrue to the same degree from the regular curriculum, a school psychologist has reported.[1] It has also been found to increase some factors of creativity in children.

Besides elementary education, it is being taught at high school, college, and graduate levels, in adult education, and in the U.S. Army. Several thousands of persons have attended seminars in France since 1962.

In many courses the principles are incorporated in the presentations of other subjects, for example, in speech (in studies of communication processes, speech behavior, stuttering, etc.), in English composition, literary criticism, mathematics, physics, journalism, psychology, etc. It is included in training courses for teachers of many subjects, and for school psychologists. In some sixth grade science classes children are learning epistemological issues through general semantics principles. Usually children are enthusiastic about such an approach, which helps them to see the relevance of their school subjects to their everyday living.

The teaching of general semantics is highly individual, and is dependent on the teacher's understanding and skill. There is as yet no formal accreditation for teachers. It ranges from distorted dilutions to brilliant and imaginative insights. The teaching must, to be successful, be more intellectually competent — it seeks to bring about new outlooks and ways of evaluating. The Institute of General Semantics is the center for teaching and for the training of teachers, and offers seminar-work-shops during the summer or at other specified dates. At such seminars, nonverbal experiencing, sensory awareness, and various visual aids and experiments are a part of the training, besides the theory. On the premise that evaluations involve all aspects of living — organismal, electrochemical, muscular, perceptual, feeling, etc., as well as verbal — the training takes these into account.

Korzybski had anticipated modifications of general semantics, or changes in emphases, and the building of new, perhaps more inclusive, systems as our knowledge increased. This process itself would be an example of "time-binding."

NOTES AND REFERENCES

1. Alfred Korzybski, *Science and Sanity: An Introduction to Non-aristotelian Systems and General Semantics*, 1st ed., 1933; 4th ed., 1958, International Non-aristotelian Library Publishing Co., Lakeville, Connecticut. Distributed by Institute of General Semantics.
2. Alfred Korzybski, *Manhood of Humanity*, 1st ed., 1921; 2nd ed., 1950, International Non-aristotelian Library Publishing Co., Lakeville, Connecticut. Distributed by Institute of General Semantics.
3. Alfred Korzybski, *Selections from Science and Sanity*, International Non-aristotelian Library Publishing Co., Lakeville, Connecticut, 1948. Distributed by Institute of General Semantics.
4. Rachel M. Lauer, "Effects of a General Semantics Course Upon Some Fifth Grade Children," *General Semantics Bull.*, Nos. 30 and 31, 106-112 (1963/64).

From the Fall 1975 Et cetera.

GENERAL SEMANTICS₁₉₅₂

Irving J. Lee

I ONCE HAD SOME LESSONS with a golf pro. He watched me swing. He took some pictures. He explained that I was more interested in seeing where the ball went than in hitting it off the tee, that I was stiff in the wrong places. He held my arms and moved me around. He demonstrated. He told me what I did when the ball was topped, hooked, or sliced. He watched me hit dozens of balls. He was doing three things: diagnosing my inept behavior, prescribing new practices, and testing my learning.

I heard Alfred Korzybski's lectures on general semantics in 1938 and wrote an introduction to the subject in 1941. But it was not until those sessions with the golf pro that I realized the strength *and* weakness of the enterprise.

The metaphor is vulnerable, but let me risk it. Korzybski was a pro, too. He was not looking at a man's stance, grip, swing, but at the way a man perceived-assumed-thought-felt-talked about anything. It was the adequacy of a man's evaluating and talking that was Korzybski's focus.

He had found a way of diagnosing and cataloguing those human actions and assertions that led to human trouble — conflict, confusion, wasted energy, misunderstanding — no matter where it happened. He evolved an analytical schema by which he could point to the over-simplifications, distortions, and maladaptive modes of talking about things, along with some devices and practices by which to overcome them.

The late **Irving J. Lee** was a professor of Public Speaking in the School of Speech, Northwestern University.

Students who took the 36-hour seminar at the Institute of General Semantics in Chicago learned about the theory and the advice. They were urged to do with them what they could. There was no clinic where one could practice the elimination of, say, any particular misevaluation under the guidance of a semantic pro. There were no situations where the learning could be tested, no way of focusing the analysis on the needs of the individual students. This is why the students were like golfers who attended lectures and then went to the links to put the content of the lectures to work. Occasionally they did, frequently they didn't. There were exceptions. Korzybski did find time to work directly in sustained fashion with a number of students about problems they brought to him. Some corresponded with him afterward. For the rest, however, there were only the lectures and the books.[1] Gilbert Ryle said that "A soldier does not become a shrewd general merely by endorsing the strategic principles of Clausewitz; he must also be competent to apply them." Alfred Korzybski died in March, 1950. He had devised and explained the principles. He had not established a training-testing program with equal thoroughness.

The Point of View

There are many reasons why it is difficult to give a capsule answer to the question, "What is general semantics?" What Highet said of William James gives just one:

> He found it impossible to make a long, sustained, orderly, authoritative speech and to unfold, stage by stage, argument by argument, proof by irresistible proof, a philosophical theory. He felt that any such speech would stiffen and cripple the essential flexibility of thought, and that any such theory must misrepresent the infinite complexities and novelties and inconsistencies of reality.[2]

Nevertheless, I have found it convenient to approach the subject in three ways.

1. As a description of a methodology of statement analysis and performance, as a set of things to do if one wished any or all of the following:
   a. The recognition and achievement of the varying degrees

of specificity, precision, and accuracy in assertion;

b. The distinction between the bewildering variety of statements which take the declarative mode since any one may be mistaken for another: verifiable and non-verifiable, factual and inferential, lie, fiction, fantasy, error, those which do and do not involve variable terms, those which label or define and those which describe, etc.

c. The recognition of the forms of oversimplification which tend to accompany talking (1) in terms of causal rather than functional relationships, (2) in additive terms about non-additive relationships, (3) in terms of symmetrical relationships to the neglect of the assymetrical, (4) in terms which split and separate what is to be found whole or inter-related, (5) in subject-predicate forms which obliterate relational factors.

2. As a description of a person's orientation, the general and specific tendencies, perspectives, attitudes a person may take in his adjustment to situations and people and in his definition of himself. These become *types of reaction* found in all degrees, variations, and combinations. If they are phrased in oppositional terms, it is for brevity only. Here the concern is with how much and under what circumstances a person reveals the following:

a. Does he ever go beyond his present premises and knowledge to face facts and theories which are different?

b. Is he disposed to listen to others to discover what "they have in mind" instead of arrogantly assuming that he knows without the investigation?

c. Does he respond in trigger-fashion without analysis of situations, or does he exhibit the control which accompanies delay-of-reaction?

d. Does he expect to find things and people alike, unchanging, or are his expectancies attuned to the possibilities of difference and process? Is his thinking in terms of fixed types, kinds, categories, or does he take account of graded variations?

e. In his moments of painful "emotion," anger, hatred, fear, shame, indignation, or envy is he aware of the object of his feeling? Does he respond to the object in its setting or is he responding to some associated label or verbal definition of the situation? Do his feelings of being afraid, hurt, insulted (which may be justified in any one situation) freeze into chronic resentments and fears as if the stimulus continued, or does he seek to fix the feelings in space-time, thus forcing re-examination and attack on the chronicity?

f. When faced with the necessity of making decisions, is he willing to experiment and act in terms of what is known, or does he take refuge in postponing action until "all the data are in"?

g. When faced with problems requiring solution does he tend to *think by verbalization*, projecting ready-made linguistic schemes onto the facts under consideration, or does he *think by visualization*, directing his attention to pictures and situations *without words*, thus involving the structural aspects unrestricted by the verbally defined categories?

3. As a set of premises, assumptions and claims, based on data available in 1933 which must be modified if new data are found:

a. That it is possible to create a general theory of sanity and human evaluation based on physico-mathematical methods which is not only internally consistent but usable and teachable;

b. That only the human class of life by virtue of its capacity to use symbols can begin where others leave off, and that upon this physical fact of interdependence can be established a rationale for a system of ethics, human relations, and feelings of social responsibility;

c. That any point of view about the behavior of human beings must start by considering them organisms-as-a-whole-in-an-environment, and that any analysis which implies a splitting must end in blind-alley over-generalizations;

d. That meanings of words or things are not merely matters of verbal definition, but are inseparably connected with "intellectual" and "emotional" states and colored by past experiences; that what something means is a composite of, at least, the cultural-psychological-logical-neurological-physiological-factors all interrelated;

e. Though a language may be used for many purposes, persuasion, poetry, polemics, etc., whenever it is used, it functions as a form of representation, a map which stands for territory inside and/or outside the person;

f. That the linguistic forms used by a people are involved in the formation of their attitudes; that a man who uses a structurally correct language will be moved to evaluations which are more appropriate than if he uses one which is structurally distorting;

g. That the creative achievements of man throughout history is evidence of human potentialities; that though we may live in a time of war and anxiety there is reason for despair only if men do not recognize the part their evaluation-talking processes play in the preservation of defeatist and destructive dogmas.

NOTES AND REFERENCES

1. The workshops of the Institute in Lakeville, Conn., are now organized to do something more.
2. Gilbert Highet, *The Art of Teaching* (New York, 1950), p. 233.

From the Winter 1952 Et cetera.

EVALUATION: WITH AND WITHOUT WORDS

Irving J. Lee

IN 1938, HITLER'S VOICE was being heard over the world, and the Wehrmacht was being readied for the march through Poland. Mussolini was still beating his breast, and Mosley was gathering courage. In this country the strident voices of their counterparts sounded strange amidst the echoes of Jefferson, of Lincoln's Inaugurals and of Wilson's 'New Freedom.' There was a threatening fervor and a rasping anger that stirred multitudes to belief in the doctrines of blood and soil, of babies for Der Fuehrer, of hatreds consuming helpless and innocent minorities. Here was a world in which a teacher of public speaking could see his art spent in the cause of perversion and destruction, debased to the misery of millions.

The great counter-chorus of Roosevelt, Churchill, Stalin, DeGaulle, Benes, was to be heard later. In 1938 they were only small voices. One felt the need of a prophylaxis, of a cleansing agent with which to sterilize the obscenities and decadent mouthings of the New Orders. I was reasonably familiar with Aristotle's Logic and Rhetoric. I had studied Blueler on dereistic thinking, Bentham on Fictions, and Vaihinger's *Philosophy of As If*. I had been exposed to John Dewey, the Robinsons, and the Thorndikes on reflective thinking. I knew about Whitehead on 'misplaced concreteness' and about Freud on rationalization.

The late **Irving J. Lee** was a professor of Public Speaking in the School of Speech, Northwestern University. This article was first presented at the meeting of the National Association of Teachers of Speech, Columbus, Ohio, December 29, 1945.

William James and Santayana were more than just names. But nowhere did I find a method, a way by which one could boldly go at the primitivism and un-reason so rapidly engulfing the world.

It was then that a colleague in the Northwestern Sociology Department told me about a little-known man, interested in mathematics and psychiatry, living in Chicago, who, back in 1933, had said that Hitler's utterances were strikingly like the pattern of the paranoid, and that in addition, this man had some interesting notions about a preventive for the poisons of irrationality. I spent the next year reading Korzybski's two books, two pamphlets, and some thirty articles. I found a method in his general semantics which filled some of the vacuum.

Korzybski made nothing I knew obsolete or irrelevant. Only a scant half-dozen of his notions had never been approximated before. But he did a great deal to reveal the restricted character of much that I knew. He provided a perspective, a means whereby some disconnected areas became related. He systematized what everyone knew piecemeal. He showed how to anatomize a developing defeatism in terms both congenial and healthy. And he put in terms that were forthright and utterly simple some methods by which I could 'think' about 'thinking,' and make sense about some of the 'non-sense' around me.

He was able to do this for me, I think, because of a peculiar interest not only in what people said but also in how they evaluated; not only in what people did, but in the character of the evaluations which accompanied the doing. That is to say: suppose a man says or does something. An observer then can look at two aspects of the situation: (1) at what was said or done, and (2) at the type of evaluation manifested.

Here is an example.

Assumptions

On a crowded bus, a soldier stood up and offered his seat to a woman. She snubbed his courtesy with the remark:

'No thank you, I don't want your seat. Anyway, you should be in Italy with my son.'

'In what part of Italy is your son located?' the soldier calmly inquired.

'I don't know,' snapped the woman.

'I wish you did,' because you might tell him to look around for my arm over there,' smiled the soldier.

It was then the woman observed that his right sleeve was empty.

Forget, if you will, all matters of grammar, rhetoric, definitions, meaning of terms, etc. Think only of the way the woman sized up the situation. Notice that she took a certain view or attitude toward the boy's wartime status. Notice that she 'felt' and 'thought' a certain way about him, that she interpreted the boy's role in terms of a certain set of premises or assumptions – in short, she evaluated in a certain pattern. What did she do? In technical terms, she identified what she saw with her assumptions or creeds about it; she confused a private knowledge of the situation with the situation itself; she took on a finality with respect to her judgment rarely justified by events, etc., etc. Her evaluation can be characterized as, say, stupid, mean, narrow, blind, immature.

Incidentally, such a pattern of evaluation has its counterpart in the drama of Chapter III, Section 3, Paragraph 8 of the official report of the Army Pearl Harbor Board, entitled 'Failure of Aircraft Warning Service to Advise of Approaching Planes, 7 December, 1941.' There are described the incidents surrounding Lt. Tyler's snappy 'Forget it,' when Pvt. Lockard reported, minutes before the fatal attack, that the oscilloscope indicated a large number of planes approaching from a direction three degrees east of north. Lt. Tyler's evaluation of the situation was of a piece with our unnamed woman's. He, too, assumed a knowledge he did not have. He, too, identified his assumptions with a more precise description of the events. He, too, acted in unreflective signal fashion. That this is not a mere academic grasping at minutiae is clear in the point the Board makes: if the Lieutenant's sizing-up of the situation had been characterized by somewhat more rigor, then 'the losses might have been very greatly lessened.'

May I invite your attention here to something so basic that

it is sometimes overlooked. The woman and Lt. Tyler were not merely 'careless,' 'inexperienced,' or 'irresponsible' in the usual sense. Their 'mistakes' were specific — but little is to be achieved by insuring that they or others do not make those particular mistakes again. Of deeper importance is the relative generality of the sort of orientation or pattern of evaluating that made these particular mistakes possible. It is only when the *pattern* of evaluating is significantly modified that we will have any substantial guarantee against such 'stupidity' in similar and in widely different situations.

Evaluations

Such an approach to Korzybski permits a quick statement of what general semantics is about. From one point of view, it is a study of the standards, patterns, and mechanisms of human evaluation wherever they occur. Korzybski, however, does not stop there. He asks: should we not do something about the woman's and the Lieutenant's evaluation so as to *prevent* such stupidity and disordering in other moments of their living? His effort to work out specific, usable, and teachable methods by which one can be trained in the means of proper evaluation is the heart of what students of general semantics study. Korzybski's great and enduring contribution to me, then, was the fact that he had evolved a means of checking the *adequacy* of our evaluations: i.e., he had a scheme by which one could describe the difference between the kinds of evaluation mechanisms which produce the degrees of survival and non-survival, of maturity and infantilism, of discrimination and identification, of the critical and the thoughtless, which human beings show. He cataloged a very large number of the patterns of evaluation which, in our time, play a role in multiplying the maladjustments, confusions, conflicts, and prejudices in daily life. And at the same time he was able to describe the approaches and techniques of those whose evaluations have led to the productive and significant contributions to our culture.

From the Spring 1946 Et cetera.

SEMANTIC ASPECTS OF LANGUAGE AND MATHEMATICS

Anatol Rapoport

THE SAYING, 'MATHEMATICS is a language,' becomes significant when we examine both the ordinary languages and mathematics as peculiarly human forms of behavior. In both cases, the behavior consists of the manipulation of symbols. The object of mathematical manipulations (aside from utilitarian computations) is a mystery to many people, and even mathematicians to not generally agree as to why they behave as they do. We shall inquire into this matter later. It is generally agreed, however, that the manipulation of the symbols of ordinary language is supposed to function in such a way that cognition of reality becomes transmissible independently of direct experience.

Rudiments of language may exist among some animals. A whole group of individuals may become cognizant of danger without direct contact with it through a warning cry of one member, who *is* in direct contact with it. But this last qualifying clause is the paramount limitation of animal languages. The fact that this limitation has been surmounted by man is significant. An animal is capable of transmitting knowledge of 'danger' or 'food' at hand but is incapable of saying,

'Last Tuesday I saw a panther with four cubs in a ravine a mile and a half northwest from here.'

Even less is an animal able to transmit knowledge acquired

Mathematical biologist and author of many books and papers on general semantics and the behavioral sciences, **Dr. Anatol Rapoport**'s first article for *Et cetera* appeared in Volume I. He was named assistant editor in 1946.

by experience to succeeding generations. Man is able to do so, and this transmitted 'knowledge' accumulates into vast systems called cultures.

That which makes possible indirect transmission of extremely complicated situations is called 'abstraction.' Certain aspects of a situation are stripped of all but very few attributes. A complex of these attributes is associated with a complex of sounds (a word). The word, when transmitted and received, is supposed to start a process in the recipient which reconstructs the situation. Of course the *entire* situation is never reconstructed, but enough of it is supposed to be reconstructed to serve the purpose of the communication.

The advantages of this system are obvious, but it often blows a fuse. How this happens is described in the literature on general semantics and allied subjects. General semantics traces these disturbances to confusion of *orders of abstraction*.

Entire cultures have become stagnant and degenerate because of the establishment of rigid behavior patterns governed by reactions to symbols. Such patterns vary widely, ranging from taboos of primitive demonologies to the intricate superstitions of high civilizations. In all cultures we find widespread evidence of preoccupation with word magic. In primitive societies patterns of behavior based on word-magic result in continued ignorance about the objective world, succumbing to disease, conquest by invaders, etc. In civilized society they result in monstrously inefficient economic anarchy, psychoneuroses, devastating wars, etc.

The aim of general semantics is in part to evaluate language as a motivating agency in human behavior. Clearly the important phase of such evaluation is the negative phase: one studies those properties of language which prevent it from functioning as it should — the pathology of language, if you will. In such a study the examination of the methods of mathematical cognition is useful for comparison, because mathematics in general does function as a language should, *i.e.*, it enables mathematicians to draw like conclusions from like hypotheses.

Let us therefore examine those characteristics of mathematics which are absent or undeveloped in ordinary language. They are (1) Postulational Method, (2) Concept of Function, (3) Explicit Delineation of Regions of Validity, and (4) Operational Definitions.

Actually all four characteristics can be included in 'Operational Method,' which governs mathematical reasoning, and contracted with the 'Substantive-Predicate Method' which governs the reasoning dominated by the structure of ordinary languages. But for clarity's sake, we shall subdivide it into the four divisions named and attempt to synthesize them later.

Postulational Method

The Greeks realized that if a system is to be constructed in which each proposition depends on propositions previously deduced and each term or terms previously defined, then the foundations of such a system must necessarily consist of unproved propositions and undefined terms. This explicit admission of the fact that certain propositions must remain unproved and certain terms undefined implied that to establish the validity of a proposition one *must* prove it, and to establish the meaning of a term, one *must* define it. However, since an endless chain of proofs and definitions is impossible, one compromises by leaving a minimum of things unproved and undefined. But what the Greeks failed to realize was the arbitrariness with which undefined terms and unproved propositions of a self-consistent system can be chosen. Somehow, certain propositions (which they could not prove) seemed to them 'self-evident' and certain notions fundamental. To start with another set of propositions, even if they were self-consistent, would have meant to deny the 'truth' of the 'self-evident' propositions.

Mathematicians, of course, realize the stifling effect of these 'self-evident truths' on the development of mathematics, precluding, as they do, non-euclidean goemetries, abstract algebras, etc. However, we are interested here not so much in the limitations of Greek mathematics, but in the limitations of language, which has its roots in the same inadequate approach to the postulational method which characterized the attitude of the West to Greek geometry. The pernicious effect of Greek geometry lay paradoxically in its brilliant success. Here was a system of breathtaking beauty and compelling 'truth,' arrived at through the power of reason alone! Small wonder that the Greeks should conclude that this method ('truths' arrived at by formal logic from 'self-evident' propositions) is to be preferred to any other. In particular, there was a deep contempt for experiment, since observations based on crude senses 'prove nothing.' This aversion for experiment is quite comprehensible to any lover of categorical conclusions based on deduction. Imagine the exasperation of a mathematician, attempting to prove a theorem of geometry, who is advised by a layman, 'Why don't you measure these segments to see if they are equal?' In itself, then, the disdain of the Greeks for experiment did exhibit a keen feeling for mathematics. Where it did most harm was in the assumption that these 'truths,' arrived at purely deductively, were truths about the objective world, and moreover that all truths of the objective world could be so deduced. The situation became even worse when the Greeks, seeing the discrepancies between reasoning and observation, postualted an 'existence' of an ideal, perfect world, of which the observable realities were but imperfect reflections.

To the modern mathematician geometry is not a natural science at all. The recognition of this fact exhibits the gulf between mathematics and the natural sciences. Only when this gulf becomes apparent can both mathematics and the natural sciences develop. On the one hand, the purely arbitrary character of the fundamental assumptions and the undefined terms of mathematics is recognized, clearing the way for the growth of generality, the most rewarding direction of development. On the other hand, science is freed from 'eternal truths' and experimental fact is placed in its rightful position of supreme authority.

Let us now turn to the role of 'self-evident truths' in non-mathematical cognition. Think of the damage done through the ages by such clichés as 'The whole is equal to the sum of all its parts.' The meanings of 'whole' and 'sum' and 'parts' are of course taken as self-evident. Try to *apply* this truth to actual situations. Are we to conclude that the magnitude of the resultant force is always the sum of the magnitudes of its components?

Are we to conclude that colinear velocities always add up to their algebraic sum? The helium atom is made of the same 'things' as four hydrogen atoms. How to explain the discrepancy in mass? Other self-evident truths have gone the same way but not before they did their part in holding back the growth of knowledge:

'Where there is motion, there is a mover.'

'A things exists only because there is a sufficient reason for its existence.'

'Causes always precede effects.'

All these maxims, so vital to philosophers and theologians, become meaningless noises in view of our present knowledge of the universe obtained from observations and controlled experiment and critical attitude to procedures. The discovery that mathematics is a *postulational*, not an experimental, system, freed man's thinking processes and delivered both mathematics and the experimental sciences from sclerosis.

Function

Function in mathematics is analogous to 'causality' in ordinary languages. But we shall see how 'function' is a very much more precise term (an operational term), and this will shed some light on the inadequacy of the notion of causality.

'Causality' in ordinary languages is riddled with anthropomorphic notions and magic. With the savage, demons 'make' misfortunes. With us gravity *causes* objects to fall. 'Laziness' and 'Lack of Ambition' *cause* poverty. So men in the pulpits attack 'lust' and 'greed,' and politicians attack 'Isms' as if they had objective existence like crocodiles.

The problem of knowing the world is not the problem of finding 'what makes it so?' but of finding sets of conditions of which we can say, 'If thus, then so.' The problem is completely solved when we can interchange the 'thus' and the 'so,' *i.e.*, when we can also say, 'If so, then thus.' When this happens, 'cause' and 'effect' become useless terms. For example, in curvilinear motion, the physicist will describe the relation between force, mass, velocity, and radius of curvature. He does not look at these elements as either 'causes' or 'effects.' It is no more true than an increase in the radius of curvature causes a decrease in force than vice versa, or than that an increase of velocity causes an increase in force or vice versa. These things are simply *related* as described. In pure mathematics finding such a set of completely interchangeable conditions is called finding 'necessary and sufficient conditions.' Some of the sharpest tools of mathematical reasoning, particularly in analysis, are directed towards these ends.

Let us now turn to the squabbles that accompany attempts to determine 'causes' and 'effects' in our world, come hell or high water. Does a 'culture' determine an 'economy' of a society or *vice versa*? Do leaders influence the collective will of a group or are they themselves influenced by it? Is a low standard of living caused by apathy of individuals or is it itself a cause? As we have seen, the physicist in his investigations usually ignores such questions of priority. He will never worry about whether a moving magnetic field causes an electrostatic field or whether the moving electric charge causes a magnetic field. The two go together. If agencies enter into the picture at all, it is the physicist himself. He can 'make' a magnetic field by moving an electric field and vice versa. The fact that in our study of society we are vitally interested in making certain conditions leads us to postulate the existence of 'agencies.' As a matter of fact, the only agencies are ourselves, and the effects of our influence depend on how thoroughly we understand the laws of motion of society, in which no agencies operate but only sets of correlated conditions. The question of causes and effects, then, reduces to a purely utilitarian question, namely, which sets of conditions can be most effectively controlled.

Suppose we find that in a society in which security is considered synonymous with accumulation of private wealth, the energies of individuals are largely directed toward such accumulation, and sets of values are established which preclude the growth of cooperative activity. And suppose that these conditions are found to be accompanied by a predominance of infantile personalities in that society, a frequency of frustration neuroses, high incidence of insanity, and crime. All these phenomena are observable. But they are all observed by people with different points of view about 'cause' and 'effect.' The man in the pulpit will ascribe the deplorable state of affairs to 'moral degeneration,' which in turn is 'caused' by loss of faith. His solution is to 'make' each individual regain faith in and fear of God. He cannot reach every individual, but he thinks that if he could, he could induce the necessary changes. Accordingly his efforts are directed to increasing church membership. The individual psychologist thinks society would become 'mature' if each individual became emotionally mature. This would happen if more people participated in cooperative effort. But he reaches even fewer persons than the man in the pulpit and often becomes discouraged. The social reformer thinks that the root of the evil lies in the fact that security depends on individual accumulation of wealth and tries to effect legislation to make security a responsibility of society. The revolutionist thinks that social reforms are inadequate so long as a class, in whose interest it is to accumulate, perpetuates itself in power. He therefore speaks in terms of class struggle and seizure of power. But seizure of power depends on organized and disciplined collective effort, of which people conditioned to grasping for individual welfare only are not capable. The vicious circle is closed.

Whatever the outcome of that hypothetical sad state of affairs may be, I think you will agree that it is worthwhile to study similar situations. It is very difficult to study society with any degree of detachment for obvious reasons. But this we must do if we wish to be successful in our studies as the physicist was successful in his. To achieve this necessary objectivity, we must imitate the physicist rather than the savage. We must not look for devils and agencies, because these are too easily found and are of no use once they are found except to make faces at. We must do as the physicist does and correlate sets of conditions. The language for expressing such correlations is the functional language of mathematics.

Explicit Delineations of Regions of Validity

No mathematical statement can be made without a more or less explicit delineation of its region of validity. In theorems these regions are defined by the conditions of the hypothesis. In definitions they are restricted to the range of operation. Thus the Pythagorean Theorem applies to certain objects in a certain universe, *i.e.*, to right triangles in euclidean space. Of other triangles and other spaces, the conclusion of the theorem is false. A function is a mathematical definition, *e.g.*,

$$y = \sqrt{25 - xw}$$

is a definition of y which states in part,

'If x is ± 3, y is 4; if x is ± 4, y is 3; if x is ± 5, y is 0, etc., for an infinity of other values of x between -5 and 5.' If y is real, no other real values of x except those between -5 and $+5$ can be included in the definition, otherwise we immediately become involved in contradictions. Thus the validity of both theorems and definitions in mathematics is lucidly restricted by the structure of mathematical language itself.

Let us see what happens in ordinary language. Aristotelian logic gives us the rules of reasoning embodied in

(1) Identity: A is A.
(2) Non-contradiction: A cannot be both B and not-B.
(3) Excluded middle: A must be either B or not-B.

These laws would be acceptable if there were anything in the objective world to which whey could be *unqualifiedly* applied. As a matter of fact, such applications are completely valid only with respect to mathematical entities[1] simply because the latter are so constructed as to *make* these laws apply. What outside of mathematics can be substituted for A and still preserve the validity of (1)? Man is Man? But Man with a capital M is an abstraction, not a reality. Even 'men' considered as 'objects' are abstractions. A minute examination of a man will reveal such a conglomeration of processes and reactions as to make any even approximately complete description impossible. As I speak before you, I become a different set of particles and processes each moment. We do not live in a world of 'objects' of which assertions can be made. Only the predominance of nouns in our substantive-predicate languages gives us that illusion. We live in a world of events, and no camera exists which can freeze these events into a picture which will stand still while we describe it. Yet the categorical majesty of 'A is A' leads people to translate it without compunction into 'Pigs is Pigs,' 'Jews are Jews,' 'Indians are Indians,' and 'You can't change human nature.'

The same considerations apply to (2) and (3). We know very well that this desk may be said to be both to the right and to the left of this chair; that Calcutta can be said to be both east and west of Karachi; that the length and mass of bodies have different values to different observers; but the tyranny of (2) prevents people from realizing many of these truths.

The corruption of (3) is the most prevalent. This abuse is what general semanticists call the two-valued orientation. Even the history of mathematics is full of man-made paradoxes and dilemmas which resulted from indiscriminate application of the Law of Excluded Middle. Numbers were thought of as necessarily either integers or fractions, blocking the study of irrational roots of equations. With the recognition of the real number system, numbers were still thought of as either positive or negative, blocking the study of complex numbers, etc.

The weakness of Aristotelian logic lies not in the principles above but in the fact that we think of the vast complexes of events as indivisible 'objects' with indivisible 'attributes' (because we designate them by individual words). We forget that no single statement made about a conglomeration of things need be valid even if deduced by formal logic from those principles. Mathematical reasoning teaches us to break up seemingly simple concepts into still simpler ones and seemingly indivisible conditions into sets of independent conditions. Thus it constantly refines its concepts by delineating regions of validity.

The most brilliant advances of science can be traced to a similar method. As long as temperature, rigidity, elasticity, mass, were regarded as properties of bodies, and bodies themselves as fragments of reality, molecular physics could not come into being. With the birth of molecules, all the properties above lost their absolute meaning, since they could be applied only statistically to large numbers of molecules, not to individual ones. More and more the physicist is aware of the necessity of giving qualified answers. Is space euclidean? Yes, within sufficiently small regions and away from large masses of matter. Is behavior of inanimate matter predictable? Yes, if matter is taken in large enough quantities. In short, it becomes clear that questions which only yesterday seemed straightforward, demanding and 'either-or' answer, today dissolve into ambiguities, which cannot be answered without a drastic revision and sharpening of concepts.

Operational Definitions

We now come to the most powerful tool of mathematical logic, the operational definition. We see the struggle to 'define terms' already in full swing in Socrates' time. Aristotle clearly stated the definition of a Definition, and he stated it is *operational terms*. That is to say, he did not apply the principle of 'definition' to defining Definition itself. Instead, he proceeded as a general semanticist or a mathematician would do. He tells us not what a Definition 'is,' but *what to do* in order to make a definition. Place a thing to be defined in a class; then name the properties which dintinguish it from other members of its class.

Now strictly speaking, every such definition would itself be operational, if the operations indicated could be performed. A definition consists of directions telling us what to do to recognize the thing defined. The weakness of aristotelian definitions lies not in the method itself but in its non-applicability in a great number of situations, its only partial applicability to others, and, most of all, in its uncritical acceptance in all situations as infallible (as, *e.g.*, people accept dictionary definitions).

Let us take some homely examples. What is a Negro? Suppose we are told (as we possibly would be by the first person in the street) that a Negro is a person with a black skin. No matter that an anthropologist or a student of 'race' will give a considerably more sophisticated definition. It will merely result in more sophisticated contradictions. On the face of it the definition is 'operational'; that is, it tells us what to do to recognize a 'Negro.' First determine whether he is a 'person,' next whether he has a 'black skin.' Assuming we know how to recognize 'persons' and where to look for 'skin,' what can we say about 'black'? A scientific definition of black immediately reveals that no skin is black; in fact there are no black objects at all in this world. Of course our man in the street will immediately correct himself and say he meant 'dark.' But how dark is dark? Let us suppose we have determined that. Yet every person in this room except myself has skin as dark as the skins of American Negroes, and our man will not call you 'Negroes.' He will say you are 'Indians.' But when we ask for a definition of that, he will be in even greater difficulties.

Of course the examples we used were quite crude. For all I know, workable definitions of 'Negro' or 'Indian' may exist. By 'workable' I mean accomplishing their purpose. Where people are determined to accomplish their purpose, they will employ 'workable' definitions. In some parts of the United States, the chief purpose of 'defining' Negroes is to bar them from certain activities. Accordingly Negroes are defined simply as 'those people whom we (the Whites) call 'Negroes.' In many of our newspapers Communists are similarly defined as 'those people whom we call Communists.' These definitions are 'workable' because they accomplish the purpose of the definer. Moreover, they are unassailable, because they are tautological. To the scientist, for whom a definition must serve the purpose of recognition, not as a means of pinning the same labels on people he doesn't like, these 'definitions' are, of course, quite worthless. Actually neither a Negro nor an Indian can be defined at all except purely arbitrarily, because no such thing exists in the objective world.

The scientist, to whom definitions must serve as tools to further knowledge, is forced to use operational definitions, where the operations consist of examining criteria, and the workability of a definition will depend on whether the operations indicated are realizable and precise. All definitions of real entities are therefore limited by the inexactness of our observations and by the fact that our words are only abstractions of these entities and not the entities themselves. In metaphysics and theology, on the other hand, the operational side of aristotelian definition was completely lost, and only its sterile grammatical structure remained.

'What is God?' asks the Catechism. And the answer is in

perfect grammatical form, 'God is a spirit, omnipotent, omniscient, and ubiquitous.'

Similarly the metaphysicist asks, 'What is Space? What is Time?, etc.,' and even the early physicists inherited the habit in their questions, 'What is Fire? What is Heat? What is Electricity?' The modern physicist has long discarded the question 'What is . . . 'and asks instead 'What does . . . ?' Nor is this in any way a retreat or admission of failure as many amateur philosophers (and some professional ones) insist, complaining that 'The physicists describe the *how*, but they will never be able to tell the *why*. They learn all about what electricity does, but they still haven't found out what electricity *is*.'

It is only the structure of our language and the pernicious thought habit of accepting definitions, which merely equate terms (as dictionary and catechism definitions do) that prevent us from realizing that *does* is the only content of *is*. Here indeed lies the greatest value of mathematics as a semantic discipline. All mathematical definitions are made in terms of operations, and the entities thus defined have *no further content* than that defined by the operations. In the development of the complex number system, negative numbers are defined by extending an operation (namely, the inverse of addition) to all ordered couples of positive integers; rational numbers are defined by extending another operation (division) to all ordered pairs of integers; algebraic numbers by extending the operation of factoring to all polynominals with rational coefficients, real numbers by extending the operation of passing to the limit to all sequences of rational numbers, etc. The same is true of functions. Functions defined by quadratures, by solutions of differential equations, by series, etc., are all examples of mathematical entities defined by operations alone. Mathematicians have long since recognized the irrelevancy to knowledge of the question 'What is . . . ?' But unfortunately this formulation and the confusion which accompanies it still haunts our thinking about what we consider with varying degrees of error as the 'real universe.'

As examples of extensions of this semantic emancipation brought by mathematics long ago to our inquiries about the universe, the advances of modern physics again stand in the limelight. The so-called difficulties of understanding the Special Theory of Relativity vanish immediately and irrevocably as soon as one begins to think of such 'absolutes' as time and space in terms of operations necessary to define them. One says, 'In order to determine the "length" of an object, one *proceeds* as follows . . . . In order to determine the time sequence of two events, one *proceeds* as follows . . . ' Length and Duration are then readings which result from the procedures, and they *have no further content*. All questions about the 'real,' the 'intrinsic,' the 'absolute' values of these quantities become meaningless.

Again the so-called dilemmas of subatomic physics are immediately resolved when one realizes that the term 'position of an electron' has a meaning only when one is able to say, 'To determine the position of the electron at a given moment, one proceeds as follows . . . ' Then, when it turns out that no such procedure can be devised (this has nothing to do with the precision of our measurements but with a much deeper question), the emancipated thinker merely shrugs his shoulders and says, 'The meaning of the term "position at a given moment" is delineated by the possibility of defining it operationally.' He does not worry about such concepts exploding any more than any physicist worries about the fact that 'elasticity' and 'rigidity' become meaningless on certain levels of observation.

Here we see the connection between the power of operational definitions (first recognized with full clarity in mathematics) and the other semantic aspects of mathematics, which can be summarized as the Operational Method. Delineation of validity is closely connected with operational definitions, because the latter, by exhibiting the operations employed, determine the region of validity. The concept of function is likewise bound up with operation: in mathematics obviously, in observation of reality somewhat more indirectly through the operations of which observation itself consists. Finally the recognition of the postulational nature of mathematics sheds light on the exclusiveness of the deductive method (also an operation) in mathematical cognition. It exhibits a gulf between our knowledge of our own inner processes (which is the only reality reflected in mathematical truths) and our knowledge of the outside world, in which observational, rather than deductive, operations are supreme. We can trace many blockings of progress of knowledge directly to the failure to realize that the conclusions of inductive reasoning are only guesses.

'All men are mortal,' goes the first exercise in syllogism; 'Socrates is a man, therefore Socrates is mortal.'

How did we get to say 'all men are mortal?' By observing that Smith has died and Jones has died, and Krishnamurti has died, etc. If 'all men are mortal' is a certainty, then the observation must have included all men, also Socrates. If it did, there is no need to prove him mortal by the syllogism. If it did not, 'all men are mortal' is only a guess, a very good guess, to be sure, worthwhile betting on, but one which can be disproved by a single counter-example.

Many modern scholasticists do not feel that way. According to some of them, the above mentioned observations lead us to a conclusion about an *inherent property* of Man (not just men), *i.e.*, Mortality. This property is inseparably bound up with the 'nature' of Man as the Pythagorean property is bound up with right triangles. This attitude reflects the insistence of metaphysics on postulating the existence of an ultimate reality, 'about' which we are getting bits of partial knowledge. In this reality there 'exist' concepts, categories, and properties, all those things which we ourselves had invented as tools to cognition. To a scientist these ghosts are useless in his work, but many scientists prefer to reserve a fond corner for them much as a sentimental woman keeps her dolls in the attic till her old age.

Most scientists are aware that the value of a language is of the same order as the value of a map. More and more natural science begins to recognize the superiority of mathematics as the language of science. This realization has come simply from the failure of introspective and syllogistic methods of philosophy and from the success of painstaking observations and quantitative descriptions.

Especially to the members of the mathematics department, much of what I have said must have appeared pretty obvious. The members of the English department, however, by whose presence I am greatly flattered, could probably profit well by acquainting themselves with some general principles of mathematics and with some mathematical technique. I understand English classes exist in order to teach people to use the English language. The question arises: 'Why should the English language, or any language, for that matter, be used at all?' I can think of two answers: (1) To establish bonds among a group of human beings; (2) To establish bonds among all human beings.

Now to achieve (1) language does not have to be a map of any reality. One can invent a most absurd Neverland, and if all the human beings in the group are thoroughly familiar with every feature of that Neverland, a bond exists between them. Such are the languages of savages (primitive and civilized) whose worlds of demons and taboos, unreal as they are, are shared by all the members. Thus, a society can exist based on a common cultural bond, even if there is no reality behind it. But such a society is doomed. Eventually they will come in contact with another society speaking the language of another Neverland, and the language of the first group will be a meaningless jabber to the others, and they will appear as another species to them, to be exterminated. The stronger will destroy the weaker.

If we consider such clashes lamentable, we should try to bring about (2). This does not at all mean that everyone should speak English or Sanskrit or Tamil, any more than it is important what colors are used for topographical and political features of maps. What is important is that the maps should all be of the same country. The question arises: What country? What set of beliefs, cultural values, ethical values, etc.? Perhaps there is an answer. The biological fact that mankind is a single species provides a hope that he can learn to speak the same language. This language will not be a map of this or that Neverland. It will be a *verifiable* language, because it will consist of 'if thus, then so' propositions. In other words, it will be a map of real territories described in operational terms. English teachers no less than mathematicians have a crucial role to play in disciplining languages into becoming instruments of human integration.

NOTES AND REFERENCES

1. Some mathematicians maintain that even with regard to some mathematical structures (3) is invalid.

From the Winter 1946 Et cetera.

MATHEMATICAL BIOPHYSICS, CYBERNETICS AND GENERAL SEMANTICS

Anatol Rapoport and Alfonso Shimbel

The Importance of 'Bastard' Sciences

IN A SOCIETY WHERE great emphasis is placed on specialization and division of labor, there is likely to develop a notion that knowledge and techniques fall into 'natural' divisions, each pertaining to some discrete, well-defined aspect of living. The general semanticist will, of course, take issue with the 'naturalness' of the divisions. Like any other classification, division of knowledge and techniques into autonomous specialties can be justified for the general semanticist only on pragmatic grounds. Instead of asking, 'What are the "natural" divisions?' he will ask, 'Given such and such classification, what can be achieved?'

The achievements of specialization are evident. Modern science and industry are so complex and the standards of scholarship so exciting that it is impossible for any one to master more than a narrow sector of knowledge. If achievements are measured by the extent to which man can know and manipulate his environment, then the pragmatic justification for specialization has been given.

However, there is also a sordid side to specialization. As Norbert Wiener has pointed out,

---

This paper was written when **Anatol Rapoport** and **Alfonso Shimbel** served on the Committee on Mathematical Biology at the University of Chicago.

A man may be a topologist or an acoustician or a coleopterist. He will be filled with the jargon of his field and will know all its literature, and all its ramifications, but, more frequently than not, he will regard the next subject as something belonging to his colleague three doors down the corridor, and will consider any interest in it on his own part as an unwarrantable breach of privacy.[1]

The notions 'your field' and 'my field' carry with them two unfortunate implications. To begin with, such 'cubicle' thinking bears a disturbing resemblance to the process of severe 'inbreeding' with its accompanying tendency to loss of vigor. The damaging results of this tendency are not too serious, inasmuch as they are confined to the devitalization of a limited number of qualified scientists and scholars.

The second implication has more serious consequences. Specialization becomes *institutionalized*. The innumerable '-ologies' provide a framework for the administrative apparatus of our institutions of learning. As is usual, the administrative structure is even more static than the conceptual hierarchies of the academicians, so that attempts on the part of non-conformists to commit 'breaches of academic privacy' are countered not only by the resentments of the 'specialists' but also by the formidable forces of administrative authority.

Such are the effects of elementalistic orientation on learning and science. The effects of either-or attitudes are no less telling and are the more profound the farther removed is a field of endeavor from the emancipated, non-aristotelian areas of physical science. In the latter it is generally recognized that a 'theory' is not 'reality'; it does not even describe reality but is only a set of directions for manipulating symbols in order to make predictions. Thus the existence of 'equivalent' theories is possible. In other disciplines, however, particularly in those dealing with human behavior, the tendency is to view each new formulation suspiciously as a 'rival' theory, whose establishment automatically invalidates and dates existing formulations. We have Marxists and Keynesians, Gestaltists and Behaviorists, Freudians, Adlerians, Jungians, and neo-Freudians. One could almost suspect that a jealous and malicious god was deliberately trying to interfere with the construction of the Tower of Science by confusing the language of the builders.

The general semanticist, aware as he is of the limitations inherent in elementalistic and either-or approaches to problems, seeks a way of unifying various points of view, of creating a new language, if necessary, for a more adequate description of the world. Therefore the general semanticist welcomes the rise of bastard sciences.

What are some of these hybrid disciplines and wherein lies the power of their method?

As an early example, one might cite euclidean geometry, the first cross between empirical mathematics and formal logic. Mathematics had existed in Egyptian and Mesopotamian civilizations merely as a description of certain experiences (measurement) and sets of rules for computation. Formal logic, as developed by Aristotle, was little more than a set of rules for making classifications. But formal logic applied to a few fundamental postulates of geometry resulted in a magnificent structure of knowledge.

Another example is the cross between algebra and geometry accomplished by Descartes on November 10, 1619. The discovery of a profound correspondence reflected in a formal isomorphism between the language of algebra and that of geometry enabled mathematicians to translate discoveries made in one field into progress in another field. As is usually the case, progress made under such circumstances is 'non-additive.'

Other examples are equally illuminating: mathematical physics, biological chemistry, physiological psychology, biophysics, etc. Two of these areas are quite new. One is *mathematical biophysics*;[2] the other has been christened *cybernetics* by Norbert Wiener and his associates and has at this time about a decade of research behind it.

These two bastard sciences are of particular interest to the general semanticist for two reasons. First, they bear out the principle that a non-elementalistic approach to any field of inquiry is likely to yield 'non-additive' dividends. Thus the general semanticist sees in the fruits of mathematical biophysics and of cybernetics a vindication of non-elementalistic methodology.

This is true, of course, of many other such cross-bred disciplines. But mathematical biophysics and cybernetics have even more important implications for general semantics. The understanding of the events in the nervous system and analogous systems *as determined by their structure* is fundamental for the understanding of *abstraction, evaluation,* and *communication,* processes of basic importance in general semantics.

Mathematical Thinking and Human Affairs

In 1923 Korzybski wrote as follows:

> If there is to be a science of human engineering, it must be mathematical in spirit and in method and if we do not possess methods to apply mathematical thinking to human affairs, such methods must be discovered. Can this be done?
>
> Let us say a word about what has already been accomplished in this direction. The latest researches in the foundations of mathematics, chiefly accomplished by Whitehead, Russell, Poincaré, and Keyser, have disclosed the insufficiency and fallacies of the traditional logic and have produced an internal revolution in logic and mathematics. Mathematics and logic have proved to be one; a fact from which it seems to follow that mathematics may successfully deal with non-quantitative problems in a much broader sense than was suspected to be possible.[3]

Elaborating this confidence in the mathematical method as a tool for studying man, Korzybski said in 1933:

> The problems of the world in 1933 are acute and immediate, overloaded with confusion, bitterness, hopelessness, and other forms of semantic disturbances. Without some means — and in this case, scientific and physiological means — to regulate our semantic reactions, we shall not be able to solve our problems soon enough to avoid disasters. The similarity in structure of mathematics, and our nervous system, once pointed out and *applied,* gives us a unique means to regulate the semantic reactions, without which it is practically impossible to analyse dispassionately and wisely the most pressing problems of immediate importance.[4]

All in all, Korzybski's conjectures (conjectures, because of the fragmentary knowledge then available of the similarity of structure between mathematics and the human nervous system) can be summarized in a few principles.[5]

1. Communication between human beings is possible.

That is to say, a language can be constructed in which the relations between events in the outside world can be symbolized in such a way that independent observers will arrive at similar symbolizations and by manipulating the symbols according to the rules of the language will arrive at similar conclusions. Korzybski cites mathematics as an example of such a language. A generalization of mathematics is any symbolic system built on structure and order relations *alone*.

2. The world is knowable.

Any symbolization of events leads us to expect that certain things will happen. But only *certain* ways of symbolizing lead to predictions which are actually verified. Such self-justifying symbolizations constitute knowledge.

3. Knowledge is the establishment of ordered structure.

The perception, interpretation, and evaluation of events is largely a neural process (although actually the whole organism is involved in the act of knowing). 'Knowledge' consists of an ordered sequence of neuromotor events.

4. Order determines sanity.

Sanity is a measure of the correspondence between the ordered structure of the neuro-motor events and the ordered structure of the world.

Knowledge as Ordered Structure

For the purposes of this discussion, the third principle will be considered first: knowledge is the establishment of ordered structure.

The naive, pre-scientific approach to the explanation of phenomena was through the invention of anthropomorphic 'agencies' which were implicitly taken to be sufficient causes. The predominant question was 'Who does it?' not 'What is being done?' And, of course, the nature of the questions determined the limitation of the answers. The quest for 'agencies' yielded a world peopled by river-gods and fates.

The reason one cannot point to a time when 'Who does it?' gave way to 'What is being done?' is that in spite of the verbal dichotomy between the two kinds of questions, the change of attitude was a gradual one. Although formally modern science can be said to be entirely based on the question in the form of 'What is being done?' yet the remnants of the 'Who does it?' attitude are still deeply intrenched in many areas of inquiry. The agencies no longer appear in anthropomorphic garb, *but they are still subjects of sentences*, whose subject-predicate structure almost forces the perpetuation of the old outlook and of its limitations.[6]

The power of the new outlook is embodied in the notion of *invariance*. The abstraction of cardinal number was perhaps the clearest and oldest example of this notion. As Korzybski, Russell, and others have pointed out, a tremendous intellectual revolution sprang from the revelation that a 'brace' of pheasants, a 'pair' of boots, a 'team' of horses, 'twins,' 'couples,' and 'duets' are all instances of a particular *invariance* which we have come to call the cardinal number 'two.' Basically the same kind of revelation underlies the law of gravity. To Newton falling bodies, tides, and the motions of the moon also appeared as instances of an invariance. It is this novel outlook which enabled him to formulate the famous inverse square law.

It is important to note that one cannot point at the 'two-ness' of two cows. Nor can one mine gravity. But it is precisely these 'intangibles' which have proved most useful in the business of scientific map-making. In counting groups of cows and stars we must completely disregard the 'nature' of the objects subject to gravitational forces in computing the effects of such forces. The things that *do* matter are not the 'nature' of the objects but the *relations* between them. Here knowledge has been reduced to structure and order.

Mathematical Biophysics and Non-Aristotelian Methods

Mathematical biophysics and cybernetics are programs of research aimed at the discovery of the significant invariants underlying the functioning of the nervous system. Rashevsky, for example, who may be considered the founder of mathematical biophysics, considers the central nervous system as an 'aggregate of a very large number of irritable elements, which all can be divided into two groups: exciting and inhibiting' and proposes 'a systematic study of the simplest cases of interaction which may occur in such an aggregate.'[7]

Thus, the method of mathematical biophysics is geared to the outlook of the general semanticist. As has been pointed out, for the general semanticist the problem of describing the world is a relation-seeking problem. The relations form a *structure* and the properties of this structure are then the properties of the world. To the general semanticist, knowledge means knowledge of structure. This is the epistemological aspect of the problem. But the general semanticist recognizes another aspect, namely, the physiological one. And this aspect also revolves about structure, namely, the structure of the nervous system. In fact, the general semanticist views sanity as a measure of the correspondence between the two structures (see Principle 4 above).

It is most important to remember that the word 'structure' as used here refers to a spatio-temporal configuration of events and not merely to the relative position of objects in space or to the connections between the neural elements. If this extension of the meaning of structure from spatial to spatio-temporal is not made, then the objections of the Gestaltists, Freudians, etc. to what they believe to be the behaviorist point of view are certainly justified. The early behaviorist view that behavior can be explained in terms of the spatial relations between the neural components of an organism rested on the tacit assumption that during an appreciable interval of time the nervous system of an organism is in a certain 'state,' which completely determines what stimulus elicits what response. The neurological basis of this assumption, as pointed out by F.S.C. Northrup, was the hypothesis that 'neurons are always put together in the nervous system to form a path in or through the nervous system which is non-circular.'[8]

This oversimplified notion is untenable in the light of (1) the principle of non-identity, (2) recent neurological findings, and (3) the theoretical investigations of the central nervous system by the mathematical biophysicists.

To begin with, the principle of non-identity, one of the corner stones of general semantics, excludes the possibility of two stimuli being 'identical' and the possibility of defining the 'state' of the nervous system over an appreciable interval of time. Secondly, the neurophysiologists (chiefly Lorente de No, Cannon, and Rosenblueth) have called attention to the importance of *circular* paths (reverberating chains of neurons) in the central nervous system. Finally, Rashevsky has shown by constructing models how circular paths may account for conditioning and gestalt phenomena, while McCulloch, Pitts, Householder, and Landahl have laid the foundations for the mathematical treatment of the spatio-temporal structure of neural nets.

This is only one example of how the broad principles of non-aristotelian methodology find a direct counterpart in the recent extension of the physico-mathematical method to psychophysiology. The work is now rapidly progressing. The Boolean algebra methods of McCulloch and Pitts are being extended to a statistical (probabilistic) formulation, which appears as a generalization of behaviorist views. It was the hope of the general semanticists that such a generalization would be found and would provide an opportunity for constructing a science of man adequate for our times. It is the task of the mathematical biophysicists actually to construct such a science.

At the time Korzybski presented the above-mentioned paper, he could report no more of this task (the physico-mathematical method applied to a science of man) than the work of Whithead, Russell, Poincaré, and Keyser, who had shown the similarity of structure between logic and mathematics. Today, a quarter of a century later, we can report considerably more.

To begin with, the physiological aspect of the problem had been outlined by Korzybski himself in *Science and Sanity*. And as *Science and Sanity* was being written, isolated investigators were already at work, laying the foundations of a physico-mathematical theory of the nervous system. We have already mentioned Rashevsky and his group, now active at the University of Chicago. Work along similar lines has been carried out by Blair (Rochester, N.Y.), Hill (England), Monnier (France), Schaefer (Germany) and others. The very tools of research which these workers employed (the physico-mathematical method) enabled them to emphasize the important aspects of the problem, namely, *invariants* rather than *agencies*.

Consciousness of Abstracting

To be sure, the point of view has not been left unchallenged. It has been pointed out that the picture of the nervous system as presented, for example, in Rashevsky's *Mathematical Biophysics*, is so abstract as to lose contact with 'reality.' It is maintained that neurons are not simply 'elements,' that the processes underlying their activity are enormously complex, that perhaps they are not even amenable to description in physicochemical terms, etc. A thorough analysis of these objections is given in the introduction to Rashevsky's book. One can see from his arguments that he is semantically sophisticated. For the sake of continuity, however, we shall briefly reproduce them here using a terminology somewhat more current in the literature of general semantics.

The objection that a formulation deals with 'abstractions' and not 'realities' is a vacuous one, because there is no such thing as a description of 'concrete reality.' No matter how minutely one were to describe a 'neuron' or the sequence of events associated with the interaction of neurons, one would not be describing 'reality' but only selecting certain aspects of it considered pertinent to the problem at hand, that is, abstracting. The question is, therefore, not whether abstractions as such are justifiable (they cannot be escaped), but which abstractions are useful. Useful for what? Useful for discovering relations to be used in constructing theories from which other relations can be predicted. The verification of predictions implied in the theories is, of course, the test of their truth. But even if the predictions fail to be realized, the framework of the theory is often such that the way to refinement and correction becomes evident and thus progress in the search for truth can be realized. Precisely this is the *raison d'être* of the abstractions made in physics. Every physicist knows that molecules are not perfectly elastic, tiny billiard balls, as they were assumed to be in the first formulations of the kinetic theory of gases. Hence the physicists were not surprised to see that experimental results often deviated significantly from their predictions. But once the 'classical' kinetic theory was developed, ways of introducing corrections suggested themselves and a steady approach to truth became possible. No physicist believes in the existence (except verbally) of 'point masses,' 'rigid bodies,' or 'continuous fluids.' Yet descriptions of events in terms of derived relations between such fictions is what constitutes physics. The physicist is at ease using abstractions, because he knows that abstraction is not reality, the word is not the thing.

Neural Nets

The value of the abstractions made in mathematical biology should be judged by the effective use to which they can be put. On the basis of Rashevsky's picture of the nervous system, it has been possible to describe *quantitatively* such relations as reaction time as a function of stimulus intensity; reaction time as a function of the interval between a preparatory 'warning' and the stimulus; acuity of discrimination as a function of the magnitude of the stimulus, and many other relations.

The approach has also been extremely useful in suggesting 'models' to account for a wide variety of 'psychological' phenomena, such as conditioned reflexes, error elimination (as observed in maze learning), logical 'thinking,' visual perception and esthetics, and some psychotic states.

Perhaps the most remarkable results of this method are to be found in the area dealing with the so-called 'gestalt phenomena.' These, as will be recalled, consist in the ability of nervous systems to appreciate a great many different stimuli as instances of 'the same thing,' that is, to recognize *invariance*.

> When a square is presented to us in various positions, we still recognize it as a square — in other words, we respond to it always in the same way although the retinal elements involved are quite different each time. Again the square may be of any color, or of the same color but of different brightness. It may be drawn in black lines on a white background or in white lines on a black background. It is still recognizable as a square.[9]

Rashevsky then proceeds to describe a model by means of which a 'neural network' can solve this problem of recognition.

Thus the structure of an abstracting system must be considered to have been given.[10]

Thinking Machines, Nervous Systems, and Negative Entropy

In the meantime, other workers, studying problems connected with the construction of electronic computers and calculating machines from the point of view of invariances involved in such devices (that is, disregarding the fact that the elements were vacuum tubes, resistors, coils, wheels, etc.) formulated analogous theories.

The two programs of research, a mathematical theory of the nervous system on the one hand and the development of electronic computers on the other, proceeded along parallel lines. As can be readily surmised, such remarkable parallelism could not long remain unnoticed. Workers from both fields soon found themselves talking to each other in a language which was a curious mixture of psycho-physiology (neurons, synapses, refractory periods, threshold, etc.) and electronics (feedbacks, vacuum tubes, amplifiers, transformers, etc.). The mathematics, however, was devoid of such specialized terminology. Its abstractions (integrals, differentials, matrices, series, etc.) were disdainfully indifferent of the uses to which they were put. They reflected the basic invariances common to both sets of phenomena.

It is said that Chinese from different provinces, unable to communicate through spoken language, nevertheless can make themselves adequately understood through writing. Psychophysiologists and communication engineers found themselves in a similar situation. Although the 'pronunciations' of their respective symbols were widely different, yet the symbols themselves (that is the mathematical expressions) were quite similar.

Thus another border area arose, concerned with problems common to communication engineering and psycho-physiology. Norbert Wiener has recently dubbed it cybernetics, a term from the Greek word for governor, an allusion to the principle of negative feedback.

The wealth of ideas outlined in *Cybernetics* (New York: John

Wiley & Sons, 1948) makes it a book of enormous interest to the general semanticist, especially if he is mathematically trained. As an illustration of the close connection between the areas of study pertinent to general semantics and cybernetics, we shall describe one of the topics discussed by Wiener, namely, the relation between 'amount of information' and entropy.

The terms 'order' and 'conditionality of response' occupy, as is well known, a central position in general semantics. The former is one of the basic undefined terms. The latter is a measure of the complexness of adjustments of which an organism is capable. In thermodynamics there exists a quantitative definition of order, or rather a quantitative definition of chaos, namely, entropy, so that a natural quantitative definition of order suggests itself, namely, the negative of entropy.

Although an adequate discussion of the entropy concept is beyond the scope of this article, nevertheless an attempt will be made to illustrate the concept by an elementary example.

Arrange a deck of cards according to suits: hearts, diamonds, clubs, and spades. Note that the first twenty-six cards are all red. Now shuffle the deck thoroughly. Examine the first twenty-six cards. Approximately half of them will be red and the other half black. Now no matter how long you keep shuffling, if you examine the first twenty-six cards now and then, the overwhelming chances are that you will find the same situation: approximately half red, half black. It is practically impossible to bring the cards back into their original order by shuffling. We say that the entropy of the deck has increased. This, indeed, is the essence of the Second Law of Thermodynamics, which implies that all natural processes tend to proceed in the direction of increased entropy (greater chaos or less order). Two different gases brought into contact will soon diffuse into each other because of the random motions of the molecules, and the likelihood that they will ever be found again unmixed is vanishingly small. Heat flows from bodies of higher temperature to those at lower temperature. It is shown by consideration of the molecular structure of bodies that this also implies an increase of chaos.

There are instances, however, where opposite processes seem

to occur. The most obvious of these are those where some 'intelligence' seems to interfere. For example, we can take a well shuffled deck of cards and shortly bring it back to its factory order.[11] Involved in such an ordering is a sequence of *decisions* (this card is black; this card is red, etc.). Presumably the decisions are events in the nervous system of some organism or in some 'servo-mechanism,' to use the terminology of communications engineers. It has been conjectured that such decisions and life processes in general are somehow connected with regions where a marked lowering of entropy is taking place. Figuratively speaking, life has been compared to a process which attempts to stem the ever-onrushing tide of chaos. To quote Schroedinger:

> What an organism feeds upon is negative entropy. Or, to put it less paradoxically, the essential thing in metabolism is that the organism succeeds in freeing itself from all the entropy it cannot help producing while alive.[12]

To be sure, a hard-headed, 'realistic' scientist may dismiss such speculations as poetic romanticising, irrelevant to scientific procedure. This austere attitude is, no doubt, a reflection of the exacting standards of modern scientific rigor. Yet let us remember that before a child learns to walk, he must babble.

Towards More Complex Organization

The early formulations of general semantics, like those of any dynamic *Weltanschauung*, are naturally full of conjectures. The recent investigations of mathematical biophysics and now of cybernetics give ample testimony to the fertility of at least some of those conjectures.

One of them is the notion of an intimate connection between knowledge and ordered structure. Wiener has succeeded in formulating this connection mathematically. From a very natural definition of 'amount of information,' Wiener derives a formal mathematical isomorphism between it and the negative of entropy, which, as has been pointed out, can be taken to be the measure of order. This formulation immediately suggests relations between ordered systems and the dynamics of knowing. Indeed, so remarkable is the parallelism between ordered systems of an 'inorganic' nature and what had long been commonly regarded as 'mental phenomena,' that the remarks of Butler's Philosopher lose their sardonic character and seem to attain a prophetic significance.[13]

Finally, the application of statistical methods to two other important classes of biological problems must be mentioned, namely, the evolution and the developmental embryology of nervous systems. If one takes the point of view that the developmental potential of an organism resides in the structure of its neural net, an obvious question to ask is how this neural net comes into being.

We have already shown how cybernetics seeks to establish a formal mathematical relation between 'amount of information' and 'amount of order.' Translated into psycho-physiological terms, the relation becomes one between 'intelligence' and 'degree of oganization,' while the analogous notions in general semantics would be 'repertoire of semantic reactions' and 'conditionality of response.'

The evidence of evolution indicates that, at least along certain lines, the development of organisms has proceeded in the direction of more complex organization of the nervous system. The authors of the present article have attempted to formulate mathematically the process of embryological development of a neural net by employing statistical and stochastic methods.[14]

Essentially the problem is this: the models of neural nets which Rashevsky, Landahl, Culbertson, McCulloch, Housholder, Pitts, and others constructed to account for various psychological phenomena, contain many frequently recurring 'units of structure,' such as cycles, convergences, divergences, cross-connections, etc. How do such structures arise? What variations can be expected between individuals, species, genera, classes, etc.? What are the invariances associated with the process of their development?

In vertebrates, the basic features of the process can be described as follows: Certain regions of the embryonic ectodermal tissue give rise to specialized cells called neuroblasts. In the course of development, each neuroblast grows protuberances (axones and dendrites) which ultimately form connections (synapses) with the dendrites and axones of other neuroblasts. Such a maze of connected neurons (adult neuroblasts) is referred to as a neural net. Certain neurophysiologists, notably P.A. Weiss, have studied the factors influencing the course of such development. In particular they have sought to determine the forces influencing the direction of growth of the axones and dendrites and the specific affinities determining the patterns which are formed by the connections.

In line with this view, the authors have asked the following question. Given an initial distribution of developing neuroblasts, what can be said about the probability of certain patterns arising *in the absence* of any organising influences? In the process of the mathematical formulation of this problem, certain parameters arise, whose variations are a measure of the 'amounts of order' of the system. Hence the growth-determining factors studied by Weiss may be associated with these parameters and integrated into a mathematical theory of neural organization.

Contributions to a Science of Man

It remains to summarize the contributions which each of the three disciplines discussed here is making toward the development of a science of man.

General semantics begins with the definition of man as a time-binding class of life. Then it seeks to establish those characteristics of the human organism on which its time-binding function depends, namely, the ability to symbolize and communicate experience. This ability is shown to be a survival mechanism which distinguishes the time-binding species from others. Furthermore, this particular survival mechanism in a sense *includes* other such mechanisms inasmuch as it implies a measure of control over them. Man, for example, by means of his time-binding activities and subsequent accumulation of knowledge, can immunize himself against certain diseases, thereby 'manufacturing' what is commonly called a survival mechanism. Finally, general semantics seeks to develop techniques of symbol manipulation which would insure the maximum utilization of time-binding and thus arrives at the necessity of formulating non-aristotelian systems.

Mathematical biophysics starts with the assumption that so-called 'mental' phenomena can be described in terms of physico-chemical events in mathematical language. Some such descriptions have been successful and have led to inferences concerning the structure of the nervous system. The study of interacting nervous systems leads to a natural extension of this discipline to the social sciences.[15]

Cybernetics seeks invariant relations among servo-mechanisms (*e.g.* nervous systems and electronic computers). These invariants provide clues to the conditions underlying the knowledge of 'universals.' Again a natural extension to social science suggests itself, namely, the consideration of the role of ideas in cultural patterns and in social organization.[16]

Social Implications

We see that each approach leads naturally to the consideration of social phenomena from the point of view of interactions of organisms with particular emphasis on the interaction of their nervous systems. One might say that *the long-range program of this approach is the investigation of the way social phenomena depend on the structure of the nervous systems of the interacting organisms.*

Wiener goes a step further by extrapolating the future development of society not only in terms of the reactions of human nervous systems with each other but also in terms of relations between human nervous systems and certain devices built by human beings. In fact, these devices can be considered extra-corporeal brains (computers, harmonic analyzers, etc.). It is not at all bizarre to think of such extra-corporeal sensoria and nervous systems as biological adaptations. Indeed, they are not confined to man. Certain species of crustacea have highly innervated pouches into which they insert grains of sand immediately upon birth. The pouches together with the sand then function as equilibrium-preserving mechanisms. These animals are certainly employing extra-corporeal sensoria.

In man this process has been going on for some time, and moreover it is *cumulative*. Wiener considers the implications of this process exceedingly important. He predicts that the 'thinking machines' will make it unnecessary to employ people for making trivial decisions. Hence if our society continues to look upon human labor as a commodity to be bought and sold, we shall eventually reach a stage where a vast majority of people will have 'nothing to sell.' They will become 'superfluous.' Wiener then is forced to the conclusion that either this superfluous population will have to be done away with or *human values will have to be measured in terms other than commercial.*

The authors feel that Wiener's predictions are as yet premature. There is not sufficient evidence to infer the inevitable devaluation of the mediocre decision-maker as such. However, the authors definitely agree with Professor Wiener that the present almost universal evaluation of human beings in terms of the market value of their services (witness the expressions, 'labor market,' 'labor monopoly,' etc., widely used in the commercial press and in orthodox economics) is fundamentally pernicious. When coupled with technological advances, it serves to aggravate the misevaluations and the semantic disturbances which form the core of our social problems.

It is a truism that advances in technology are often accompanied by social ills and catastrophes because of the lag that exists between technological invention and social adjustment. It could be easily imagined that the thinking machines may likewise carry with them potentialities of social disintegration. Whether or not this disintegration can be avoided is an interesting question, but it will not be discussed here. Rather we should like to examine some of the more obvious adjustments of human behavior which will have to accompany the development of thinking machines.

Some of these adjustments have already imperceptibly diffused through our culture. Switchboard girls, comptometrists, I.B.M. operators, etc., are all people who have been trained in the use of extra-corporeal 'nervous systems.' Wherein consists their training? It consists in being able to ask very simple but *meaningful* questions. To be sure, the questions are not asked by the usual form of communication. But neither are mathematical equations stated in 'every day language.' Yet the formulation of a problem as a mathematical equation is essentially a formulation of a question in the most meaningful and manipulable form. And so is the operation of a thinking machine. The development of thinking machines implies primarily a growth of the repertoire of questions which may be meaningfully put to them. Hence, the training of people employed in operating these machines is essentially a training in *a new kind of communication.* This aspect of machine manipulation may seem ludicrous to those who associate contemporary technology with the frustrations of monotonous 'assembly line' labor. The authors venture to suggest that these frustrations are due not so much to the super-organized character of our production as to the disorganized character of our competitive society. A mathematician 'discoursing' with a mammoth differential analyzer does not feel frustrated.

It takes skill to ask meaningful questions. The history of knowledge is largely a development of the ability to ask such questions and the recognition of their importance. Contrary to this striving for objective cognition run the partialities, wishful thinking, social involvements and superstitions which encumber our communicative process. The thinking machine (at least at this stage of its development) has no ideology. Moreover its 'sanity' is measurable in terms of its performance.

The semantic implications of mathematical biophysics and cybernetics are pointing a way to a measure of our own sanity. How meaningful are the questions we ask ourselves and each other, and to what degree do we let 'static' distort our answers? Perhaps we can eventually manage to keep ourselves at least as sane as our extra-corporeal nervous systems. With that minimum of sanity (i.e., the effective use of our problem-solving potential at all levels of complexity) we may begin to hope for a fuller realization of what Korzybski has called the 'manhood of humanity.'

NOTES AND REFERENCES

1. Norbert Wiener, *Cybernetics*, New York: John Wiley, 1948.
2. A research unit in mathematical biophysics was formed at the University of Chicago in 1935. It is now organized as the Committee on Mathematical Biology.
3. A. Korzybski, 'Fate and Freedom,' as quoted in *The Language of Wisdom and Folly*, Irving J. Lee, editor.
4. A. Korzybski, *Science and Sanity*, 2nd edition, p. 273.
5. Not to be confused with the 'non-aristotelian postulates.' The authors believe these principles to underlie the 'jumping off' platform of Korzybski's formulation. In the course of the formulation, he arrives at the necessity of constructing a 'non-aristotelian system.' The non-aristotelian postulates are then offered as the foundations of the system.
6. For a fuller discussion of the consequences of anthropomorphism in scientific questions see A. Rapoport, 'Newtonian Physics and Aviation Cadets,' *Et cetera*, 1.154 (1944).
7. N. Rashevsky, *Mathematical Biophysics*, University of Chicago Press, rev. ed., 1948.
8. F.S.C. Northrup, 'The Neurological and Behavioristic Psychological Basis of the Ordering of Society by Means of Ideas,' *Science*, April 23, 1948.
9. N. Rashevsky, *Mathematical Biophysics*, revised edition, p. 448.
10. The general semanticist will immediately recognize in the schematic representation of Rashevsky's model a neural counterpart of the Structural Differential. Subsequently McCulloch and Pitts and later Culbertson constructed other models.
11. This illustration is not meant as an example contradicting the Second Law of Thermodynamics inasmuch as the system considered is not isolated. It is brought out merely to show that the processes where an 'intelligence' interferes may seem to tend toward decreased entropy whereas they tend toward greater entropy when 'left to themselves.'
12. E. Schroedinger, *What Is Life?* Compare this definition with Goethe's Mephistopheles' definition of himself as the antithesis of the creative principle:

> I am the Spirit that Denies
> And justly so: for all things, from the Void
> Called forth, deserve to be destroyed.
> 'T were better, then, were naught created.

and his admission of failure:

> How many have I made away with!
> Yet ever circulates a newer, fresher blood.
> It makes me furious, such things beholding:
> From Water, Earth, and Air unfolding,
> A thousand germs break forth and grow . . .

13. *Cf.* Samuel Butler, *Erehwon*.
14. *Cf.* various articles on the statistical approach to the theory of the nervous system by A. Rapoport and A. Shimbel in the *Bulletin of Mathematical Biophysics*, Vol. 10, 1948.

15. *Cf.*, for example, N. Rashevsky, *Mathematical Theory of Human Relations.*
16. As Northrup suggests in the above mentioned article, 'our problem of determining the relation between cultural factors and biological factors in social science becomes, in part at least, that of determining the relation between the processes of biological systems and the responses of people to particulars which embody universals.'

From the Spring 1949 Et cetera.

TOWARDS A UNIFICATION OF PHYSICS AND PSYCHOLOGY

Michael E. Gorman

It is precisely here, in an improved understanding of our mental relations to nature, that the permanent contribution of relativity is to be found. We should now make it our business to understand so thoroughly the character of our permanent mental relations to nature that another change in our attitude such as that due to Einstein, shall be forever impossible.

— P.W. Bridgman[1]

IN THE ABOVE QUOTATION, Bridgman is suggesting that the most significant contribution of a major change in the laws of physics would be a better understanding of our psychological relationship to nature. In the light of the strict line of demarcation traditionally drawn between the subject matters of physics and psychology, this idea may seem somewhat surprising. Of course, readers of this journal will recognize in A. Korzybski's *Science and Sanity* an attempt to do just what Bridgman is suggesting, i.e., to apply the findings and methods of such scientific revolutions as relativity to an "improved understanding of our mental relations to nature." In fact, Korzybski had little patience with disciplinary boundaries and even proposed a broad science of man he called General Anthropology that "would include all disciplines of human interest from a special

---

Michael Gorman is in the Department of Psychology at the University of New Hampshire.

anthropological and semantic point of view."[2] The purpose of this essay, however, is not to evaluate Korzybski's system; rather, it is my intent to show the arbitrariness of the distinction between physics and psychology and to point to some lines of convergence that promise an eventual unification of the two.

Historical Perspective

To investigate, briefly, the origins of the split between the physical and psychological universes, we must go back in time at least as far as Galileo Galilei, the famous physicist/astronomer of the early 1600s. It was he who first expressed, in modern form, the distinction between primary and secondary qualities. Galileo called "primary" such qualities as shape, motion, hardness, and number, whereas he considered phenomena like color, heat, pitch and taste secondary. According to his systematic view, primary qualities alone were properties of the "real" world; the secondary qualities represented the subjective reactions of the perceiver to that external world and were therefore derived from the primary. In short, Galileo — and later philosophers like Descartes and Locke, who echo similar opinions on this point — would argue that all the impressions produced by the senses and the mind are secondary, that beyond them lies a "real" universe composed of sizes and shapes, numbers and motion.

It is these quantifiable primary qualities that have become the subject matter of physics; all the supposedly unmeasurable secondary, subjective qualities have been banished from physics and left for the "less reputable" science of psychology. Since Galileo's time, and partially due to that great man's efforts, physics has made spectacular progress, including such important advances as Newton's all-encompassing gravitational theory, Maxwell's elegant equations describing electromagnetic fields and Einstein's theory of relativity. Psychology, on the other hand, has stumbled forward awkwardly — it has no grand syntheses or fundamental laws. But is such a comparison fair, in the light of the fact that the early physicists eliminated from their field and assigned to psychology exactly those aspects of the universe they found the most difficult to measure, i.e., the secondary qualities? As the philosopher of science E.A. Burtt notes, ". . . it does seem like strange perversity in these Newtonian scientists to further their own conquests of external nature by loading on mind everything refractory to exact mathematical handling and thus rendering the latter still more difficult to study mathematically than it had been before . . . mind was to them a convenient receptacle for the refuse, the chips and whittlings of science, rather than a possible object of scientific knowledge."[3]

While it would have been difficult — if not impossible — for physical science to develop without setting some limits on the kinds of phenomena it would incorporate, Burtt's point is well-taken: psychology has been left with "the refuse, the chips and whittlings of science." But psychologists, by refusing to accept the distinction between primary and secondary qualities, can avoid the trap that has been laid for them. For that distinction is more semantic than realistic; those qualities that physics regards as primary are, psychologically speaking, the most abstract. Such characteristics as size, motion and number are what Korzybski would call higher orders of abstraction: they are derived from, not prior to, our immediate experience, which is a haze of colors, tastes and feelings from which we construct concepts like length and motion for descriptive purposes. Therefore, these "primary qualities" are psychological abstractions, not physical realities that exist independently of consciousness.

To take this argument a step further, the data base of physics actually can be seen as part of the subject matter of psychology, in that the very invention and conduct of physics itself are acts worthy of psychological study.[4] What does it say about human beings that they developed physics in the way that they did? How do its concepts, its way of characterizing the world, reveal the basic workings of the consciousness that designed it? Psychology and physics are both products of the human imagination, both abstractions from the same reality; to see them as distinct disciplines dealing with totally different aspects of the universe is, therefore, a hopelessly inadequate viewpoint.

Recent Developments in Physics That Point Towards a Unification With Psychology

Interestingly enough, in this century a number of problems have arisen in physics that imply a breakdown of the strict observer-observed distinction and suggest that psychology may yet play an important role in the understanding of phenomena hitherto labeled as "physical." A few examples may serve to illustrate.

Before the turn of the century, it seemed fairly clear that light and other electromagnetic phenomena propagated in the form of waves. A classic demonstration of this fact involves simply passing a beam of light through a diffraction-grating: an unmistakable wave-pattern results. But in 1905, Einstein proposed that, even though light propagates as a wave, in its interaction with matter it behaves like a particle. He provided solid empirical evidence by mathematically accounting for the photoelectric effect; further experiments verified that light does, in certain situations, behave as though it were made up of particles.

All of which left physics in a bit of a dilemma: light could not both be made up of waves and particles. The famous physicist Niels Bohr argued that this apparent contradiction in the nature of light stemmed from "the impossibility of any sharp separation between the behaviour of atomic objects and the interaction with the measuring instruments which serve to define the conditions under which the phenomena appear."[5] In short, Bohr implied that light does not exist as an entity separate from the observer; on the contrary, the fact that light appears as a particle in certain situations and as a wave in others is an unavoidable result of an interaction between the phenomenon and the measurements made by the perceiver. As the eminent historian of science Gerald Holton notes:

> The study of nature is a study of artifacts that appear during an engagement between the scientist and the world in which he finds himself. And these artifacts themselves are seen through the lens of theory. Thus, different experimental conditions give different views of "nature." To call light both a wave phenomenon and a particle phenomenon is to over-simplify matters. Our knowledge of light is contained in a number of statements that are seemingly contradictory, made on the basis of a variety of

experiments under different conditions, and interpreted in the light of a complex of theories. When you ask, "What is light?" the answer is: the observer, his various pieces and types of equipment, his experiments, his theories and models of interpretation, and whatever it may be that fills an otherwise empty room when the lightbulb is allowed to keep on burning. All this, together, is light.[6]

Another example of the ways in which recent physics has had to take account of the characteristics of the observer as well as of the observed is Heisenberg's uncertainty principle, which essentially states that the very process by which one locates an elementary particle in space and time with increasing precision has the inevitable side-effect of making the determination of its momentum increasingly imprecise. In cruder and simpler terms, the more one knows about where a particle is, the less one knows about how fast it is going and vice-versa. No improvement in measuring techniques can overcome this uncertainty: it is a fundamental principle of the universe, a necessary aspect of the relationship between the observer and the observed. As Fritjof Capra argues:

> The fundamental importance of the uncertainty principle is that it expresses the limitations of our classical concepts in a precise mathematical form. As described previously, the sub-atomic world appears as a web of relations between the various parts of a unified whole. Our classical notions, derived from our ordinary macroscopic experience, are not fully adequate to describe this world. To begin with, the concept of a distinct physical entity, like a particle, is an idealization which has no fundamental significance. It can only be defined in terms of its connections to the whole, and these connections are of a statistical nature—probabilities rather than certainties. When we describe the properties of such an entity in terms of classical concepts—like position, energy, momentum, etc.—we find that there are pairs of concepts which are interrelated and cannot be defined simultaneously in a precise way. The more we impose one concept on the physical "object," the more the other concept becomes uncertain, and the precise relation between the two is given by the uncertainty principle.[7]

The problem Capra is pointing to is akin to what Korzybski would call a confusion of orders of abstraction: concepts derived from classical physics, based on "our ordinary macroscopic experience," cannot provide a completely accurate picture of events on the sub-microscopic level. What Heisenberg's principle accomplishes is a quantification of the relationship between such higher order abstractions as position and momentum and the lower-order events they seek to describe. Again, "reality" emerges as an interaction between the observer and the observed. As Korzybski himself notes, "The Heisenberg theory has succeeded in formulating (verbal) structural methods which are best suited to represent the experimental facts which underlie physics, as well as being structurally in accord with the working of the human nervous system."[8]

Still another striking example of the intimate relationship between the observer and the observed is the manner in which developments in "pure" mathematics have provided a "language," or logical system, capable of describing the new picture of the physical universe that has emerged from modern physics. The classic case is that of the non-Euclidean geometries, which were developed as exercises in abstract mathematical reasoning, an exploration of the possibilities left open by an unprovable postulate of Euclid's regarding parallel lines. Einstein, many years later, found that these same geometries provided an excellent mathematical description of the characteristics of the space-time continuum. In short, a development in pure mathematical thought was later found to correspond with the structure of reality. Other examples of the surprising connection between abstract mathematics and advances in physics abound. As the famous physicist Eugene Wigner notes, "The enormous usefulness of mathematics in the natural sciences is something bordering on the mysterious and there is no rational explanation for . . . this uncanny usefulness of mathematical concepts."[9] He cites as an illustration the use of the imaginary numbers in quantum mechanics and says, "It is difficult to avoid the impression that a miracle confronts us here (i.e., in the agreement between the properties of the hypernumber $\sqrt{-1}$ and those of the natural world)."[10]

So, mathematics and physics seem to flow together in an extraordinary harmony, even though the former is apparently more of an abstract invention of the human mind than the latter, which relies heavily on constant checking of its concepts against an experimental reality. But even this "experimental reality" does not exist outside of consciousness; it is, in its own way, as much a product of the human imagination as mathematics. As Wigner argues, "When the province of physical theory was extended to cover microscopic phenomena, through the creation of quantum mechanics, the concept of consciousness came to the fore again: it was not possible to formulate the laws of quantum mechanics in a fully consistent way without reference to . . . consciousness."[11] Is it so surprising, then, that mathematics — a product of creative human thought — should provide insights into the nature of the physical universe? For "thought" and "the universe" are intimately related; they are not separate, distinguishable entities. Mathematics may yet provide the key to a lawful expression of this relationship, a set of equations that link the observer and the observed into a scientific whole.

One of Einstein's greatest dreams — and the cherished dream of many physicists who have followed him — was the construction of a unified field theory that would reveal the fundamental connections between the four apparently distinct forces recognized by modern physics: the gravitational, electromagnetic and subatomic strong and weak forces. As two physicists noted in a recent article concerning a unified field theory: "There is no obvious reason why nature should be so complicated, and perhaps the most ambitious goal of modern physics is to discover in the diversity of particles and forces a simpler underlying order. In particular, a more satisfying understanding of nature could be achieved if the four forces could somehow be unified. Ideally they would all be shown to have a common origin: they would be viewed as different manifestations of a single more fundamental force."[12] In the same article, these two authors provide a promising outline of a possible ground on which such a unification could be achieved; it is within the range of modern physics.

Beyond the unification of physics, however, there lies an even more exciting possibility — that of a unified theory that would incorporate both the characteristics of the observer and the observed, that would make even Einstein's dream of a special case of a more general theory that would cut across the arbitrary boundaries separating psychology and physics. Certainly, this kind of a unification can at best be glimpsed hazily on the scientific horizon, especially given the fledgling state of modern psychology; however, it is not impossible and would represent an advance as stupendous as any that has been made in the history of science so far.

The Importance of a Unification of Physics and Psychology

Aside from the scientific and philosophical considerations mentioned above, there are other important factors that demand the inclusion of a psychological dimension in the study of the "physical" universe. One of the inevitable by-products—and motivating factors—in the evolution of science has been a similar growth in technology. Unfortunately, this kind of technological achievement, marvelous though it is, poses a grave threat to the future of the human race simply because it has not been accompanied by a similar increase in psychological understanding. As one of the characters in C.P. Snow's novel *The Search*, a young physics student arguing with one of his peers about the limitations of their science, puts it:

> But when I said you ought to put human beings first, that didn't mean anything at all. The how of human beings—every village gossip has been doing that since talking started. Now I know what I ought to have said. It's the why of human beings you've got to understand, Arthur. Or else you'll be giving all your science to a mob of children. Whatever they do with it, they won't know why. We can never trust them. Unless they know the why about themselves, then everything in the world is like giving a child some poison and telling it to go and play in the kitchen.[13]

The scientific revolution has produced breathtaking syntheses, marvelous glimpses into an orderly universe—but it has also succeeded in placing nuclear weapons in the hands of "a mob of children." For without an understanding of ourselves, that is exactly what we are: a "mob of children," equipped with advanced tools we can use either to destroy or create. If, as

Bridgman and Korzybski suggest, science can help us "to understand . . . the character of our permanent mental relations to nature," then in science lies the germ of a great hope for the future. But such an understanding cannot occur until the "split between the worlds," between subject and object, is transcended. It is in this sense that a unification of physics and psychology becomes essential.

NOTES AND REFERENCES

1. As quoted in A. Korzybski, *Science and Sanity* (Lakeville, Conn.: The International Non-Aristotelian Library Publishing Company), 1958, p. 648.
2. *Ibid.*, p. 39.
3. As quoted in Brian D. Mackenzie and S. Lynne Mackenzie, "The Case for a Revised Systematic Approach to the History of Psychology," *Journal of the History of the Behavioral Sciences* 10 (1974): 330. This article is an especially good source for information regarding the effect on psychology of the "splitting of the world" into primary and secondary qualities.
4. In fact, Korzybski would argue that physics and mathematics are just the kinds of things psychologists should be studying. As he puts it, "It was already emphasized that the existing 'psychologies' are animalistic or metaphysical, because either they disregard one of the most unique human characteristics, such as the behaviour called mathematizing, or they indulge in speculations on, and in, el terms. It was suggested that no human 'psychologist' can actually perform his official task unless he is an equipped student of mathematics." (*Science and Sanity*, p. 289).
5. As quoted in Gerald Holton, *Thematic Origins of Scientific Thought*, (Cambridge: Harvard U. Press, 1973), p. 119.
6. *Ibid.*, p. 120.
7. Fritjof Capra, *The Tao of Physics* (Berkeley: Shambhala, 1975), pp. 159-160.
8. Korzybski, *Science and Sanity*, p. 716.
9. Eugene P. Wigner, "The Place of Consciousness in Modern Physics," in *Consciousness and Reality*, ed. by Charles Muses and Arthur M. Young (New York: Outerbridge and Lazard, Inc. 1972), p. 139. Of course, Korzybski would explain this "uncanny usefulness of mathematical concepts" by arguing that mathematics is a language with a structure similar to that of the human nervous system. (See *Science and Sanity*, Chapter 19, pp. 287-311). As Korzybski's thesis leads into some fairly knotty issues, especially given advances in physiological psychology since the publication of *Science and Sanity*, I have avoided discussing it, although I feel a certain sympathy for his viewpoint. But certainly he would see mathematics as a system which transcends the subject-object duality, in terms of it ability to characterize invariances in relations. For, as

he notes, "It seems that relations, because of the possibility of discovering them and their invariance in both worlds, are, in a way, more 'objective' than so-called objects" (*Science and Sanity*, p. 285).
10. Wigner, "The Place of Consciousness in Modern Physics," p. 140.
11. *Ibid.*, p. 133.
12. Daniel Z. Freedman and Peter Van Nieuwenhuizen, "Supergravity and the Unification of the Laws of Physics," *Scientific American* 238 (1978): 126-143.
13. C.P. Snow, *The Search* (New York: Charles Scribner's Sons, 1934), p. 44.

From the Winter 1978 Et cetera.

III.
APPLICATIONS IN DAILY LIVING

SENSORY AWARENESS

Charlotte Read

IN SPEAKING OF 'sensory awareness' I refer to the work developed, and so named, by Charlotte Selver, which has become so influential particularly during the past few decades. Why is this approach important in training ourselves through general semantics? It offers a way of learning to *experience*, to internalize through increased awareness of our usually unconscious ways of perceiving and moving, behaving and speaking, what we try to achieve through general semantics methods, sometimes less successfully, through verbal means. We discover what it feels like to be 'silent on non-verbal levels,' to come in contact, through our senses, with what our words represent, to get in touch with the 'territory.' We practice being more in touch with ourselves-in-action, rather than clinging to some image or idea we may have of ourselves, we learn to allow and trust our organism to establish its own inner order rather than imposing what we may have learned we ought to do. This work toward increasing sensitivity becomes a study and practice for each of us in relating ourselves throughout the day to our environments, to our daily tasks, to other people, and to our deepest feelings, as we learn to quietly feel through whatever we undertake, finding out what each situation asks of us. It is thus of central importance to a theory of evaluation such as general semantics, where body mind, intellect-emotion, etc. are not split, and awareness of ourselves as living organisms becomes as important as our verbalizing.

When I discovered the work about 1955 I immediately felt it so important for persons interested in general semantics that it became an integral part of the seminar programs of the Institute ever since then. For many years there was almost nothing written on the subject. Now, finally, a book has appeared called *Sensory Awareness: The Rediscovery of Experiencing* (Viking Press, 1974), in which the work is beautifully, understandingly and clearly written about by Charles Van Wyck Brooks, student and husband of Charlotte Selver, and for many years her collaborator in teaching. Since there is much misunderstanding and often superficial interpretation of 'sensory awareness,' this authentic book is most welcome in showing the discipline in its historical perspective and in its seriousness and depth. The pioneering efforts of Charlotte Selver in this country beginning in 1938, based on the work of Elsa Gindler in Germany, has been largely responsible for the popularity of this type of awareness at growth centers and other centers throughout the country interested in the whole person.

Whoever has known the difficulties of putting into words some deeply felt experience, or who has had some practice in 'sensory awareness,' will appreciate Mr. Brooks' extraordinary achievement. He meets the challenge, shows the many facets of the work, leads the reader to the threshold of experiencing through descriptions of experiments in classes, questions raised, and through the attitudes conveyed in what he says. One may learn by reading and then — most importantly — by trying out for oneself. The book is a blend of clarifying, philosophical, poetic, autobiographical statements, permeated with Charles Brooks' wit and delightful humor. Its message is enhanced and strengthened by the many photographs which convey more than words could.

The name 'sensory awareness' in my opinion is not inclusive enough, and tends to be misleading. The subtitle of the book, 'The Rediscovery of Experiencing,' places the emphasis on awakening our usually smothered ability to experience each moment anew, as we could when we were babies or very young children. Long-shut doors may open, our world appears in fresh perspective, and our explorations can lead us to unexpected insights about ourselves, we can become more whole, more fully alive.

From the September 1976 Et cetera.

MUSIC, THE DISCIPLINE OF SILENCE

Stewart W. Holmes

I

IT HAS BEEN SAID that 'silence is golden.' Probably this nugget of wisdom was first painfully dug up by some pithecanthropic Socrates who sat dismally on a stone in front of his cave while his skin-clad Xanthippe hurled bones at his head. But at some time or another a more positive value was seen in remaining silent, a value that caused men in the Himalayas and in the Pyrenees, in the hills of Palestine and in the deserts of Egypt, to live for long periods of time with their tongues still.

To speculate as to what exactly happened inside these practitioners of silence is not our purpose here. We may simply note that the benefits must have been in some measure equivalent to the sacrifices involved in living so unaverage a life. What we do wish to note here is a modern call to silence, the reasons for it, and a relatively ready and easy way to practise it.

This call is formulated in a non-aristotelian system of evaluation which we call 'general semantics.' 'Semantics' comes from the Greek word signifying 'meaning'; Korzybski uses this term to indicate the whole system of organismal processes by which we react meaningfully to our surroundings. The aim of general semantics is to help people train themselves in sane reactions, train themselves to accept the reality principle, as some psychiatrists put it. To accomplish this, we must come as close

---

Stewart W. Holmes is a teacher and author of textbooks on general semantics.

as possible to seeing things as they are rather than as we may wish to see them. 'Our actual lives,' Korzybski writes, 'are lived entirely on the objective levels, including the unspeakable "feelings," "emotions," etc., the verbal levels being only *auxiliary*, and effective only if they are translated back into first order unspeakable effects, such as an object, an action, a "feeling," etc., all on the silent and unspeakable objective levels. In all cases of which I know at present, where the retraining of our *semantic reactions* has had beneficial effects, the results were obtained when this "silence on the objective levels" has been attained, which affects all our psycho-logical reactions and regulates them to the benefit of the organism and of his survival adaptation.'[1]

Of all God's children, only human beings go crazy in impressive numbers. Likewise, only human beings use such symbols as words. Misuse of words would seem to be a factor in the conditions producing many types of unsanity. And indeed, it is a prominent factor if we understand by the term 'misuse of words' the inability to make our world of ideas and our world of actual things correspond in a workable map-territory arrangement. The trouble is that we can affect our surroundings relatively little; we have to learn to adjust ourselves to them. But we can shape our verbal world, the maps inside our heads, in any way we wish. If we are not careful, we wishfully convince ourselves that 'everybody's out of step but Jim,' that our personal maps are always right. Then we are likely to come to grief. One way to keep from coming to such grief is to train ourselves to recognize the thing as a thing and the word as a word and to remember that the twain never meet and become one.

Many young wives have reason to train their husbands thus. For example, the husband sees an unfamiliar dish on the table. 'What's that?' 'Bread pudding. There's a war on, you know.' 'Oh,' says he, reacting to his meaning of the word *bread pudding*, 'I don't like bread pudding.' And then the young lady, being a good psychologist, maneuvers her husband into trying *her* bread pudding, into reacting to the thing (which is what will nourish him) rather than to the map-memory inside his head called *bread pudding* (which could never build an ounce of tissue).

This homely illustration of the necessity of reacting *wordlessly* to the *thing*, of continually adjusting the map inside our heads to fit the dynamic, ever-changing territory outside, may serve to point to the heart of what Korzybski means by 'retraining our semantic reactions.' The only fair way for our guinea pig to eat his bride's bread pudding is for him to put aside his old prejudices against such a dish, to react to it on the 'objective level.' Such a healthy reaction will become automatic when he makes automatic the realization that the word is *not* the thing and that, of the two, the *thing* is the more important. Except metaphorically, we cannot eat our words.

Such differentiation of these two levels of abstraction will lead in turn to differentiation of other levels of abstraction: thing, impression, word, and then descriptions and inferences in ever more generalized terms. Thus, whether we deal with the disposition of a bread pudding or of Bessarabia, we shall be adjusting our private maps to the public territories as closely as our acquaintance with things and facts permit.

To achieve this retraining, Korzybski postulates as most important 'silence on the objective level.' To effect this primary discipline he uses a three-dimensional diagram of the orders of abstraction which he and his students look at and manipulate *without speaking*. Training in silence cannot be gained through the use of words. Lectures and books are verbal. We can be told about 'silence' and we can talk about it — as we are doing at the moment — but if we think this trains us to be silent before a thing, we delude ourselves. No more can we learn to play the piano by reading a book of theory.

Yet most people, especially those who are learned in the academic, verbal world, find it difficult to react to anything in silence, to react without forming words audibly *or inaudibly*. The three-dimensional diagram referred to above (called by its author 'the structural differential' and by the irreverent, 'the semantic rosary') is of tremendous value in learning to differentiate between the various orders of abstraction and in wordlessly reminding ourselves of the correct thing-word relationship. But the writer has found another practice to be as helpful as it is pleasant in achieving the habit of reacting wordlessly to an event. This is simply—listening to music.

II

I say 'simply.' Perhaps it is not so simple, in one's home, at least. Very few people seem to be able to listen to music with undivided attention. They must be eating or drinking or talking or reading or playing cards or doing any one of a hundred things at the same time. This is not what is meant here by 'listening to music.' Nor is *outward* quiet alone sufficient, if inwardly you are reviewing the day's activities or shaping fine phrases with which to impress your co-listener when the selection ends. Nor even is an interpretive play of the imagination allowed if you conjure storm clouds out of one phrase, a quiet meadow with a faun chasing a nymph out of the next. For training in silence, no transposition of sounds into picture *or* words is allowed while the music is being played.

The realization must be understood and confirmed that whatever you say that music is, it is *not*. If you substitute a word for a musical phrase, you are experiencing your word rather than the composer's music.

To express what is meant positively rather than negatively is difficult, since—and this is the important point—the value of the experience is its very wordlessness. The type of music which I have found best adapted both to my pleasure and to the 'discipline of silence' is chamber music. This music is almost purely structural. 'Bodiless,' Spengler called it. It is related closely to mathematics, also a bodiless form of symbol. It is significant that the fugal style was worked out at the same time that Liebnitz and Newton were discovering the infinitesimal calculus and the four point movement was evolved when Euler was formulating functional analysis. Spengler, in his historical analysis of the arts of form, speaks of chamber music as 'our deepest and most intimate kind of music. . . . Certain it is that the violin is the noblest of all instruments that the Faustian soul has imagined and trained for the expression of its last secrets, and certain it is, too, that it is in string quartets and violin sonatas that it has experienced its most transcendent and most holy moments of full illumination. Here, in *chamber music*, *Western art as a whole reaches its highest point*.[2]

Such music is alone amongst all the arts in that it affords a communication at once to our highest 'cortical' centers by reason of its high degree of abstraction and also to our 'sub-cortical' centers, since it is a direct, objective experience of sounds which imitate nothing in the world of nature. A possible exception to my generalization is modern art, for which Oliver Bloodstein claims something similar. 'In a painting we can be made to "visualize" structure, to experience it apart from a great many incidental concomitants, and to experience it on sub-cortical levels.... By re-translating our higher order verbal abstractions of relations and order into simplified but direct manifestations which can be visualized and felt, modern art affords immediate, sub-cortical experience of essential structure.'[3]

To divorce everything you see in a modern painting — bits of glass, eyes, profiles, umbrellas, serpentine lines — from all recollections of other pictured or actual bits of glass, eyes, etc., seen elsewhere is to many people extremely difficult. That amount of effort is practically nonexistent when you listen to a Beethoven string quartet whose sounds resemble neither the meowing of a cat nor the squeak of a door nor the bark of a dog nor anything else one has ever heard outside the world of music.

III

It must be admitted that this advantage is also the chief reason for the lack of popularity of chamber music. If people insist on making verbal noises about the music they hear, or insist on conjuring up pictures, they will find music which discourages such practices to be disagreeable and annoying. A little persistence will cure this if the subject genuinely wishes a semantic re-training. And without this latter condition, there is no hope anyway.

'Immediate experience,' writes Korzybski, 'always unspeakable, is strictly connected with the lower centres. In the translation of experience into higher order abstractions and language, the unspeakable character of experience is lost, and a new neurological process is needed to re-translate these higher order abstractions into new lower order abstractions, and thus fully and successfully complete the nervous cycle. . . . If the translation is made into the language of lower centres, namely, into "intuitions," "feelings," "visualizations," the higher abstractions gain the character of experience."[4] In chamber music this cycle of translation is rendered unnecessary. The experience itself is at the same time on the unspeakable level and also on that of the higher order abstractions. The music charms us by the mutual relationships of its sounds; we are made feelingly, intuitively, aware of complex structure at the same time (and partly, at least, because) we are experiencing our 'most transcendent and most holy moments of full illumination.' In the world of the mystical experience, no saint's words, no picture or statue of the world's greatest artists can possibly convey the intense feeling of holy at-oneness with archetypal Humanity in its most Christ-like state that the third movement, *Molto adagio*, of Beethoven's fifteenth *Quartet in A Minor*, affords the listener who will be *silent*. His nervous system is affected directly by the order embodied in these bodiless vibrations whose only meaning is in that very order.

Music, then, I call the Discipline of Silence because listening intently and wordlessly to chamber music first, avoids the use of words as in lectures and books; second, discourages the use of words by the extreme immateriality of the subject; third, makes it easy to check the rise of words or other symbols to consciousness because it consists of vibrations that have only a remote relationship with objects in our ordinary experience; fourth, offers the almost unique opportunity to avoid the cycle of translation and retranslation from lower to higher to lower order abstractions by presenting us with a dynamic symbol of the universal order which is itself an experience of order and structure. We are affected in a way extremely beneficial to our organism, since our impression of order and of the primacy of the thing level has directly the character of experience.

Last but not least, the pill is sugar-coated. To enjoy the art of our 'culture' at its best while our nervous system is being recanalized sounds almost like too much of a psychological bargain to be true. The test will be in each reader's own experiences.

NOTES AND REFERENCES

1. Korzybski, Alfred, *Science and Sanity, An Introduction to Non-Aristotelian Systems and General Semantics.* Lancaster, Pa., 1933. p. 35.
2. Spengler, Oswald, *The Decline of the West.* Alfred Knopf, New York, 1932. I, 231.
3. Oliver Bloodstein, 'General Semantics and Modern Art,' *Et cetera,* I, 16 (August, 1943).
4. Quoted in Bloodstein, *op. cit.*

From the Autumn 1945 Et cetera.

BODY LANGUAGE: NONVERBAL BEHAVIOR AS A COMMUNICATIVE STIMULUS

Phillip V. Lewis

MAN IS A MULTI-SENSORIAL being who occasionally verbalizes; the real language is behavior.[1] Touch, tone of voice, facial expression, rate of speech, propinquity with colleagues, relaxation or tension in posture speak in clear tones. The adage, "What you are speaks so loudly I cannot hear what you say," is beginning to be of practical value. Pride, presumption, antagonism, jealousy, competitiveness, love, friendliness, and kindness are being heard by others. Our real message is being sent loud and clear. We are communicating by *body language*.

Thus, new terms are being found in the literature — kinesics, instrumental affiliative functions, ingratiation tactics, gesticulations, paralinguistic cues, semiotics, or extralinguistic areas. These terms have now become of interest to a new group of scientists — "ethnologists." Ethnology is a branch of anthropology dealing with the cultural and environmental differences of various people. Recently, enthnology has been given a new dimension — nonverbal communication or body language.

"Body language and kinesics are based on the behavioral patterns of nonverbal communication, but kinesics is still so new as a science that its authorities can be counted on the fingers of one hand."[2] In fact, "there has been relatively little systematic investigation of the information" that may be transmitted

---

Phillip V. Lewis is on the faculty of Administrative Services and Business Education, Oklahoma State University, Stillwater.

by nonverbal behavior, kinesics, or body language.[3] Research on body position and facial expression "has had to deal with a phenomenon that is continuously occurring, has no readily apparent unit of measurement or method of evaluation, and is both difficult and expensive to record."[3]

Communicative behavior research has increasingly focused on the verbal interpersonal transactions rather than the nonverbal. Most of us speak at least one oral language, but everyone speaks body language. Communication analysts tend to agree that perhaps most "of the expression of emotional and motivational states occurs on nonverbal levels,"[4] and is communicable "by facial and paralinguistic cues, although the cues themselves seldom have been identified."[5]

The conclusion of the research that has been conducted is revealing: whether we are sitting, walking, lying down, or standing still, we are communicating information about ourselves to those around us.

> During the course of the day we blush, sweat, gasp, choke, cough, twitch, squirm, scratch, blink, fidget and wiggle. As Freud said, "betrayal oozes from every pore." A suppressed smile, a lifted eyebrow or a wrinkling of the nose can serve as a barometer of how the speaker feels about what he is saying or, alternatively, how he is reacting to what is being said.[6]

One's ability to communicate with others goes far beyond the ability to write or speak well.

We communicate with words but not with words alone. The following formula depicts the proportion between our words and the other parts of our communication:[7]

 7 percent   words only
38 percent   tone and inflection
55 percent   facial expression, body position, and gestures (body language)

Our body language seems to convey our frame of mind with the same accuracy as our most carefully selected words. Therefore, every move we make may reveal our origins, attitudes, and health, or even the state of our psychological balance. A furrowed brow, pursed lips, the pointed index finger, head-wagging, the "horrified look," hands on hips, arms folded across chest, wringing hands, or patting another on the head are typical reactions to what is being said or heard.[8] Everyone constantly reacts in a conversation, but words are only a portion of it.

To understand body language one has only to think of gestures. Gesture is our first speech; it shapes and clarifies our thoughts. Try, for example, to describe a spiral staircase without using your hands. Gestures reveal "the conscious and, more importantly, unconscious images of our minds. They are mostly instinctive and not under our conscious control. Gesture is our adaptive response to exterior situations and stimuli."[9]

Narcotic squads are watching body language for possible users and pushers of dope. Detectives are students of body language to discover shoplifters or determine if a suspect is lying. Studies are being made of the unconscious widening of the pupil when the eye sees something stimulating. In fact, body language is more and more a factor to pay attention to—the basis of techniques for dealing with other people.

To know something about body language is to master another technique for more effective communication in certain situations. The following are some examples that should aid in decoding body language.[9]

1. Pulling one's ear is a gesture of interest—"Tell me more."
2. Closing and opening fists—fight-or-flight conflict.
3. Hands in pockets or behind back represent fear of contact or exposure to others.
4. Clenched fist(s) is a desire to convince others.
5. Arms intertwined or held close to chest is a defensive gesture; be prepared to do a lot of convincing.
6. Arms extended straight over head is a symbol of power and authority, love of limelight.
7. Hands together while sitting or standing suggests an attempt to hold oneself together.

While these habitual "languages" should aid in decoding nonverbal communication, they must be "taken with a grain of salt" or judged in the situational context. Body language is by no means an exact science, although it "is as rich, unlimited, and varied as mankind itself, and we are just on the threshold of discovering its infinite variety."[9]

NOTES AND REFERENCES

1. Birdwhistell, R.L. Kinesic analysis in the investigation of emotions. In *Expression of the Emotions in Man*. New York: International Universities Press, 1963.
2. Fast, Julius. *Body Language*. New York: Simon and Schuster, Inc., 1970.
3. Ekman, Paul. Body position, facial expression, and verbal behavior during interviews. *Journal of Abnormal and Social Psychology*, 1964.
4. Birdwhistell, R.L. Paralanguage 25 years after Sapir. In *Lectures on Experimental Psychiatry*. Pittsburgh: University of Pittsburgh Press, 1961.
5. Dairtz, F.R. *The Communication of Emotional Meaning*. New York: McGraw-Hill, 1964.
6. Feinberg, Mortimer R. Sabotage by body language. *Business Management*, March, 1971.
7. Mehrabian, Albert. Communication without words. *Psychology Today*, 1970.
8. Harris, Thomas A. Analyzing the transaction. In *I'm OK – You're OK: A Practical Guide to Transactional Analysis*. New York: Harper & Row, 1969.
9. Fiel, Maxine Lucille. What His Hands Tell. *Mademoiselle*, November, 1970.

From the September 1973 Et cetera.

FASHION: THE SARTORIAL COMMUNICATION REVOLUTION

Paul Lippert

THE LATE MIDDLE AGES of European culture was a time of incremental change behind the façade of a crumbling social order. Through the cracks in the feudal establishment seeped the first drops of a new era which promised to burst forth in a flood of new ideas, inventions, explorations, social relations, and untold economic growth. Our historians depict a society that had plainly exhausted its possibilities and could do nothing but give way to its replacement.[1] It is at this time that a developing merchant class was helping to build the trade relations, productive capacities, and other prerequisites upon which the future system of capitalism was to be based.

As these forces of social transition gathered strength and began to act upon society, they spurred the growth of new technologies (hard and soft) which encouraged, hastened, and directed this change. The invention of a particular grouping of these technologies and the effects considered to be directly related to them has been labelled the Communication Revolution. Most prominent in this group of inventions are the printing press, the utilization of the phonetic alphabet in the vernacular for mass literacy, the ability to reproduce graphic illustrations, the use of perspective in drawing, the adoption of Arabic numerals including zero, and, after the eighteenth century when the transition can be said to have been more or less completed, photography, moving pictures, and the various electronic media.

Paul Lippert is Managing Editor of *Et cetera*.

The purpose of this paper is to describe and account for the radical change in another medium of communication during this transition in Western Civilization to the modern era which deserves to be considered as an integral part of this Revolution. I am referring to the medium of clothing and its communicative transformation through the development of fashion.

First of all, it must be made clear that fashion, as I am using the term, refers not merely to the fact that a particular mode of dress is thought desirable by any particular group of people but to a process whereby the forms that clothing takes are constantly changing, where different modes compete with, replace, and blend with one another. Clothing has always been used for some expressive function,[2] but fashion is the mechanism by which particular forms are singled out as appropriate for particular social conditions.

It has been argued that fashion has the power to act as a barometer of the social climate, similar to the way that the other mass media have been observed to mirror the course of the culture. James Laver, the noted British art historian, was overwhelmed by the thought of this expressive power. In his *Taste and Fashion*, a book which describes the evolution of Western dress from the French Revolution to the outbreak of the Second World War, he remarks that fashion is, ". . . something very mysterious, as if the Time Spirit were a reality, clothing itself ever in the most suitable garments and rejecting all others. One is almost driven back on the mystical conception of Zeitgeist, who determines for us every detail of our lives, down to gestures, turns of phrase, and even thoughts."[3]

But even if one does not agree with the assertion that fashion may serve as a summary of the essential qualities of a culture, surely it may be conceded that clothing plays a communicative role *within* a society in regard to status and sexuality. With this acknowledgement we may proceed to describe the genesis and some of the effects of the Sartorial Revolution.

It seems that Western Civilization is alone in its development of fashion (although, this Western concept has spread to nearly every culture on the globe). Other cultures, from hunter-gatherer societies to the more technologically advanced Chinese and Moslems, never developed this need for constantly changing modes of dress which seems so natural to our society. Using China as a representative of non-Western cultures, Bell draws this distinction with a simile which brings to mind McLuhan's opposition between visual, linear and acoustic, "allatonce" cultures: "Western costume is like a river: throw in a novelty and it will flow downstream. Chinese costume on the other hand is like a pond: that which it floats it keeps." Thus when a relatively short-lived novelty, the pigtail, was imposed by the Manchus on Chinese culture, it remained an integral part of dress for nearly three hundred years.[4]

Fashion was equally absent from our own culture up through much of the Middle Ages. Its beginnings have been traced back as far as the thirteenth century but become more apparent with the importation of large quantities of exotic clothing from Byzantium and the Levant and the influence of these imports on native dress.[5] From there on the speed at which the predominant styles of dress change accelerates along with the accelerating growth of trade and the size of the merchant and artisan classes. But it was not merely the availability of more numerous and varied goods which caused this. There was a social change of a much more fundamental nature taking place.

In almost all known societies the predominant elements of clothes symbolism have been the expression of hierarchic status of one form or another and sexuality.[6] As the standards in these two areas and the classes which they form have tended to be quite fixed in almost all societies prior to our own, their expression in clothing has been equally static. Indeed, as should be well known, the leaders of societies have been quite attentive to the use of clothes symbolism as a means of imposing and maintaining their desired social order, much the same way as other media or symbol systems such as language, writing, or the mass media may be controlled to political ends.

This use of clothing style as a means of maintaining the symbolic hierarchy was well known to the leaders of medieval Europe. Similar to the manner in which the Catholic Church maintained its guardianship over the written word as a means of preserving the symbolic order of society, the feudal aristocracy enacted rather strict sumptuary laws which regulated the dress of the various classes. These laws went so far as to specify exactly what dress was appropriate for each social class. But as the class of the bourgeoisie took form and strengthened, the feudal standards of propriety and the laws which enforced them lost their effectiveness. In their exuberant desire to outshine the knights, the merchants symbolized their growing economic and political power in their clothes. For dress is the most immediate and personal outward symbol of one's world view and social position.[7]

This aspect of clothes symbolism as the expression of social hierarchy and status is perhaps best understood by Veblen. According to his theory of conspicuous consumption, the major determinant of the dress of all the classes in society is the display and emulation of pecuniary power.[8]

But how are we to account for the constant style changes? Why would a triumphant bourgeouisie not in turn impose its own specific dress standards in place of those of the vanquished aristocracy? In answering this we must keep Veblen in mind, but it is necessary to go beyond him in order to note a peculiarity of this new dominant class.

Throughout history, the ruling classes of the various societies as have existed can be categorized as either priestly, warrior, or some combination of the two. Although much of their distinction has always been pecuniary, the primary basis of their superior position in the social hierarchy has been their pugnacity and/or imputed divine endowment. However, in capitalist society, whose upper strata are filled essentially by the mercantile class, the chief determinant of social position is economic success in a more or less competitive marketplace. This marketplace, being relatively fluid and open to constant shifts in power when compared with military and religious domination, allowed for the opportunity of patterns of status to be challenged constantly. The new social order, at least in principle, would allow the people of the lower social strata to compete with those in the upper strata — and each other — for positions at the top. And such a society, which is itself capable of constant change, is necessary in order to have changing fashions.[9] For it would seem natural that any competition or imitation in status or hierarchy should be reflected in dress habits, and, as I shall now try to show, it is precisely this competitive imitation which makes fashion possible.[10]

So, given a situation where all classes are relatively free to compete in economic spheres—including dress—with their superiors, the chic bourgeois turns to the coutourier for new, and singularly expensive, modes of dress in order to maintain her social distinction. But alas, within a short period of time almost exact copies of her priceless creation have been made by the second rung dressmakers in slightly less expensive fabric. These in turn influence the cut of the more common dresses and the patterns bought by women who make their own dresses. With the advent of mass production and centralization of clothing manufacture, this diffusion could take place in as little as a few weeks. And so Madame, upon seeing her maid dressed in a somewhat shoddy but rather stylistically accurate knock-off copy of her original, will soon tire of the dress and will feel compelled to buy another plus outré.

The more that rigid class distinctions in style disappear, the more does the struggle for chic become a means of maintaining the sartorial hierarchy.[11] But what drives the ever-increasing pace of fashion change onward is the fact that the closer more people come to achieving the standards of chic, the more that those standards become vulgar, and the sooner they are replaced with new, more unattainable standards. Although fashion abhors the independent singularity of sartorial expression that would allow one to break free of her tyranny, she is equally threatened by too successful conformity to her demands.[12]

This constant diffusion of the cultural traits of the upper class through the common medium of fashion might be seen as similar to the observed cultural equalizing effect of the other mass media, especially television. Just as the same modes of dress are spread throughout the population in the form of the same styles (although unequal quality) of clothing, so are popularized versions of the cultural traits of the more reputable elements of our society presented in our daily television fare. This process of diffusion and emulation can also be witnessed in the mass marketing of commodities through the mass media.

The addiction to novelty which can be seen in the constantly changing fashions of our times is mirrored in our equally fickle mass media entertainment. This likeness may be attributed to their common occurrence in a competitive market where that which ceases to sell the most is immediately replaced with that which does. Also, the power of both types of media — clothing and TV — to quickly and thoroughly saturate the culture with any particular new piece of content must surely cause the public to tire of it all the sooner.

The constant drive for novelty has as a consequence pushed both the fashion and other mass media to engage in what has been called "conspicuous outrage."[13] Pursuing the need to shock and titillate, both fashion and the electronic media must constantly strive to go just beyond the bounds of propriety. This is as true of the cavalcade of sexual and horrific material that we view on television, in movies, etc. as of the bizarre contrivances of fashion and its tendency to shift its focus from one erogenous zone to another.

It can also be said that both the electronic media and the medium of fashion have a tendency to distort or destroy our sense of history, our awareness that the present is but a step in the progression of time. Both concentrating almost exclusively on the here and now, the two kinds of media cause us to see the past through the strongly distorting lens of present tastes and biases. Television and the other modern media are continually altering any historical material or classic literature that they might carry in order to make them "relevant to today." Likewise, there is an analogous tendency for the costume described in literature, presented in plays, movies, paintings, and even sculpture to veer from historical accuracy in order that it may come into line with prevailing aesthetic standards. For this reason a number of artists, notably Reynolds, have expressed a preference to exclude the fashionable details of dress from their works.[14]

By undermining our society's standards and shifting its perspective at a dizzying pace, fashion and the electronic media do not provide the type of experience that is conducive to a mature, well-integrated outlook on the world. When everything is "the absolute most" the day it is introduced, and then loathed or forgotten, we are encouraged to be at the mercy of the moment, like children.[15]

But perhaps most significant about fashion, like the other mass media, is its ubiquity. Exerting their influence toward international cultural homogeneity yet constant change, fashion and the electronic media create an experiential environment which influences our behavior, helping to shape our sexual appetites and erotic imaginations, our view of history, and our aesthetic tastes.[16] The trends of fashion, as well as the daily doings of the other mass media, command us to "get with it" with a force unsurpassed by any other cultural institution. It was undoubtedly under the spell of fashion that Herbert Spencer said, "The consciousness of being perfectly dressed may bestow a peace such as religion cannot give."[17]

And so, if it can be recognized that fashion, as a medium spawned by the Communication Revolution during Western Civilization's emergence from the Dark Ages, plays an important role along with the other media in the symbolic order of our society, we might proceed to learn how to read its messages and observe its influence on our social behavior. But we must be forewarned that fashion may have no less an effect on one who studies it than on those one studies, for, as a prominent social scientist once noted,

> 'Seest thou not, I say, what a deformed thief this fashion is? How giddily he turns about all the hot bloods between fourteen and five and thirty. . . . ?
> 'All this I see, and I see that the fashion wears out more apparel than the man. But art not thou thyself giddy with the fashion too, that thou hast shifted out of thy tale into telling me of the fashion?'

NOTES AND REFERENCES

1. See Barbara Tuchman, *A Distant Mirror* (New York: Alfred A. Knopf, 1978).
2. J.C. Flugel, *The Psychology of Clothing* (London: The Hogarth Press, 1950), pp. 17-8.

3. James Laver, *Taste and Fashion* (London: George G. Harrap and Company Ltd., 1945), p. 199.
4. Quentin Bell, *On Human Finery* (New York: Schocken Books, 1976), pp. 59; 93-4.
5. *Ibid.*, pp. 60; 113-4.
6. Flugel, *op. cit.*, pp. 25-33.
7. Max von Boehn, *Modes and Manners*, tr. J. Joshua (London: Harrap, 1932), p. 215.
8. Thorstein Veblen, *The Theory of the Leisure Class* (New York: The New American Library, 1953), pp. 118-131.
9. Bell, *op. cit.*, pp. 113-5.
10. Paul Henry Nystrom, *Economics in Fashion* (New York: Ronald Press, 1928), pp. 25-6.
11. Laver, *op. cit.*, p. 203.
12. William Hazlitt, *On Fashion, Complete Works* (1933), Vol. XVII, p. 51, cited in Bell, *op. cit.*
13. Bell, *op. cit.*, p. 203.
14. *Ibid.*, pp. 68-83.
15. Bernard Rudofsky, *Are Clothes Modern?* (Chicago: Paul Theobald, 1947), p. 230.
16. Bell, *op. cit.*, p. 62.
17. Rudofsky, *op. cit.*, p. 88.

From the Spring 1981 Et cetera.

DO YOU KNOW HOW TO LISTEN?

Wendell Johnson

IN A FUNDAMENTAL SENSE, psychological counselors and psychiatrists operate a good deal of the time as professional listeners. Over the years, particularly since Freud, they have learned the hard way that for listening to be effective certain principles or rules must be observed.

Two of these principles are essentially those emphasized by Professor Steer's findings: stay relatively relaxed and hear the speaker out. The psychologists have elaborated and supplemented these basic rules, however, in several ways. As developed by these professionals, the procedure of the good listener seems simple, sensible — and most unusual. The great contribution of the late Dr. Sigmund Freud lay not only in what he discovered about human personality but also in the *method* by which he discovered it. In fact, one need not subscribe to Freud's theories in order to admire his methods. Fundamentally, this method grew out of Freud's discovery that in order to get to know and understand the patient it is necessary for the doctor to refrain from giving advice, to abstain from moral judgments, and to listen patiently and for a long, long time while the patient talks as freely as he will and in extraordinary detail. This was certainly something new in medical practice, and the fierce opposition to Freud arose not only out of the shocked sensibilities of the lay public, but also out of the outraged pride of a medical

---

The late **Wendell Johnson** was a Professor of Speech Pathology, University of Iowa.

profession accustomed to giving orders rather than giving painstaking attention to anything and everything the patients might want to say to their physicians. In effect, Freud was telling the doctors to button their lips, to be humble, to stop lecturing their patients, and start learning from them.

For all practical purposes, this was the beginning of the modern development of listening as a fine art. Freud's beginnings were substantial and they have been extended by many who followed him. Of these, Professor Carl Rogers of the University of Chicago, is one of the most widely known. His book, *Counseling and Psycho-therapy*, published in 1942, may be viewed as a handbook for anyone who would become an effective listener. Perhaps the one word that sums up Rogers' listening method most aptly is the term 'permissive.' What it means in practice is that the client (a term Rogers prefers to 'patient') is fully *permitted* to say whatever he likes without fear of blame—or danger of misdirective approval. The counselor confines his remarks mainly to *restating what the client has said* (although usually in slightly different words), so that the client feels not only that he is being listened to, but that he is being genuinely understood.

The procedure is commonly referred to as nondirective counseling. It tends to have two important effects. It encourages the client to speak freely and fully. For this reason, and also because of the attitude the counselor must maintain in order to listen in such a fashion, it tends to make for an unusual depth of understanding of the client by the counselor. This colors the entire relationship beneficially with constructive efforts so far as the client is concerned. The general principle pointed up by all this is that not only does effective listening have its rewards, but also to be listened to permissively and at length has generally good effects. It is an ancient wisdom that talk is curative; a modern refinement is that talk is most curative when done to a permissive listener.

Another significant contribution to the art of listening has been made in recent years by general semantics. General semantics is by no means exclusively concerned with the art of listening. It provides a general approach to problems of evaluation, stressing the rudiments of scientific method, so formulated as to be useful from moment to moment in daily living. The contributions it makes to the art of listening are to be found especially in certain key questions it encourages the listener to ponder as he attends to any speaker.

The first of these questions is particularly potent, although it may sound drably familiar at first glance to be too obvious to warrant special attention. It is simply this: What does the speaker mean? The word to be scrutinized in this question is 'mean.' Generally speaking, we take for granted that what the speaker means by what he says is precisely what we would mean if we were to say the same thing. We forget that the meaning of a word is not in the word; it is in the person who uses it or responds to it. And people differ. So it is that a word means different things to different persons, in different contexts, under different circumstances. The skilful listener, therefore, starts with the attitude that he doesn't know what the speaker's words mean to the speaker, and that in order to find out, as well as he might, he must attend to the context and the circumstances. He exercises the further attitude that any interpretation he may make of the speaker's words will be his own interpretation, not necessarily universal, and that he must take full responsibility for it himself.

Because he has such attitudes, the semantic listener demands a great deal of the speaker. What he demands primarily is that the speaker operate with similar attitudes. It falls upon the speaker, therefore, to take special pains to make his own meanings as clear as possible, to choose his words well — and to distrust them, to suspect them of vagueness and ambiguity, to suspect his own interpretations of them of being personal and private, in need of painstaking clarification. It is positively startling to imagine what might happen in future political campaigns for example, if all the listeners in this country were to insist that the candidates leave no statement unclarified beyond reasonable question.

This what-do-you-mean? attitude can be cultivated to an extraordinary degree, and as developed by certain students of general semantics its effects in promoting clear-headedness is marked. If the attitude ever takes hold on a national scale, advertising is going to have to undergo a major operation, if indeed, it will be able to survive at all. Radio commentators, professors, editorial writers, politicians, and other word-hucksters will be caught woefully short of syllables if ever the school children of this country are taught to recognize and demand significant clarity in verbal discourse.

After a general semanticist has discovered what you mean, he also wants to know what reliable factual observations have been made—or could be made how, when and where—in order to verify your statements. In other words, his second question is, 'How do you know?' He wants to know what you are talking about in a down-to-earth, factual, seeing, hearing, smelling, tasting, touching sense. He wants to see the data. He wants photographs. He is asking for a demonstration. He is saying, 'Show me.' At the very least, he wants a diagram. As he listens to your words, he insists on being able to visualize what they might refer to. He is the most demanding listener the world has ever known.

This does not mean that he is intolerant of 'abstractions' and generalizations. He insists upon them no less than other listeners do. It is only that he insists, also, that they be defensible. He merely asks, quite reasonably, that evidence supporting them be produced, or if it can't be he wants to know the procedures whereby it might be obtained. Before he takes your check he wants to know that it actually represents money in the bank. He asks not only that your statements be clear — that they refer to something unambiguously — but also that they be valid. A true statement is necessarily clear, but a clear statement is not necessarily true. In the immortal words of the University of Chicago's grand old professor of physiology, Anton J. Carlson, the general semanticist is continually asking, 'Vat is de effidence?'' It is question that promotes extremely efficient listening.

A third basic semantic question is this: 'What is the speaker leaving out?' This encourages the extraordinary art of listening for what the speaker does not say. What he does not say turns out, as a rule, to fall into one of three general categories. He may leave out important factual details; he may fail to draw certain possible conclusions, while overstressing the ones he favors; and he may neglect to develop the implications of the conclusions he does draw. The good listener, then, hears far more than the speaker says; he hears what he might have said, too. And what he might have said not infrequently renders what he does say inadequate, irrelevant, or misleading.

The good listener realizes that there are no exhaustible subjects — certainly not the subject of good listening. But one more point remains to be emphasized. It is that in order to listen effectively, one must disregard symbols of authority, in and of themselves. A speaker's family name, his title, academic degrees, the uniform he wears, the name of his sponsor, or the banners that flutter about him as he speaks are not necessarily 'effidence' of the reliability or validity of his remarks. Moreover, the quality of his voice, the color of his skin, the slant of his eyes, his height, weight and apparent age guarantee nothing with respect to the wisdom or foolishness of what he says. Truth can be lisped, stuttered, or twanged through the nose just as well as it can be molded by a meticulous Harvard or Oxford tongue. It can be mispronounced. It may be ungrammatical. Whether it comes in a satin case or a paper bag is a matter of no importance.

So much, at least, we know with reasonable certainty about the art of listening. It is a simple, difficult and neglected art. It does not 'come naturally' — although it might if our education did not prevent it. Our education, however, shows signs of blowing up a rain, so to speak. In courses in general semantics, speech, the psychology of language, and in other, sometimes unlikely, courses, in a steadily increasing number of colleges and universities, an ever larger number of students are being taught how to listen so as to come out by a different door from that wherein they went.

What is being taught to these students — and what has been presented here — may be summarized quite briefly: In order to cultivate the art of listening, one must at least relax and hear the speaker out — with a permissive understanding attitude, disregarding the speaker's symbols of authority, or lack of them, all the while asking, 'What does he mean?' 'How does he know?' and 'What is he leaving out?'

As Stuart Chase once remarked concerning the rudiments of straight thinking, so one may say of the principles of effective listening: they are not hard to learn, they are just unusual. In the meantime, our need to learn them and apply them is becoming more and more urgent. As the world grows more ominously voluble by the hour, the words we hurl at each other are no more confusing and maddening, or clarifying and calming, than our habits of listening permit them to be. Until they reach our ears they are mere sound waves, gentle breezes, harmless as a baby's breath. It is through the alchemy of listening that they become transformed into the paralyzing and convulsant toxins of distrust and hate — or the beneficent potions of good will and intelligence.

In this fact lies our gravest warning and our greatest hope. The Pied Pipers of Doom will prance away down the road, each one a clown tootling to himself, not until — but just as soon as — we have cultivated an appreciation of finer music.

From the Autumn 1949 Et cetera.

THE POWER OF WORDS

J. Samuel Bois

WHEN THE JUDGE SAYS to the bride and groom standing before him, "By virtue of the authority of the State I pronounce you husband and wife," the words "husband" and "wife" establish a new set of relations between the man and the woman who are there. Henceforward they will cohabit, enjoy the possession of each other's bodies, share a common name, and begin to weave a joint pattern of life made of experiences, aspirations, purposes, and responsibilities. Society accepts the relating power of the words pronounced by its duly appointed official. He establishes a new relationship between two members of that society, and this new set of relations is immediately integrated in the web of relationships that hold together the group to which the spouses belong.

This web of relationships differs from one cultural group to another. Interracial marriages that are accepted and respected in certain states of the Union are considered felonies in some others. It may also differ from one generation to another in the same cultural group. The old formula, "I take thee for my husband (or wife) until death do us part," does not express any longer the mores of our culture. It would be more descriptive of the present state of affairs to say, instead of "until death do us part," something like "until divorce do us part," because a provision is now made in our legal system to terminate the marriage relationship prior to the death of either partner.

An appointment to a new position, an election to a public

The late **Samuel Bois** was an Industrial Psychologist, author and long-time teacher of general semantics at Viewpoints Institute in Los Angeles.

office, and, in the old days, a consecration performed according to the rites of the established religion, create a new set of relations that gives to the person thus appointed, elected, or consecrated new privileges and responsibilities. In the Catholic Church, which assumes that her jurisdiction covers eternity as well as time, priests are ordained *in eternum*. Once a priest, always a priest, and forever a priest. The rationalization behind this was that the ordination confers a "character" that adheres to the soul of the ordained and transforms him into a different individual. As with many old formulations that we are apt to dismiss as obsolete, this rationalization contains a kernel of truth that is quite acceptable. In his world as he experiences it — and as his co-religionists experience it — the young priest is "really" different from what he was before his ordination. Parishioners much older than he see him as "father of their souls," and both he and they react accordingly.

Not all statements are as portentous as those of the marrying judge, the appointing authority, the official election recorder, or the ordaining bishop; but it remains that all propositions assert relations and involve evaluations that are either proposed or accepted. To name anything is to determine where it belongs in the scheme of things that constitutes our experiential world, the only world in which we have our being and in which we function. Once we accept a word as proper to designate a person, a thing, a situation, or an operation, we adopt implicitly as real and effective all the relations that this word has with other words in our universe of discourse. If we purposely change our manner of talking about anything, and keep that change until it becomes an established habit, we change the very structure of the world in which we live.

When we talk to ourselves or with others about a situation, a problem, or a plan for the future, we are conducting a thought experiment, and the only aspects of the situation that we can manipulate, combine, or rearrange in this experiment are those for which we have labels. The grammatical relations among these labels determine to a larger extent than we realize the meaning we attach to the conditions they describe. Phenomena for which we have no label are not likely to be taken into account; phenomena that our language relates incorrectly will appear illegitimate, puzzling, or undesirable. A simple example is what Hayakawa calls the fallacy of the transitive verb. When I say "I hit the ball," the transitive verb "hit" conveys the meaning that I do something to the ball, and that the result depends on how well and how hard I hit. But if I say "I teach the boy," the transitive verb "teach" establishes between me and the boy a relation that is different. The result will not depend exclusively — or mainly — on my skill and energy. If I take the verb-object relation to be the same in both cases, as grammatical common sense implies, I may come to a bitter disappointment and look in the wrong direction to remedy the situation.

To the reader who might find this example too simple to warrant our attention, I suggest that he read the article from which I take the following quotation. He will see that research psychologists themselves have yielded to the transitive assumptions of the verb "to communicate."

> The model held by the general public ,and by social scientists when they talk about advertising, and somebody else's propaganda, is one of the exploitation of man by man. It is a model of one-way influence; the communicator *does* something to the audience, while the communicator is generally attributed considerable latitude and power to do what he pleases to the audience. This model is reflected — at its worst — in such popular phrases as "brainwashing," "hidden persuasion," and "subliminal advertising [p. 319]."[1]

In 1947, when I was practicing psychology in Montreal, a young woman came to me for advice. Early in the War she had completed her high school and joined the CWAC (Canadian Women Army Corps). Her parents, whom she described as "rigid, domineering, and old-fashioned," had been utterly opposed to her joining the Army, and she had grabbed that opportunity to get away, in a socially approved manner, from a situation that had become unbearable. While overseas she had met an Air Force officer whom she married while still in the service. At the time she came to see me, he was taking his Master's degree in engineering at McGill University. They had a baby girl, and they were very happy, except for the fact that she had practically no contact with her parents who were living out West, had never forgiven her for joining the Army, never approved of her marriage, and ignored the very existence of the baby when they did as much as answer her letters. The father had retired, and they were aging rapidly. She was worried about them.

That summer, her husband Jack insisted that she go home for a visit, and do her best to mend a situation that he felt had no reason to continue indefinitely. She was their only child, and she had nothing to be ashamed of. Why not try at least once to make them see that they could be proud of their daughter, of her husband and child.

She agreed with him, but she wondered how she should go about it. From past experience she knew that her parents were not likely to change an attitude they had maintained for so many years. She often thought that it might be better to let the thousand miles lie between her and them rather than run the risk of a face-to-face clash that might mean a final and permanent break. If she went, it was mostly to please Jack, who felt that it was her "duty" to go.

We quickly came to the conclusion that it was a good idea to go, provided she could make the trip an experiment in managing herself under trying conditions. I suggested that we rehearse the actual experience by going through a thought experiment.

She was an accomplished typist and a fluent writer. I directed her to type for me two or three pages of solid text, describing her father and mother, the house they lived in, their neighbors and acquaintances, their habits and behavior, but all along avoiding reference to them as *Dad* or *Mom*, as she was doing while talking to me about them. "What else can I call them?" she said. "They are my father and mother, are they not?" "They are," I agreed, "but they must have another name, a name for the public outside the home. What do people in your town call them?" "People of their generation call them Fred and Marion. When I write to them, I address my letters: Mr. and Mrs. Fred Smith." "Fine! From now on, here in my office and whenever you write to me about them, we shall call them Mr. and Mrs. Fred Smith, or Fred and Marion. Write about them as a newspaper reporter would. Type your essay without ever using the words Dad or Mom; and bring me your rough copy, where you will have crossed out those two words whenever you let them slip under your fingers.

She did as directed. The first page had many corrections, where she had crossed out Dad or Mom and replaced them with the more formal Mr. or Mrs. Smith. The second and third pages were almost free from such errors. When she brought her work to me we had a long conversation during which I corrected her mercilessly whenever she said Dad or Mom. Eventually she broke into tears. "Doctor, you are hurting me!" she cried. "You are making me destroy something within myself, and it hurts!"

It was mental surgery, indeed, but she wanted quick results, and I felt she could stand it. I let her weep a while and encouraged her to continue. She volunteered to write another essay, which came out without any misprint. This time we had a pleasant talk about her coming trip and about how she would address them when she first met them. "Of course," I said, "you will call them Dad and Mom when you meet them first and all during your stay, but between now and then, keep talking to yourself about them as Mr. and Mrs. Smith."

Before leaving she accepted my suggestion to see the whole thing as an experiment, with better than even chances of success but no more. She had her doubts, but was ready to give it an honest try.

After she had spent two full weeks with her parents, she wrote: "I thank you very much for making possible this vacation with a fine old couple, Mr. and Mrs. Smith. They are not at all what I had known them to be. We are getting along fine."

You may call this autosuggestion, self-hypnosis, self-fulfilling prophecy, or whatever. I see it as simply projecting onto the silent level of feelings and attitudes the full meaning of the language we choose to use. This projecting mechanism keeps functioning all by itself, whether we are aware of it or not. It does too often reinforce the hold of cultural shibboleths that we repeat without questioning them, but it will just as easily make possible new orientations, observations, and transactions, if we are wise enough to use it in a creative manner.

It works for groups as well as for individuals. As an industrial consultant I found that, instead of being preachy about the need of teamwork in committee meetings and task force projects, we could obtain better, quicker and more lasting results by calling the members of the group—and by having them call themselves—*participants* instead of *members*. It seemed as if the very definition of the word *participant*—and of its relatives: *participation* and *participate*—eventually became an active phase sequence in the nervous system of each individual member and guided his behavior in a subtle manner.

There was another word that we learned to eliminate from the current vocabulary—the word *problem*. We found that it usually involves many assumptions. When you were given a problem to solve in mathematics, you were given *all* the pertinent data, and, if you knew the rules and applied them correctly, you reached the *one* good solution. All other solutions were wrong, of course. In business, you practically never have *all* the pertinent data; there is no *one* solution that actually solves the problem. So, instead of saying "I have a problem," they learned to say "I wonder what is most expedient in this situation." There was less anxiety, more constructive thinking, and the batting average for "good" decisions went up.

In clinical psychology, the damaging and depressing words are legion. Take the word *guilt* as an example. It has a definite cluster of implications and connotations that are stirred up the minute we choose it as the suitable label to describe an action. To plead guilty in a court of law is to accept blame and punishment. To call that uneasiness and displeasure with oneself about something that one has done or failed to do a *guilt* feeling is to open the door to a multitude of culturally accepted accompaniments of pleading guilty. If, instead of feeling *guilty*, you simply state, "I do wish it had happened differently," you may be in a better condition to mend the situation.

Of all forms of life, man is the only one who actually creates the world in which he lives, and he may well people this world with very disturbing ghosts. It is often against such unwelcome ghosts that the counselor has to wage war, and not against the conditions that the client wishes could be changed by the sweep of the professional magic wand.

If we have no name for a phenomenon that occurs within us, we are apt to ignore it, or we describe it to ourselves so inadequately that we miss its particular significance. "A large proportion of human behavior follows nameless channels which have no language symbols, nor any kinds of signposts whatsoever [p. 130]."[2] These nameless channels operate as powerful controls on our thoughts, feelings, and behavior. They are outside the field of logic, since logic has to use words and symbols, and these phenomena have no names nor symbols by means of which they can be inserted in a syllogism or an equation.

If words are lacking to bring out of the dark phenomena the presence of which we have good reason to infer, what of the potentialities we expect to emerge under the relentless formative tendency of the evolutionary process? When it comes to cultural evolution, this general formative tendency is embodied in the urge that we feel in our better moments to create a world where it will be "natural" for the best that is in every one of us to come out and flourish. This calls for a skill that we have to get busy developing without delay. It is the skill of moulding our behavior after a pattern of words chosen deliberately.

This is a new field for research and experimentation. Whoever feels that the views expressed in the present essay deserve serious consideration as a working hypothesis may find it worthwhile to experiment with them and improve on them as he goes along. By planning a change in the network of communications that link us with our fellow humans, and by maintaining this change for a sufficiently long time, we might bring about a corresponding change in the network of affective relations that make life happy or miserable and that bring about clashes and wars, or cooperation and peace.

What of *potentialities* and *development* instead of *crisis* and *survival*? What if we took in earnest the statement of Albert Szent-Györgi: "If you have an *opponent*, regard him as your *associate* in finding the best solution with good will and mutual respect [p. 26]."[3]

NOTES AND REFERENCES

1. Bauer, Raymond A., The obstinate audience. *American Psychologist*, May 1964.
2. Kelly, George A. *The Psychology of Personal Construct*, Vol 1. Norton, 1955.
3. Szent-Györgi, Albert. On education. *The Minority of One*, December 1964.

From the September 1972 Et cetera.

SEARCHING FOR THE RIGHT WORD: THE SEMANTICS OF HETEROSEXUAL RELATIONSHIPS

Nicholas Johnson

LOVE, SEX, MARRIAGE, and other aspects of relations between men and women have occupied a major portion of the attention of humankind since the beginnings of recorded history.

How then do you explain our frustrating search for the right words to describe today's heterosexual relationships?

Oh, we have a language for marriage relationships that seems to be adequate enough. In fact, it's more than adequate. It totally dominates our vocabulary of relationships.

Marriage deserves a rich vocabulary. Even as an "option" for men and women, it's still the dominant choice for old and young alike. But its overpowering influence on the language of relationships seems excessive.

Everything is defined in terms of the married state. Before marriage, one is "single" — that is, not married. Subsequently one may be "engaged" to be married to one's "fiance/e." Preliminary "engaged to be engaged" relationships, such as "going together," "going steady," or being "pinned" are consistent with this perception of the inevitability of marriage.

For those who have attained marriage, the vocabulary includes "husband" and "wife," and such colloquial but equally precise expressions as "better half," "old man," and "little lady." We even have an elaborate vocabulary for differentiating "in-laws."

Nicholas Johnson, FCC Commissioner 1966-73, teaches Law at the University of Iowa and creates Educational Television programs.

There is an after marriage language. To say that individuals are "separated," "divorced" or "widowed" is to define their status in terms of the *absence* of marriage. We then create a language of "ex" or "former" marriage—"my former husband," or "my ex-mother-in-law."

It is not the purpose of this article to analyze the reasons increasing numbers of men and women are unmarried. (There are now 52 million single adults.) Partly it's the 1947-57 baby boom; partly it's the high death rate (44% of the 16 million singles' households are occupied by widows). The divorce rate per thousand population has increased ten-fold from 1890 to 1980 (but seems to have levelled off)—26% of the singles' households are occupied by separated or divorced persons.

David Riesman says it's a form of narcissism—"Something's missing and that is connectedness." The Bank of America sees singles as a "market." Economist Eric Thor: "It's a misconception to continue thinking of the traditional American unit as a family of four." The fact is that more and more Americans are single by choice, as well as by chance, and that sociologist Frank Ferstenberg probably states our confusion about the phenomenon most accurately: "Some view it as society's liberation—and others as society's dissolution. It's a double-edged sword."

Whatever the causes and consequences may be, the fact is that the vocabulary of marriage is simply irrelevant for millions of Americans today, and that nothing has sprung up to take its place. To talk about an individual's status *without* reference to the language of marriage becomes difficult and ambiguous, if not ludicrous. We are left with words and phrases like "date," "lover," "couple," "colleague," "friend," "boy friend," "mate," "partner," "lady friend," "my man," or "roommates." The California Welfare Department's word is URAM (unrelated adult man). The Census Bureau's tongue twister is POSSLQ (person of the opposite sex sharing living quarters). The Swedes have a word for "personal relationships including sexual intimacy"—"samlevnadsundervisning." They seem to be managing all right with it, but it took us twenty years to feel comfortable with "ombudsman," and with a ratio of 22 letters to nine it would be the year 2030 before Americans would stop choking on "samlevnadsundervisning."

None of these words is quite adequate to convey reasonable expectations of behavior on the part of the man or woman involved—let alone the behavior of others toward them. "Friend" can refer to anything from the equivalent of a spouse to someone met only moments before. "Roommate" can cover everything from a stranger sharing rent to an intimate friend sharing sex.

For a man and woman to share sex is a matter of great consequence in defining their relationship—for them, and for others. But how it helps define it is not altogether clear, especially if one knows little about the sexual habits of the individuals involved. If they and their friends have tended to live with exclusive sexual ties over sustained periods of time it means one thing. If they participate in sex with multiple partners, or their sexual relations, while exclusive, are shortlived, the significance of sex in their "relationship" is a different matter.

Of course, sex is far from all there is to opposite-sex relations. "Caring," "love," "companionship," "intellectual compatibility" and "shared interests"—to name but a few factors—are also important to others' evaluation of a relationship.

"Love and marriage," to borrow from the song of the same name, do not always "go together like a horse and carriage." Neither do sex and caring.

If Rose is having a tennis party it may make more sense to include Joe's steady tennis partner, Sue (with whom he has never had sex), than either his wife (from whom he has been separated for four months) or Dizzy (a current partner in bedlock whose most outstanding qualities are neither athletic nor intellectual).

Parents may well be more interested in their children's opposite sex friends, whom their kids really care about, than in their offsprings' casual sexual partners (if any).

Who really cares what labels we put on relationships? What difference does it make?

For many purposes, of course, the relationship makes no difference.

When Vic introduces you to Terry at a cocktail party it makes little difference whether Terry's relationship to Vic is that of daughter, wife, colleague, lover, or someone he just met at the party a few minutes ago. You and your spouse can enjoy superficial conversation with the two of them, and quickly pass out of each other's lives forever.

Your waitress in a restaurant may be enjoying a mutually satisfactory incestuous relationship with the chef (her father) for all you know or care — so long as the food is well prepared and served.

Even when there is a need to know, we can live and communicate without a precise vocabulary of relationships. We can gesture, ask questions, and use poetry and long descriptive paragraphs rather than individual, one-word labels — and that's what we tend to do.

"How well do you know Betty?"

"We grew up in the same small town together — but we're just really good friends."

• • •

"I saw you and Tom together."

"Yeah, I work with him."

"Is that all."

"Well, we like each other a lot, but I've never been to bed with him, if *that's* what you mean."

What difference does it make? It's both academic and practical.

A general semanticist might take an academic interest in why a matter of such urgent import to so many people in our culture would go so long with such an obviously inadequate vocabulary. Whole new languages — for computers or space travel, say — seem to spring up rapidly and effortlessly elsewhere when needed. Why not here?

The practical difference it makes concerns the individuals involved; those who would like to establish relations (of whatever kind) with members of the opposite sex; and parents, friends and others who must deal with "couples" socially. The misunderstandings, hurt feelings, confusion and catastrophes are seemingly infinite.

No one wants to go around unnecessarily labeling people and then reacting to such labels. General semantics makes an effort to free us from such behavior. But all couples seem to search for some labeling of their relationships, to govern their expectations of others and themselves.

To preserve individuals' rights of privacy, most of the examples in this article use fictitious names, however much they may draw upon the experiences of friends. But the California *Marvin* case is firmly on the public record. Actor Lee Marvin and Michelle Triola lived together for six years without being married, and then went their separate ways. He had no expectations. She did. In this instance the absence of adequate labels (or contractual understandings) led to a $1.5 million misunderstanding and lawsuit.

Being "honest" may not always be adequate. The fact that one partner is totally open about his or her sex with additional individuals may simply not be heard or internalized by the other, who wants a monogamous relationship. To live for the moment, ask no questions, and let all encounters evolve as they will is a romantic but dangerous way of interacting. And it is a way that is inconsistent with some kinds of satisfactory relationships.

Tom and Liz are college students who enjoy each other's company, occasionally study or play tennis together, but do not have a sexual relationship. Tom thinks he wants Liz as his wife, but has not told her. He's shy, and his religious background is such that he's had only one or two sexual experiences. He is hesitant to approach Liz sexually. Liz likes Tom a lot, but hasn't the slightest interest in marrying anybody. She is very casual about her sexual relationships, and hasn't approached Tom sexually only because she now has as many lovers as she can handle.

How can one define this relationship — except as "short lived"? Ultimately Tom and Liz will talk things over and either change their feelings and behavior or go their separate ways.

In this example, the difference made by our inadequate language of relationships affects only Tom and Liz — so far.

But what of their acquaintances? Bill wants to date Liz, and have sex with her, but has no interest in marrying her. He has no reason to believe her relationship with Tom is "serious," having seen her with a number of other fellows. Will Tom be offended if Bill asks Liz for a date? If Tom learns Liz and Bill had sex together? Did Bill have any reasonable means of knowing Tom's probable reaction—short of asking Tom directly?

Sue is having a party at her parents' summer home to which she is inviting couples who are engaged or "going together." She wants to invite Liz (whose sexual habits are unknown to Sue). She knows how Tom feels about Liz, but doesn't know they haven't slept together. Should she also invite Tom? Should she plan on putting them up in the same bedroom, or ask one (or both) first?

Tom's parents are on campus for a football game, and he introduces Liz to them for the first time. Later Tom's mother asks, "Just who is she, Tom? Someone serious?" How should Tom describe the relationship?

Children of single parents now constitute 20% of all American children. They have to deal with their parents' opposite sex friends, too. If they are living with their mother youngsters may welcome (or dread) the prospect of a new "Daddy" for Mother. And how are they to deal with Dad's women friends—what one teenager refers to as his father's "girl of the week"?

Willa is recently separated. Michael, her young teenage son, is very protective. Jerry came over to work on Willa's car, and stayed for dinner. Afterwards, Michael wanted to know what was going on. "Who is Jerry?" he asked. All Willa could do was to try to explain how Jerry and Laverne love each other, that he was only being friendly and helpful with the car—and hope that Michael would make the inference there was nothing to worry about.

What if Wally, who lives in New York with his wife Alice, spends weeks at a time on business in Chicago, where he enjoys a close, but non-sexual relationship with Beverly. Beverly is a former college classmate of Wally's whom Alice has only once met. Yvonne lives in Chicago. She knows Wally and both Alice and Beverly. Yvonne is planning a cocktail party in Chicago. She wants to invite Wally. Does she also invite Alice (who probably can't come), or Beverly (who can), or both, or neither? What word describes Beverly's relationship to Wally?

How would your answers differ if (1) Beverly and Wally had had a sexual relationship before (but not after) Wally's marriage to Alice? (2) Only once or twice since Wally's marriage? (3) Repeatedly since the marriage, but clandestinely? (4) Repeatedly and openly?

From our own experience, that of our friends and fictional accounts, each of us knows of an almost infinite variety of heterosexual relationships.

There are unmarried couples who live together with far more stability, happiness and sexual fidelity than married couples.

There are individuals who seem almost totally consumed by brief, but intense, love affairs — one after another.

Some seek marriage and family life with grim determination. Others avoid it with an equal sense of purpose.

Multiple sexual partners may be a natural and open way of life, or a clandestine maneuver requiring intricate logistics, duplicity and cunning.

Some couples break up and get back together again with such regularity that their friends come to accept it.

And, of course, anyone is capable of changing attitudes, practices, partners, and lifestyles at any time — as a temporary aberration, a permanent substitution, or a gradual evolution to something else.

Of course, marriage can be equally volatile. Either spouse can have an affair, fall out of love or radically decrease or curtail sex with the other. Unless they are "separated" or "divorced," however, they are still "husband and wife." Family, friends and colleagues will treat them accordingly. There is a cultural code of behavior for married couples that may be either followed or broken, but in either case is done so knowingly. There is no need to inquire into the actual relationship between a husband and wife, sexual or otherwise. The labels permit us to behave according to presumptions.

There is no comparable set of presumptions for relationships other than marriage, in large measure because those relationships have not even been named or defined.

Remember the line from the song, "You were only fooling, while I was falling in love"? Tom probably would be crushed if he knew of Liz's attitudes about sex and marriage. And yet neither is deliberately misleading the other. Tom just assumes, as a matter of course, that Liz probably wants to get married, that she evaluates men as potential husbands, and will have few if any sexual experiences before marriage. Liz assumes that Tom is just interested in good times, and has no more interest in marriage than she does.

There are, of course, instances for deliberate manipulation, misrepresentation and deceit. For some, interpersonal relations with members of the opposite sex are, almost by definition, a "game" between untrustworthy combatants—in which one "scores" by obtaining sex through guile, or by teasingly obtaining sexual interest which is subsequently spurned.

A far more common experience, however, especially following the increased efforts towards "openness" since the 1960s, is unintentional misrepresentation.

The wedding ring is a marvelously efficient non-verbal definition. It says: "I'm married." Unless accompanied by outrageously flirtatious behavior, one can fairly safely assume the wearer wants to keep opposite-sex relationships on a businesslike, or a friendly but superficial level.

One of the qualities of life without formal "marriage" ties—a quality which makes it attractive to some, and unsettling to others—is the excitement (or confusion) of any opposite-sex encounter. Meeting a stranger on the street, at work or a party can be limited to a brief exchange, or expanded into a new acquaintance, friendship, brief "love affair," or a more long-lasting relationship. That's the practical version of the songwriter's romantic vision: "Some enchanted evening / You will see a stranger / Across a crowded room. . . . "

If one is married and wearing a wedding band, opposite sex encounters begin with an unspoken introduction built upon thousands of years of definitions and expectations of behavior. If one is not, ambiguity is rampant. At what point is one obliged to strive to remove the ambiguity?

Ed meets Susie at a cocktail party. Now you can't go around a social gathering saying, "Hi-I'm-Susie-and-I'm-now-divorced-with-one-child,-not-interested-in-getting-married-again,-not-yet-'going-with'-anyone-'serious'-and-am-open-to-seeing-if-you-and-I-are-compatible" — although some come close.

If Susie's "partner" (whatever that may mean) is present at a party or other gathering he can be sought out and introduced by her — but as what, and with what effect? Is "My friend, George" someone Susie works with, "dated" for the evening and is trying to ditch, or has been sharing an exclusive sexual relationship with for five months? Is Ed supposed to assume that Susie is being genuinely friendly by introducing George, or trying to give Ed a message that she's not available?

Assuming Susie is open to getting together for coffee or lunch, the subject of her "relationship" with George can be broached at that time. "Oh, we've just broken up," or, "George? He's one of the most delightful gays I know. We've been friends for years" clears the air.

But the couple themselves — now, let us say, Ed and Susie — need a vocabulary, level of reasonable expectations, and behavior code for their own relationship as well.

Assume Ed and Susie start sleeping together. At what point is Susie obliged to tell Ed that she's still in love with George and wants to "get back together" with him? Or that she has sex with Pete once or twice a month when he's in town? That she regularly has sex with more than one partner? That she only has sex with men she potentially could marry, Ed's only the third, and she's crazy in love with him?

Is Ed obliged to stop having lunch with an old girl friend? To tell Susie about her?

For the participants to stop repeatedly during the course of an evolving relationship to discuss it at length can be quite disruptive. It's like checking your yogurt culture while it's multiplying, pulling up a seedling tomato plant to examine the roots, or asking the coach after every few plays how the game is going.

On the other hand, to fail to discuss what's going on — both within and outside the relationship — can be equally disastrous. The matter of permanence, commitment, exclusivity, and the holding out of the relationship as that of a "couple" needs to be discussed, at least loosely agreed upon, and revisited periodically as it may evolve or regress. And this difficult task is in no way eased by the failure of our language to help us label and talk about it.

By now Susie and Ed have spent three of the last five nights together. They've had lunch twice during that time. He calls her every day, and sent flowers on their one-month "anniversary." Yet Susie's miserable. Why? Ed still "sees" his old girlfriend, Helen.

"I thought you loved me."
"I do."
"I thought you were 'my man.' "
"I am."
"Then why do you see Helen?"
"Because we're friends."

Susie thinks the relationship with Ed carries the implied agreement that neither will spend time with opposite-sex people who either have been (or could become) sex partners. Ed isn't looking for sex with Helen, or anyone besides Susie, but doesn't think he's agreed to preclude it. Both could be reasonable in their expectations.

Two years later Susie (and Susie's friends) think Ed is being somehow less than honorable because he's still not interested in getting married. Ed feels he's been very open about his disinclination to marriage in general and to marrying Susie in particular, and that he is being unfairly criticized.

Some couples in love, whether or not living together, and even though not "engaged to be married," are headed down a track that will likely end in marriage (so long as the relationship "works out"). Other couples — with seemingly similar patterns of behavior — are not. Yet we have no way to label this difference.

Why this failure in the evolution of our language?

In part, it's a matter of time. The need for a new vocabulary of relationships is fairly recent in the history of verbal evolution. We've heard of the yam-eating Indians with eighty or more words to describe their favorite varieties. What we don't know is how quickly those words developed. How long did the tribe struggle along with "yam" before someone undertook to make the language as diverse as the diet?

But much of the delay and resistance seems to me to be cultural, almost political. To label something is to recognize it, and thereby give it a measure of approval. It's like sending an Ambassador to China or legalizing marijuana. To come up with words for "couple-with-sex-exclusive," "couple-with-sex-non-exclusive," "one-of-pattern-of-'love affairs,' " and so forth, is to risk social acceptability. It's a threat to the cultural acceptance and dominance of marriage, and to all who have made a commitment to that institution.

Finally, some of those who live other-than-marriage-track lives seem to enjoy the ambiguity of their verbal limbo. Part of their joy in an evolving relationship is that it *is* undefined. Definition carries commitment — to *something*. Ambiguity does not. They may not know the other person well enough to label their feelings. They may prefer to let the relationship evolve into something better — or break it off — rather than backing themselves into the most accurate label for their current status ("an affair," "acquaintances"). They may want to avoid the *Marvin* problem of economic obligations. Loving and living arrangements may carry other economic or professional sanctions — failure to get a job or a promotion. The recognition of a relationship may create family or social pressure to marriage (for want of an alternative label) — married individuals Russell Baker has recognized as the "victims of a failure in English."

It is even possible that the failure to define or label our relationships is a form of semantic maturity. It may be an effort to avoid the realities as well as the overtones of dominance, or possessiveness, inherent in an expression like "my girl." It may be evidence of an awareness that we do need dates and indexes — lover[1] is not lover[2], Ed and Susie$_{1975}$ is not Ed and Susie$_{1979}$. Every relationship between a man and a woman is unique, is known best only to them (and to them not very well), and changes over time. Whatever may be the dangers of operating without adequate labels, they may pale compared with the dangers of operating with them. A relationship is made up of actions, conversations, activities together, shared living quarters or other resources, feelings and emotions, shared background, friends, expectations, and so forth. Those can (and under some circumstances should) be verbalized. But the search for labels may be less useful than the creation of poetry and song.

So where is the pressure to change to come from? In the political arena, such an absence of constituent group support would lead most elected officials to conclude the problem can't be solved, the bill will never pass the legislative body.

There is no reason to believe the politics of semantics is any different. If so, we may continue to interact without a language of relationships for some time to come. And we may even be better for it.

From the Spring 1979 Et cetera.

THE MAKING OF A NONSEXIST DICTIONARY

Alma Graham

THE FIRST DICTIONARY to define *sexism*, to include the phrase *liberated women*, and to recognize *Ms.* was a wordbook for children published in 1972 by American Heritage Publishing Company. *The School Dictionary* contains 35,000 entries, which were selected after an unprecedented analysis of 5 million words encountered by American children in their schoolbooks.

When the task of compilation began in 1969, we could not predict that the dictionary would be the first ever published in which lexicographers made a conscious effort to correct the sex biases that exist in English as it is commonly used. But the computer revealed a pattern that we who were editing the dictionary could not ignore: in schoolbooks, whether the subject is reading, mathematics, social studies, art, or science, males command center stage. Boys and girls may go to school in equal numbers; they may be graded for equal achievements; but the computer had tipped the scales on the side of male supremacy.

In some ways the American Heritage computer was no different from any other. It was stupid. Though it devoured reams of printed matter — 10,000 passages of 500 words each culled from 1,000 books and magazines — it couldn't read. To the computer the "lead" in flaking paint was no different from the "lead" in a play, and a "row" of cabbages was the same as a "row" between lovers. Fortunately, this lack of discrimination was

---

Alma Graham is Executive Editor of the Dictionary Division of American Heritage Publishing Company.

unimportant, for in addition to alphabetizing all its words and ranking them by the frequency of their usage, the computer's unprecedented contribution was to deliver 700,000 citation slips, each of which showed a word in three lines of context. By using these slips, the editors could see each word as it is used in sentences that schoolchildren read, and we could in turn write definitions that schoolchildren could comprehend.

The original objective in using a computer was this obvious one of gaining access to primary sources. Peter Davies, the editor in chief of *The School Dictionary*, was the first to recognize what else the computer had delivered. To Davies, the vast body of words was a reflection of the culture talking to its children. He suspected that if imaginatively used, the computer could also supply a profile of what was being said between the lines.

For example, Davies noticed that when adults write for one another, they refer to young children as *children* almost as often as they call them *boys* and *girls*. When writing books and stories for children, however, adults use the gender words *boy* and *girl* twice as often as the neutral words *child* and *children*. When the culture talks *to* its children, it is careful to distinguish them by sex. Moreover, no matter what the subject being taught, girls and women are always in a minority. Overall, the ratio in schoolbooks of *he* to *she*, *him* to *her*, and *his* to *hers* was almost four to one. Even in home economics, the traditional preserve of the female, the pronoun *he* predominated by nearly two to one.

It was suggested that some of those excess *he*'s might apply not to boys and men but to the unspecified singular subject, as in: a person . . . he; a student . . . his; someone . . . him. To check this out I made a survey of pronoun citations from an earlier, experimental sampling of 100,000 words. Out of 940 citations for *he*, 744 were applied to male human beings, 128 to male animals, and 36 to persons such as farmers and sailors who were assumed to be male. Only 32 referred to the unspecified singular subject. The conclusion was inescapable: the reason most of the pronouns in schoolbooks were male in gender was because most of the subjects being written about were men and boys.

In the real world, there are 100 women for every 95 men. Yet in the books read by schoolchildren, there are over seven times as many men as women and over twice as many boys as girls.

Then another oddity came to light. Despite the preponderance of the words *man* and *boy* in textbooks, the word *mother* occurs more frequently than the word *father*, and the word *wife* is used three times as often as the word *husband*. Women, it would seem, are typecast in the supporting roles that refer to their relationships to men and children.

Might this fact simply imply that in the world of the elementary school the mother is seen as the chief parent? The situation changes when the subject words analyzed are not *mother* and *father* but *daughter* and *son*. An examination of citation slips showed that four times as many sons and daughters are referred to as the children of a male parent (Jim's son; the landlord's daughter) as of a female parent (her son; Mrs. Greenwood's daughter).

Other kinship-term citations revealed still more about this schoolbook never-never land. Two out of every three mothers are mentioned in relation to male children. Father references are even more extreme: four out of every five fathers are fathers of a male. And there's more bald bias: twice as many uncles as aunts, and of those aunts, four times as many have nephews (Charley's aunt) as have nieces (Nelly's aunt); sons outnumber daughters by better than two to one, and every single firstborn child is a son.

Where have all the young girls gone?

It seems clear that they have grown up and have been given (or taken) in marriage — because in schoolbooks wives are three times as numerous as husbands, showing that the speakers or main characters are males. Furthermore, many other words besides *husband* serve as counterparts of *wife*. Farmers' wives and farm wives (but no farm husbands) appear in the citations, as do diplomats' wives and Cabinet wives.

Obviously, the basic imbalance in male/female pairs was far more than simply a numbers game. The 700,000 computer citation slips contained the evidence that boys and girls were also being taught separate sets of values, different expectations, and divergent goals. Boys in the schoolbooks ran races, rode bicycles, drove fast cars, and took off in spaceships for Mars. Girls, on the other hand, were less concerned with doing than with being. After reading, "He was the manliest of his sex and she was the loveliest of hers," a child would say that the word comparable to *manly* was *lovely*, not *womanly*. In the sentence, "The men are strong, virile, and graceful, and the girls often beauties," we note that girls, not women, are paired with men and that *virile* is parallel to *beautiful*. A feminine figure, a feminine voice, and a feminine laugh are no match for masculine prerogatives, masculine egos, and masculine drives. The "mannish uniform" of a female general in the Chinese Army is condemned by the very adjective that describes it, but three modifiers commend "a very feminine dream gown."

If this new dictionary were to serve elementary students without showing favoritism to one sex or the other, an effort would have to be made to restore the gender balance. We would need more examples featuring females, and the examples would have to ascribe to girls and women the active, inventive, and adventurous human traits traditionally reserved for men and boys.

Our new archetypal woman took form gradually. Each of the editors writing and reviewing word entries had special moments of insight and decision when we recognized her presence among us. Mine came at the word *brain*, where a computer citation asserted "he has *brains* and courage." In what seemed at the time an act of audacity, I changed the pronoun. "She has *brains* and courage."

As the number of word entries grew, the new woman made her way from example to example, establishing her priorities, aspirations, and tastes. She was "a woman of dedicated political *principles*." She "made a *name* for herself" and "everyone *praised* her good sense and learning." When she "*plunged* into her work, her mind began to *percolate*" (not her coffee), and "she *prided* herself on her eloquence" (not on the sheen of her freshly waxed floors).

Her appearances in the dictionary were widely separated,

of course. Her brothers and traditional sisters continued to surround and outnumber her, example for example. But she had arrived, and from A, where at *abridge* she quoted the 19th Amendment, to Z, when "she *zipped* down the hill on her sled," her spirit, character, and credentials were never in doubt.

As the feminists—male and female—who had brought her into the lexicon cheered her on, "her *determination* to win" was bolstered by our "*devout* wish for her success."

Men in the dictionary examples continued to be active and daring, competitive and combative; but the liberated man could be vulnerable, too. He might be "striving to attain *mastery* over his emotions," but he was not disgraced if "his resolve began to *waver*" or if "tears *welled* up in his eyes." Like the new woman, he had a freer choice of careers than heretofore: "He *teaches* kindergarten" and "he *studies* typing at night."

Ms. was the word we watched with the greatest degree of interest. Some of us favored adopting it right away, but a problem arose over its pronunciation: it was an abbreviation that anyone could write but that no one could say. Arguments over "miz" or "mis" or "em es" continued through the summer. Then, in October, Bruce Bohle, our usage editor, urged that we enter *Ms.* in the dictionary as an abbreviation whether or not the title could be pronounced with ease. Thus supported, I wrote the definition and Peter Davies provided a note explaining the parallel with *Mr.*, the derivation from *mistress*, and the pronunciation possibilities.

<u>Ms.</u> or <u>Ms</u>   *An abbreviation used as a title of courtesy before a woman's last name or before her given name and last name, whether she is married or not.*

At the same time that womanpower in the dictionary was beginning to be felt, consciousness of woman's powerlessness in the language was rising. As a lexicographer and feminist, I had started a notebook on sexism in language, collecting examples of ways in which men and women were classified as human beings by being labeled with male or female words.

One method used in this socializing process is a tactic I called "my-virtue-is-your-vice." Since men and women are supposed to be polar opposites, what is considered admirable in one has to be contemptible in the other. If a woman is commended for the gentle qualities that make her *feminine*, then a man must be condemned for any similar show of softness with the epithet *effeminate*. A man's teams are *womanish*; a woman's uniform *mannish*. The lessons to be learned by both male and female are clear: biology is not only destiny; it is character and personality.

Another trick of socialization is to label what we consider to be the exception to the rule: the *woman* doctor, the *male* nurse, the career *girl* (the phrase *career man* is restricted to government service). The term "feminine logic" illustrates the most negatively sexist use of the modifier tactic since it implies non-logic or lack of logic. Because *logic* unmodified is assumed by men to apply to men, a woman who thinks logically is said to have "a masculine mind" (a supposed compliment that serves as a questionable exception to the my-virtue-is-your-vice rule).

Then there is the "trivializing tactic." This tactic operates through female gender forms, such as *poetess* and *usherette*, and through the put-down process that turns *liberationist* into *libber*, just as it once turned *suffragist* into *suffragette*.

The tendency in the language that I called "praise him/blame her" is still another device. From Eve and Pandora on, the female has been held responsible for evil and assigned to a semantic house of ill fame. Titles of honor illustrate the point particularly well. *Queen*, *madam*, *mistress*, and *dame* have all acquired degraded meanings, whereas *prince*, *king*, *lord*, and *father* are exalted and applied to God — for even God is thought of as a male and is called Him.

Most pervasive of all is the phenomenon I called the "exclusionary tactic." Here the possibility is simply not considered that the person or persons being addressed or discussed might be female. A typical example is the loan application that reads: "Full Name. Wife's First Name and Middle Initial. Your Present Employer. Wife's Employer. Your Monthly Salary. Wife's Income (if any)." But the exclusionary tactic employed most tellingly is the constant, careless overuse of the word *man* in its extended senses. When speakers refer to "the leading man in the field," to "the man whose book sells half a million copies," or to "the man they would most like to see as President," they effectively rule out the possibility of a female authority, author, or candidate.

To fight these sexist habits of language, *The School Dictionary* had to avoid gender assumptions that other dictionaries imposed more through custom than necessity. *Youth*, one dictionary said, is "the part of life between childhood and manhood." *Youth*, we said, is "the time of life before one is an adult." *Sex*, itself, we defined straightforwardly, with impersonal examples, avoiding a rival dictionary's use of "the fair, gentle, or weaker sex" and "the sterner or stronger sex" dichotomy.

While we were working our way through the alphabet, other word watchers were already speaking out. In Venice, California, Varda One (formerly Varda Murrell) was analyzing and commenting on a phenomenon she called "Manglish." We could not counter her criticism that dictionaries give less space to *woman* than to *man*. This is not the fault of the dictionary makers, but of a language in which the same word denotes both the human species as a whole and those of its members who are male. In English, contradictory propositions are true: a woman is a man; a woman is not a man.

If a woman is swept off a ship into the water, the cry is "Man overboard!" If she is killed by a hit-and-run driver, the charge is "manslaughter." If she is injured on the job, the coverage is "workmen's compensation." But if she arrives at a threshold marked "Men Only," she knows the admonition is not intended to bar animals or plants or inanimate objects. It is meant for her.

In practice, the sexist assumption that man is a species of males becomes the fact. Erich Fromm certainly seemed to think so when he wrote that man's "vital interests" were "life, food, access to females, etc." Loren Eiseley implied it when he wrote of man that "his back aches, he ruptures easily, his women have difficulties in childbirth. . . ." If these writers had been using *man* in the sense of human species rather than male, they would have written that man's vital interests are life, food, and access to the opposite sex, and that man suffers backaches, ruptures easily, and has difficulties in giving birth.

At every level of achievement and activity—from primitive man to the man of the hour—woman is not taken into account. Consider the congressman. He is a man of the people. To prove that he's the best man for the job, he takes his case to the man in the street. He is a champion of the workingman. He speaks up for the little man. He has not forgotten the forgotten man. And he firmly believes: one man, one vote. Consider the policeman or fireman, the postman or milkman, the clergyman or businessman. Whatever else he may be, he is by title a man, and if his employer feels that he is "our kind of man," he may become "our man in the home office" or "our man in Algiers."

From Wordsworth's line "The Child is father of the Man" to the recent New York subway poster "Give a kid a job and help mold a man," a woman is a possibility everyone tends to forget.

When a culture makes adulthood synonymous with manhood, a girl can never reach adulthood at all. There is a clear demarcation between the words *boy* and *man* that does not exist between *girl* and *woman*. A boy greatly increases his stature when he becomes a man, but a girl loses status and bargaining power when she loses youth. So females are in effect encouraged to cling to girlhood as long as possible. Nor is this reluctance to grow up surprising when one considers the largely negative connotations attached to the word *woman*. To take defeat like a man is to accept it stoically like a good sport. To take defeat like a woman is usually understood as meaning to weep.

The American Heritage School Dictionary defines sexism as "discrimination by members of one sex against the other, especially by males against females." In order to avoid sexism in language that has come to sound "natural" we devised logical sex-blind substitutes. When referring to the human species, the dictionary employs the term *human beings*, not *man* or *men*.

In our efforts to reduce the super-abundance of words referring to the male, we found it was possible to use the word *person* or a more specific substitute instead of *man*. The best man for the job is the best person or candidate; a 12-man jury is a

12-member jury; a real-estate man is a real-estate agent; and machines are used for work formerly done by people or by human beings — not by men.

To avoid unnecessary use of the pronoun *he*, we frequently shifted from the singular to the plural. Instead of saying "insofar as he can, the scientist excludes bias from his thinking," it is easy to change to *they, scientists*, and *their*. Plural pronouns desex themselves. The use of *one* is also convenient. A breadwinner, for example, can be "one who supports a family or household by his or her earnings."

Because of our conscious efforts, the nonsexist dictionary is as free of discrimination against either sex as the reformist editors could make it. But as proud as we are of our lexicographers' revolution, writing a nonsexist school dictionary is only the barest beginning. Most schoolbooks still reflect the assumptions of our sexist society. As writers and teachers and parents, we have an obligation now to weigh our words, to examine them, and use them with greater care. Children of both sexes deserve equal treatment, in life and in language, and we should not offer them anything less.

From the Spring 1974 Et cetera.

THE BELIEF IN MAGIC

Wendell Johnson

AFTER PEOPLE HAVE learned all that they can learn about something that needs to be done, about a solution to a problem that only needs to be put into effect, they often find it hard to take advantage of their new learning. They find it difficult to change even when change would be highly desirable and they *want* to change. I think that the most pervasive and fundamental of these obstacles to change and growth is a complicated condition we can call by a simple name (or a simple-sounding name), "a belief in magic."

I think we *all* believe in magic. I think this fact is probably more fundamental than anything talked about by Freud — although he did talk about magic sometimes, usually by indirection.

What do I mean by a belief in magic? Well, let's be simple about it. When we were very young and something went wrong — when we broke a toy or bumped or heads — we learned that Daddy would fix it or Mother would kiss it away. This was no innocuous learning. We learned it very well. We were taught in this way to believe in magic, and the magician was father or mother.

Then we got measles or mumps. The doctor was called and he said we should be good and take pills and a cherry-flavored syrup. We weren't taught very much about what was going on

---

The final lecture of the late **Wendell Johnson**'s introductory course in general semantics at the University of Iowa was an event students always looked forward to. This transcription from a tape-recording was prepared for publication and edited by J. Albert Southern and S.I. Hayakawa.

inside our bodies. We weren't taught anything to speak of about the chemistry of the pills, the cherry-flavored syrup, and practically nothing about the relationship, if any, between these and the measles or the mumps. We were taught to take the pills and wait—and the magician was the doctor.

In the curious and hazardous business of teaching that I am engaged in, the basic problem I have is that those who come to me to learn tend to react to me as if I were a magician. This is their disease, their maladjustment from which their other maladjustments in large measure, I think, develop. The gravest problem I have is that I might get caught in this delusion—as I think many do who work in this business—and begin to think myself a magician and to believe in my own magic.

How do I know that those who come to me believe in magic? They differ, of course; some believe in it very much and some only a little. I am talking about averages. How do I know they do? For one thing, I know by their expectations. You would be surprised how many students come to the University of Iowa simply because the Speech Clinic is here. They stutter, but they do not come to me until the last semester of their senior year, usually a month or two before they are about to go into the world to look for a job. Then they ask, "How soon can you cure me?"

You may think this funny, but it happens very often. I've had a number of girls come to me a month or so before they were to be married. "Can you cure me? I'm going to be married in June." It takes one some time to catch on to what is going on. At first, it all sounds innocent enough, as if there were nothing to be explained: they came when they were able to, you assume. Then you begin to realize that they all could have come much sooner. And they would have come sooner if they hadn't believed in magic—if they hadn't believed that sometime, somewhere, someone would be able to do something. Daddy will fix it or Mother will kiss it away. And until there is a real need to have it fixed, there's no need to bother Daddy.

I have had many parents come to me and say, "Willie is entering school in about four or five weeks. How soon can you cure him? We wouldn't want him to enter school this way. He's been this way for quite a while." I have to be very careful not to sound unsympathetic or unkind. I think one of the important parts of a teacher's or physician's skill is his capacity to understand this sort of thing: to be sympathetic, and to realize that this is the best some people can do. I think anyone who works with people needs to study a great deal of cultural anthropology. What I am talking about goes back to the Stone Age, I am sure—this belief in magic.

How do I know these people believe in magic? I am also talking about their assumptions regarding methods.

I suppose the question I am asked most often when people find out that my specialty is the study of stuttering is, "What about hypnotism? Can you cure stuttering with hypnotism?" The next most frequent question is, "What about the new drugs?"

What about hypnotism? Do you want to be hypnotized? Is this the way to maturity? You want to use my mind? You don't want to use yours? Hypnotism is, among other things, incantation. What goes on while your mind is filed away?

Here is an anthropological—what? I was going to say goldmine, but I don't mean that. I think I mean swampland. What about hypnotism? What about the new drugs? These drugs are the cherry-flavored syrup—it is an elaborate form of Mother kissing your troubles away. What are you doing when you give a person who has some kind of trouble a happiness pill? Is it therapy, or is it postponing therapy? Does he become a more mature person able to deal with the world and with himself? Ought you never to be anxious about anything? Should you just go around happy? Is "happy" the word we should use here? Are these people happy—or just indifferent? I take it for a sign of a belief in magic when people ask for hypnotism or drugs.

You would be surprised how many of the people who come to me have been to faith-healers, mineral springs, fortune-tellers. At first this fact is merely a curiosity, but after you have been in this business for twenty-five or thirty years, it becomes one of the basic facts. They seem to want—and by "they" I mean not all, but the majority—the pat answer. "What *is* stuttering,

Doctor?" The slick trick, the quick result, the secret. What is the *secret* of your success?

Over many years of practice, there are two things you get tremendously impressed by. One is the apparent belief on the part of many patients in incantation — the magic of the doctor's words. Hardly ever does anybody ask, "What did the doctor *mean*?" "What did he *know*?" "What did the doctor *say*?" Does the patient believe that he will get better because the doctor said words over him? He acts as if he does.

Another thing you get impressed by is the apparent belief in the physical presence. People will tell you, "I've been to Rochester. I've been to Johns Hopkins. I've been to Iowa City. But I've still got that pain in my back. I've been to your Speech Clinic, but I still stutter."

The physical presence! You would almost believe sometimes that these people think the walls have a special kind of substance that emanates rays. But you've got to find the right place. If they only come to a certain room, a certain office, with a certain name on the door. Names are important. All of this goes back to the Stone Age. All of this is fundamental to our culture. How anyone can work effectively with people without a rather wide knowledge of history and culture, I don't know. I don't really think one can.

People also have an almost unaccountable lack of information that is available. Very few have ever read a book dealing with the problems they are troubled with. Even more interesting are those who have. Have you ever had occasion to question such people about a book they have read? Usually they don't remember the date of publication or the publisher. They know almost nothing about the world of publishers and publications; which publishers might be more dependable than others; what there is about a book that might give you a clue as to its dependability. They seldom know the author, or anything about him. They almost never can tell you what the author said.

On the subject of speech correction (or other therapies), there is information available. It is quite easy to get. But very few make any kind of systematic effort to get it — by writing to the American Medical Association or the American Speech and

Hearing Association or the American Psychological Association. They almost never have written to the nearest university. When you try to find out why they came to this particular speech clinic, you discover it was by word-of-mouth: Uncle John heard somebody talking about it down at the store. It's almost a lottery. It's an accident that they come at all. Hardly ever have they even gone to their own doctors for this kind of information.

These are some of the observations which make me think that an enormous number of people believe in magic. They surely do not believe in information. They surely do not know much about the methods used for obtaining information. I take it as a reasonable hypothesis that they don't see the value of seeking information, because they believe in magic.

Daddy will fix it. Mother will kiss it away. So why know anything about it?

But mainly I notice how they talk about their problems. "It" is something they "have." "It" is something that exists more or less independently of them. They talk about "it" whether "it" is their allergy or their stuttering or their ulcer or their backache. "It" comes and goes. "It" gets worse. They sometimes think "it" will go away, as if they were talking of something quite independent of themselves and their thinking and behavior.

This kind of language is animistic. It is a language that animates what they are talking about, giving it a life of its own, an activity of its own, a will of its own. The language of these people is also either-or-ish or categorical. They *are* stutterers or they *are not*.

And there is the magic: if they *are* stutterers, *that* is why they stutter.

They talk this way. Not just stutterers, but everybody! I just happen to work with stutterers. I have friends who work with ulcer patients, others who work with allergy patients. No difference.

What might be done about all of this in the last seven minutes of the semester? Well, I have waited until now to ask this question, because this is what we have been answering all semester. This is fundamentally what the course is for, in case you haven't been entirely clear on this up to now. The course has been designed to make for a kind of facilitation of one's reorientation; to counteract the belief in magic; to make it possible for the individual to become more aware of his language as a factor in his knowledge and understanding. It has been designed to make one more aware that one's language does tend to put words in one's mouth, ideas in one's head, and spooks in one's world.

Thus, as an individual learns to talk with more care and awareness of the effects of what he is doing while he talks and abstracts and projects, you find that he talks less and less about what he *is* and what he *has*, and he talks more and more about what he *does* and how he *feels* and *when* and *where*. He talks less about what happens *to* him and talks more about what he *does*. He talks in terms of *degrees of change* and improvement rather than magical transformations, categorical changes. Because he can understand improvement rather than transformation, his expectations become more realistic. Not "I am" or "I am not" a stutterer, but I do *more* or *less* of what I have been doing.

As expectations become more realistic, the individual encounters less disappointment and discouragement and confusion. He therefore has less need for rationalizations and compensations. He has less need for defensiveness, and therefore is able to be cooperative and understanding of other people.

Such an individual comes to depend more on himself and less on Daddy and Mommy and the Magician. He begins to have what we call, in a curious phrase, "a mind of his own." Why did we ever think of such a phrase? A mind of his own? Whose else? Unless he believes in magic and is under a hypnotic spell.

The child begins to grow up. He takes increasing responsibility for what he knows, for what he doesn't know, for what he says. He no longer says, "I can't help how I feel, can I?" This is the voice of a child. A mature person helps how he feels. He takes responsibility for how he feels. He takes responsibility for what he does. If he stutters, *he* is doing it; it is not happening to him. If he is afraid of other people, *he* is the one who is tensing and cringing. He takes responsibility for himself. Then he becomes able to help others take responsibility for themselves.

If you want to be a parent, teacher, or doctor—or anyone who presumes to help others—an important question to ask yourself is, "What is help?" Help is something you do that enables others to become mature, to take responsibility for what they say and do and think. They can be themselves because they can take responsibility for themselves. If you are going to be a parent, teacher, or doctor, rather than something I would call a magician, this, so far as I know, is how you become one.

Well, we are not done, but the hands of the clock tell us we are done. So we will end the course with a word we always have to use to end things: *et cetera.*

From the Fall 1968 Et cetera.

IV.
COMMUNICATION IN THE LARGER SOCIETY

THE TASK OF THE LISTENER

S.I. Hayakawa

THE WORD-MANIPULATING professions have of necessity grown in importance with increasing economic interdependency in a technological world. The more industrialized society becomes, the more carefully must human effort be coordinated — and this coordination is achieved by language. The more interdependent society becomes, the more communications there must be. The need for everyone to be understood (or at least to be heard) by other persons, by other classes of society, by people of other faiths, occupations, other economic interests, other nationalities, is a direct outcome of this vast social interdependency which industrialization has created.

The result of this vast need for communication created by the modern world is familiar to us all. The citizen of today, Christian or Jew or Mohammedan, financier or farmhand, stockbroker or stockboy, has to interpret more words a day than the citizen of any earlier time in world history. Literate or semiliterate, we are assailed by words all day long: news commentators, soap operas, campaign speeches, newspapers, the propaganda of pressure groups or governments — all of these trying to tell us something, to manipulate our beliefs, whether about the kind of toothpaste to use or the kind of economic system to support. We are told these many things sometimes for our own good, and sometimes for the good of those who

---

S.I. Hayakawa is the founder and editor of *Et cetera*. This article first appeared in *Communication in General Education*, edited by Earl James McGrath, U.S. Commissioner of Education (Dubuque, Iowa: William C. Brown Company, 1949).

tell and not for ours. We are living in a time when millions of dollars are spent each day by people who want to make up our minds for us.

It is natural that this kind of climate should generate widespread scepticism. Confronted by the clamor of a thousand contradictory voices, our tendency is to say 'Let's not believe anybody!' We therefore have many sceptics in the modern world — people who simply refuse to believe anything. In my own experience I have found that such sceptics belong to two large groups: first, there is the working class group of sceptics, who tend to disbelieve all newspapers, all the propaganda of the employing classes, and most of the propaganda of their union leaders. They are left believing, by and large, only what they learn from face-to-face contact with people whom they have learned to know and trust.

The second class of sceptics is found among those who are themselves in the word-manipulating professions. They have seen, or been party to, so many phony publicity stunts, slanted news stories, deceptive political campaigns, or ill-advised public relations drives, that they take a kind of professional pride in not believing anything. I should also include in this class of sceptics some academic people of my acquaintance who are so clever that they see through everything: the logical weaknesses of the arguments for capitalism or against it; the weaknesses of the arguments both of theists and atheists; the shortcomings of science and the shortcomings of the alternatives to science. These sceptics of the word-manipulating class are perhaps in an even sadder state than the working-class sceptics, because the latter at least continue to believe in each other as partners in work, and they believe in the realities of their work. When a man digs potatoes, he does not doubt the reality and validity of potatoes. But the sceptic of the word-manipulating class is sceptical above all things of the validity and worth of his own work, because if all communications are suspect, so are his own. This conviction leads to the kind of disintegration into cynicism (and sometimes drink) not uncommon in the journalistic profession, in advertising, in politics, and (we are forced to admit) in academic life.

But the problems of the sceptic, whether naive or sophisticated, are the problems confronting everyone who lives in an age of the loudspeaker, the power of press, and the mass circulation media. How does anyone find the needle of legitimate meaning in the haystacks of nonsense? How does one find the few cuts of real beefsteak hidden somewhere, we hope, in the carloads of baloney? It is in this situation that, in our time, the science of semantics has arisen. Briefly stated, semantics is the study of the relationships between symbol and reality, between language and behavior, between words and their consequences.[1] One of the basic questions of semantics, then is, 'What *kinds* of meaning can language convey?'

If I may simplify (or oversimplify) the answers given to this question in semantic literature, a useful way of classifying the functions of language is to divide them into four.[2] First, there is the *informative* function, an example of which is found in such a sentence as 'The car is in the garage.' The 'truth' of an informative statement is determined by looking *beyond the words and at the facts*. In other words, one looks into the garage to see if the car is there.

Second, there is language that is used to set up language. This I shall call (after the terminology of Charles Morris) the *systemic* use of language. Before we can say, 'The car is in the garage,' we have to come to some agreement as to what we shall call 'cars,' 'garages,' and so on. Systemic language gives *information about our linguistic systems* so that information about the world may be conveyed. Language is not merely names, but systems of names and named relationships. (The number system, for example, is a system of consecutive sound-clusters socially agreed upon as being applicable in certain, pre-established *order*.) The 'truth' of systemic statements is determined by *logical consistency*.

Third, there is the *directive* function of language. A statement of the kind, 'No parking,' says nothing descriptive about the world. It simply tries *to control future behavior*.

Fourth, there is what may be called the *expressive* or *valuative* function of language, in which one expresses preferential feelings toward something: 'That's a lovely hat you have on,' 'The free enterprise system is the finest system on earth.'

This, however, is the barest skeleton of our system of classification. Language being infinitely rich and complex, and human beings being endlessly resourceful in styles of saying things, we rarely have the four uses of language in simple, clearly recognizable form. Some of the complexities can be exemplified in a few sample sentences drawn from everyday life; the full complexities can, of course, only be studied in whole pages of rich and thoughtful prose or verse. But here are some trivial samples:

'*Magic Baking Powder contains no alum.*' This statement is on the surface informative. It has valuative connotations, however, since it is implied that inferior baking powders contain alum. It has also a directive function, suggesting that you buy this kind.

'*Bill is a communist.*' Although this statement is systemic in form, it can, depending on context, be used informatively, directively, or valuatively.

'*Best motor oil.*' Ordinarily valuative, but in technical discourse where such criteria as the Society of Automotive Engineers' standards are previously agreed upon, this statement can be informative.

'If you spell it backwards, it spells "Nature's."' This is, I suppose, a systemic statement, but it is certainly used for its valuative and directive implications.

One logical consequence of this fourfold distinction of the functions of language is that there are at least four different meanings possible for the expression 'talking sense.' We must all talk some kind of sense in order to be believed. One can talk sense informatively, systemically, directively, or valuatively. Each function of language has its own criteria of meaningfulness. In order to examine these, let us look at these four uses of language at their highest development, since obviously the most important linguistic events do not remain forever at the simple-minded levels of discourse quoted in the examples above.

The sum-total of all the verified statements made in carefully refined informative language—information about the earth, stars, animals, plants, society, digestion, health—constitute the body of knowledge which we call science. What we call 'good reporting' and 'accurate description' are also high products of the informative uses of language. It is the concern of the scientist, whatever his field, to describe accurately, to report well, and to increase the number, the scope, and the generality of his verifiable statements. In one sense of the term, the scientist's language represents *one* kind of semantic ideal.

But before the scientist can talk sense at all, he has to set up a vocabulary and a language. For this reason, systemic training is part of the training of a scientist: he has to learn chemical symbols, mathematics, systems of notation, systems of weights and measures, all of which are special refinements of language. Logic is also a systemic discipline; it tells what statements may legitimately follow what other statements — it says nothing at all about the informative truth of statements as they apply to the world outside of language. Mathematics is also pure systemic discourse. It sets up languages of a variety of structures, enabling specialized accurate discourse about an indefinite number of actual or imagined situations. Grammar, too, is a systemic discipline, and it is a sound tradition that insists that all students be taught grammar. However, there is something radically wrong with the way it is ordinarily taught. The effect of systemic discipline is normally to make discourse possible. But the effect of usual grammatical instruction is to paralyze students so that they become afraid to use their own language.

I have said that logical consistency is the important criterion of talking sense in a systemic language. In practical terms, such consistency means, in our own utterances, that what we say at one moment should bear a recognizable relationship to what we say at other moments. Unless some consistent relationship exists internally among the many utterances we make from time to time, we shall not be talking sense.

Directive discourse, at its highest generality, is what we have traditionally called 'ethics' and 'moral ideals.' Religions, too, are powerful systems of directives, giving us commandments about our attitudes and behavior. Another class of directives is law, which is the body of directives agreed upon by the members of any given society as necessary to be obeyed if that society is to continue to function. Still another class of directives is exemplified by advertising and propaganda.

How does one talk sense in directive utterances? Every directive, it seems to me, implies a promise, whether trivial or grave, whether limited or general. Certain satisfactions are promised as the result of obeying. The person who talks sense in directives is he who predicts accurately the consequences of following his directives.

The highest development of valuative utterance is to be found in literature: the novel, the drama, poetry. Excellence in valuative utterance means that sensitive and subtle valuations have been made, exploring new areas of feeling, making new perceptions possible, enlarging human experience; it also means that the writer has not only managed to state his perceptions, but has also made the reader or listener know what it feels like to make such valuations. This, perhaps, is the ultimate magic of language: that Joseph Conrad has been to sea, and that we should feel, reading his novels, something of what he felt; that Shelley felt in the west wind a powerful symbol of his personal aspiration to be 'destroyer and creator,' and that we should, reading his poem, feel something of his revolutionary spirit.

I am not saying that literature and poetry are simply valuative, but that valuative content is a major ingredient. There are certainly systemic elements in all of art. The differences between a rambling narrative and a novel is that the latter is given an additional dimension by the fact that the novelist has ordered his events into a system of symbols that have a structure and a consistent set of internal relationships.

One criterion of the meaningfulness in valuative utterance is what we ordinarily call 'sincerity,' which simply means that when a man says, 'My heart leaps up when I behold a rainbow in the sky,' these words should stand for some kind of actual pleasurable excitations going on in the speaker's nervous system. Valuative language, like scientific language, must be refined and elaborated in order to make finer distinctions possible. The scientist cannot be limited, in his discussion of temperature, to the two words, 'hot' and 'cold.' Similarly, whatever some of our less articulate friends may believe, valuative utterances cannot be limited simply to such terms as 'swell' and 'lousy.' Literature performs the function, among others, of constantly refining valuative language, so that finer distinctions of valuation become statable.

As stated at the beginning, the task of the citizen today, to an unprecedented degree is to distinguish sense from nonsense, confronted as we are by the greatest deluge of words that human beings have ever faced. And because of the profound interdependency of the modern world, the penalties of not being able to distinguish sense from nonsense are severe. If employers believe a great deal of nonsense that is told them about labor unions, or if union members believe a great deal of nonsense about employers, the consequences are grave enough to involve the entire community. If we are told about the British experiment in socialized medicine solely through the nonsense of extreme partisans for and against socialized medicine, there will be no way in which we can profit from British experience. Even more seriously, if a time ever comes when nonsense crowds out all or almost all sense from radio, journalism, and the mass media, so that people are thrown into complete confusion, the word-manipulating professions, by having betrayed their basic trust of communicating accurately and well will have created the conditions under which civilization will no longer be able to survive — because civilization depends on communications faithfully made and therefore to some degree heeded. How to tell sense from nonsense is a crucial problem, therefore, to the listener, in order to insure his own survival, and to the speaker and writer, in order that they may faithfully perform their tasks.

How, then, does one distinguish sense from nonsense? I believe that there is a general method in which we can be trained in this useful art. It is simply that we be trained to talk sense ourselves. Those who have disciplined themselves to talk sense can tell whether or not others are talking sense, in the same way that people who have played baseball (even if unskillfully) can understand a professional ballgame better than those who have not.

Let me explore some of the implications of this principle for academic life. It is clear, first of all, that no department of knowledge has a monopoly in talking sense, since there are at least four different kinds of sense. There is a tendency among some scientists to believe that they alone talk sense, while philosophers and literary people talk sentimental nonsense. Philosophers and literary people retaliate by holding that what they talk is a 'higher wisdom,' while the utterances of scientists are merely 'instrumental' knowledge for which exaggerated claims are made. Nevertheless, it is clear that since all of us, in everyday living, have need of all four kinds of sense, it is absurd for the scientist, the politician, the logician, the philosopher, or the poet to claim that his words are more important or more meaningful than those of other occupations. In semantic theory we see the true unity of all knowledge. Valuative discourse must be based on knowledge of the world as it is, which knowledge is a function of informative uses of language. Science, which is the accumulation of informative statements, although often claiming not to deal with values, is itself based on some of the most general values in existence, such as the preference of truth over error, of generality over the cataloguing of unrelated data, of intellectual cooperation over concealment and secrecy. Society itself does not exist except by virtue of commonly agreed-upon directives. And all other functions of language are made possible because each of them is refined by means of systemic disciplines. The four functions of language are therefore profoundly interrelated, and no one can afford not to avail himself of the resources of all of them. Those who fail to avail themselves of the accurate informative language of the medical profession are left at the mercy of the inaccurate information of patent-medicine ads. Those who fail to heed the highest directives of philosophy and religion obey instead the narrower directives of one's own special interest group, one's social class, or one's gang. Similarly with valuative utterances: those who fail to refine their valuations through contact with the best in literature, philosophy, and ethics, evaluate none the less, but they do so with the valuative clichés of the Hearst editorial, the drugstore greeting card, the movie fan magazine, Gabriel Heatter, and the *Saturday Evening Post*. Those who think they can live without science live by pseudo-science. Those who think they can live without poetry live by pseudo-poetry. A thorough understanding of semantic theory has the effect in education of cutting across departmental lines, unifying professions across disciplines formerly regarded as distinct and separate.

I shall not go into detail about the ways in which semantic theory affects education within the various subject-matter disciplines, but I shall sum them up in one sweeping generalization. In order to train our students in talking sense, we must first and foremost set them the example. When we inform, we must give the criteria by which our information may be checked. When we teach linguistic systems, we must demonstrate the need of special languages. When we direct, we must show reasoned grounds in social convention or in practical consequences of following our directive. When we evaluate, we must evaluate sensitively, earnestly, sincerely.

These are difficult prescriptions, because we are all caught in a semantic environment in which the rewards of life go not necessarily to him who talks sense, but to him who talks fast. Many of us have learned that technique and have practiced it successfully for so many years that we have forgotten that any other formula exists. As Wendell Johnson has said, 'Every speaker is his own most interested and affected listener' — and many of us in education have talked so plausibly for so long that we have come to believe what we say.

Furthermore, in certain branches of knowledge nonsense has been institutionalized, so that we have to memorize large amounts of it in order to get our advanced degrees. The reader may take his choice of examples on this point: according to logical positivists, much of philosophy is institutionalized nonsense; according to Veblen, most traditional economics is nonsense; according to Jerome Frank and Felix Cohen, so is much of law; according to Thurman Arnold there is much traditional nonsense to be found in political science.[3] I feel that I memorized much nonsense in literary criticism and theory for my degree in English. But whatever these areas of institutionalized delusion may be, we who are trained in them have invested too much of our lives in them to start doubting their validity in middle age. So we go on talking.

Let me sum up. The task of communication arts today is desperately urgent. We all have so much to learn, so much to understand, so much to unlearn, in order to function in the modern world. Whole new areas of new knowledge in science, technology, and social thought have opened up in the past few decades. We are called upon in addition now to understand the peoples of all parts of the earth if we are to live at peace with them. More than ever, everybody needs to know more and valuate more adequately, and if we remain stupid and ignorant about the implications of modern technology and about the nature of the peoples of Russia and Asia and Europe and the Middle East, there will be a terrible price to pay.

Communication — accurate, meaningful communication — is urgent. Yet, as we all know, meaningless and misleading communication floods the newsstands, all but monopolizes the airwaves, and is rapidly taking over television. In order to sort the sense from nonsense — in order that people may begin to protest the nonsense that crowds almost all else off the mass media, there needs to be developed a public passion for sense. And it is this passion that we must develop in our courses in communication.

Edmond Taylor, the war correspondent who wrote *Richer by Asia*, says in that book that the real enemy of mankind is the delusion inside the heads of so-called normal men. By delusion, he means what I have called nonsense — but especially the nonsense we talk to ourselves *and believe*. The delusions of the mentally ill are sufficiently obvious to be guarded against, but the shared delusions of normal people: the delusions Russians have about America and Americans have about Russia; the delusions whites have about Negroes and Negroes have about whites — these are dangerous because they are not known by those who hold them to be delusions. Freeing the world of delusion is then a fundamental task of peace: undeluding Europe about Asia, Asia about America, America about Europe; undeluding Russians about America and Americans about Russia; and perhaps most important of all, undeluding Americans about America and Russians about Russia. When the myths are cleared from the people's eyes the world over, we may finally see each other not as hobgoblins but as men. But where does one start clearing up the delusions the whole world suffers from? Taylor says that one of necessity starts with oneself: 'Any victory over delusion in a single mind is a blow struck at the accumulation of group delusion which is the main cause of the world's disunity.'

Communication is a mediatory art. Mediation, more often than not, means clearing up people's delusions about themselves and others so that human cooperation can begin. The teaching of communication cannot stop, therefore, with the inculcation of such verbal skills as merely enable the writer or speaker to be more agreeable or plausible or persuasive, and enable the listener or reader to follow the meaning of what is said. It must go beyond these skills to a philosophical and ethical perception of the role of communication in human life. For the only settling of human conflict by other than communicative means is resort to force. And we can no longer afford to use force.

NOTES AND REFERENCES

1. A major aspect of this study is the contrast between healthy and pathological reactions to symbols (including the linguistic) drawn by A. Korzybski in *Science and Sanity: An Introduction to Non-Aristotelian Systems and General Semantics* (Lancaster, Pa., 1933). See also Wendell Johnson, *People in Quandaries* (New York: Harper, 1946); Irving J. Lee, *Language Habits in Human Affairs* (New York: Harper, 1941); Hayakawa, *Language in Thought and Action* (New York: Harcourt, Brace, 1949).
2. See especially Charles Morris, *Signs, Language, and Behavior* (New York: Prentice-Hall, 1946).
3. See Rudolf Carnap, *Philosophy and Logical Syntax* (London: Kegan Paul, Trench, Trubner, 1935); Alfred J. Ayer, *Language, Truth and Logic* (New York: Oxford U.P., 1936); Thorstein Veblen, *Theory of the Leisure Class* (New York: Modern Library); Jerome Frank, *Law and the Modern Mind* (New York: Brentano, 1930); Felix S. Cohen, 'Transcendental Nonsense and the Functional Approach,' *Et cetera, A Review of General Semantics*, II (Winter, 1944-45), 82-115; Thurman W. Arnold, The Symbols of Government and *The Folklore of Capitalism* (New Haven: Yale University Press, 1935 and 1937).

From the Fall 1949 Et cetera.

PROPAGANDA

Neil Postman

OF ALL THE WORDS WE use to talk about talk, *propaganda* is perhaps the most mischievous. The essential problems its use poses, and never resolves, are reflected in the following definition, given by no less a personage than the late Aldous Huxley:

> There are two kinds of propaganda—rational propaganda in favor of action that is consonant with the enlightened self-interest of those who make it and those to whom it is addressed, and nonrational propaganda that is not consonant with anybody's enlightened self-interest, but is dictated by, and appeals to, passion.

This definition is, of course, filled with confusion and even nonsense, both of which are uncharacteristic of Huxley and only go to show how *propaganda* can bring the best of us down.

To begin with, Huxley makes a distinction between "good" and "bad" propaganda on the basis of the cause being espoused. If what we are told is good for everybody, then propaganda is "rational." If it is bad for everybody, it is nonrational. But how are we to know what is good and what is bad for everybody? In most instances, this is far from self-evident, and not even an Aldous Huxley can say for sure what is enlightened and what is not. Moreover, the information we might need to decide the issue is often not available to us. Suppose, for example, a television commercial tells us that a certain drug will help to relieve nagging backaches. That would appear to be in every-

---

Neil Postman is Editor of *Et cetera* and professor of Media Ecology at New York University. This article is excerpted from his book, *Crazy Talk, Stupid Talk*.

body's self-interest, thus, rational propaganda. But let us also suppose it is later discovered that in addition to relieving nagging backaches, the drug also relieves you of a healthy liver. Was the commercial "good" propaganda at the time you heard it or was it "bad"? Perhaps it was "good" when you heard it but *became* "bad" when you learned of the drug's side-effects. But since it was never in anybody's self-interest to use the drug, then wasn't the commercial "bad" propaganda to begin with?

And now let us suppose that in combination with another substance, the drug is rendered harmless to your liver. Will a commercial for the drug (with Secret Formula X-gy added) now be "good" propaganda? Then suppose . . . Well, you can begin to see the problems here.

But they are simple ones compared to those raised by a television commercial which tells us to vote for a political candidate. How would we know *before* the candidate is elected if it is in everybody's self-interest to vote for him? Indeed, how would we know a year after his election if it *has been* in everybody's self-interest? People continually disagree over such matters, and we would be left with a definition of propaganda that says: What I think has been good for me is "rational." What you think has been good for you is "nonrational." But Huxley does give us a hint, although a misleading one, of how we may resolve the problem. He says that nonrational propaganda "appeals to passion." He says nothing about the type of appeal made by rational propaganda, but we may assume he believes it appeals to the "intellect." Here Huxley has, of course, moved to another ground, and is offering a definition based on the type of appeal, not the goodness or badness of the cause. But as he has it here, this shift only results in more confusion. What do we say of "propaganda" that appeals to our passions but in an enlightened cause? And what of propaganda that appeals to our intellect but for a cause that is not consonant with everybody's enlightened self-interest?

There are two possible ways out of this dilemma, as far as I can see. The first is to stop using the word "propaganda" altogether. Huxley himself seems to suggest this in another part of the book, from which I earlier quoted. He says:

In regard to propaganda the early advocates of universal literacy and a free press envisaged only two possibilities: the propaganda might be true, or it might be false. They did not foresee what in fact has happened . . . the development of a vast mass communications industry, concerned in the main neither with the true nor the false, but with the unreal, the more or less totally irrelevant.

I infer from this passage that Huxley does not quite know how to classify "totally irrelevant" messages except to say that they are nonrational because they distract people from seeing the "truth." Of course, they also distract people from seeing "falsehoods," and perhaps on that account, Huxley might think, as I do, that the word "propaganda" causes more misunderstanding than it resolves.

But if the word is to remain with us, then I suggest we pick up on one of Huxley's ideas and use "propaganda" to refer not to the goodness or badness of causes but exclusively to a use of language designed to evoke a particular kind of response. We might say, for example, that propaganda is language that invites us to respond emotionally, emphatically, more or less immediately, and in an either-or manner. It is distinct from language which stimulates curiosity, reveals its assumptions, causes us to ask questions, invites us to seek further information and to search for error. From this perspective, we eliminate the need to distinguish between good and bad propaganda (except in the sense that "good" propaganda works and "bad" doesn't). We eliminate the need to focus on causes and actions and the precarious issue of which ones are in whose enlightened self-interest. And we eliminate the need, which thankfully Huxley does not bring up but which others have, to distinguish between language that persuades and language that doesn't. Since all language is purposive (even, I am told, the language of paranoid schizophrenics), we can assume that talking is always intended as some form of persuasion. Thus, the distinction between persuasion and other types of talking does not seem to be very useful. But the distinction between language that says "Believe this" and language that says "Consider this" is, in my opinion, certainly worth making, and especially because the techniques of saying "Believe this" are so various and sophisticated. Here, for example, are two pieces of propaganda, according to the way in which I have defined the word. The first is of a fairly obvious species, and I think three short paragraphs of it will be about all you can take. It was published in *The Indianapolis Star* in 1968, about the time the Vietnam War was heating up, and was called "A Letter From a War Veteran":

> It was too bad I had to die in another country. The United States is so wonderful, but at least I died for a reason, and a good one.
> I may not understand this war, or like it, or want to fight it, but nevertheless I had to do it, and I did.
> I died for the people of the United States. I died really for you; you are my one real happiness. I died also for your mom and dad so that they could go on working. . . . For your brothers so that they could play sports in freedom without Communist rule. . . .

It goes on like this for several paragraphs, in the course of which God comes into the picture, along with Dad's retirement, vacations, and several other sure-fire winners. There is, in my opinion, not much to say of interest about this piece of propaganda because it is so obviously constructed to evoke Indianapolis passions in favor of the war. This is not to say that there were no arguments for waging the war, only that no arguments were presented here in any form, and there is no pretense that there are. The rhetorical devices are, so to speak, all up front, and I confess to a certain admiration for the boldness of their sentimentality. Even the admen on Madison Avenue would be ashamed to try to pull this off, and I can't help thinking that there must be something very curious going on in Indiana if this could be done as late as 1968.

But the next species of propaganda is another matter. In fact, perhaps in a special way, it illuminates the difference between Indiana stupid talk and New York stupid talk. This one was widely circulated among intellectuals in New York City when it was the fashion to elevate revolutionaries to sainthood.

The propaganda was intended to give us some background information on George Jackson, who was for a time a charismatic leader in the movement for black liberation. We are informed that Jackson was a choirboy, that his father was a post office employee, and that Jackson subscribed to conventional values when he was young. We are also told that the circumstances of Jackson's first serious crime were these: One night a friend whom Jackson had invited for a ride in his car ordered him to stop at a gas station. The friend went inside and stole seventy dollars; then he told Jackson to drive away. Although Jackson was convicted for robbery, we are led to believe that he was entirely innocent. The following paragraph telling of Jackson's early life was included in the piece as part of our background information:

> When Jackson was 15, still too young to drive legally, he had a slight accident in his father's car, knocking a few bricks out of the outside wall of a small grocery store near his home. His father paid the damages, the store owner refrained from pressing charges, but he was still sent to reform school for driving without a license. Three years later, shortly after his release from reform school, he made a down payment on a motorbike, which turned out to have been stolen. His mother had the receipt and produced it for the police, but Jackson was sent back to reform school, this time for theft.

I believe that this paragraph is one of the great propagandistic passages of all time, and is deserving of being included in the *Joseph Goebbels Casebook of Famous Boondoggles*. Let us do a small explication of it:

> When Jackson was 15, still too young to drive legally . . .

Well, now, what does this imply? That Jackson was a competent driver, but that the laws governing these matters are unreasonable? Why not, "still too young to drive"? Who or what is in need of correction here, Jackson or the Motor Vehicle Bureau?

> . . . he had a slight accident in his father's car, knocking a few bricks out of the outside wall of a small grocery store near his home . . .

The diminutives are almost oppressive: a *slight* accident, a *few* bricks, a *small* grocery store. One almost expects to read that someone's *trivial* leg was *barely* fractured. And what is a slight accident, anyway? Dislodging even a few bricks from an *outside* wall (It wasn't, for God's sake, an *inside* wall!) doesn't

212

sound awfully slight to me. And why are we told it was "near his home"? Are we being led to believe that he had only driven around the block?

Best of all is the phrase "in his father's car." Does this imply that George really had nothing to do with the accident, that it happened *to* him while he was innocently sitting in his father's car? Why not, "He had a slight accident when he stole his father's car"? Or did George's father approve of his taking the car?

> His father paid the damages. The store owner refrained from pressing charges, but he was still sent to reform school for driving without a license.

The "still" is a wonderful piece of propaganda here. It leads us to believe that everything had been settled to everyone's satisfaction, but that the police and the courts were simply being vindictive. After all, it was a *small* crime, and George *was* a choirboy. Why the big deal?

> Three years later, shortly after his release from reform school, he made a down payment on a motorbike, which turned out to have been stolen.

First of all, I'd like to know how "shortly" after his release. It sounds as if George was in reform school for almost three years. Is this true? And why is the information being kept from me?

Second, the word "down payment" is simply marvelous. It conjures an image of a responsible businessman engaged in a wholly legitimate transaction. But George obviously didn't buy the motorbike at Macy's. He must have bought it from someone on the streets who was giving him a "real bargain." But, the "turned out to be stolen" suggests that choirboy George never suspected, not even for a moment, that anyone could traffic in stolen property. Where did George grow up, in Beverly Hills?

> His mother had the receipt and produced it for the police, but Jackson was sent back to reform school, this time for theft.

The implication here is that the evidence George's mother produced should have been enough for any reasonable policeman. But apparently it wasn't. What was the evidence against George? Was he convicted of theft without a trial? What did the police have to say at the trial? We are told nothing, left with the impression that George was possibly framed and certainly the victim of a system that was out to get him.

Let me stress, in case you have gotten the wrong impression, that I do not know much about the late George Jackson, and some of what I do know evokes my admiration. What I am talking about is a method of propagandizing which attempts to conceal itself as information. The response that is asked for here is, "Believe this. You are being given all the information you need to know." But I can sooner believe that a soldier would go to war for Mom's apple pie than that a friend of George invited him for a ride, "ordered" him to stop at a gas station, held up the place, and told him to drive away, while all the time George thought his friend was only going to the bathroom. I would guess that you couldn't get away with that kind of stuff in Indianapolis . . . In New York, it's easy.

Each end of the political spectrum has, I suppose, its own favorite style of propaganda. The Right tends to prefer gross, straightforward sentimentality. The Left, a sort of surface intellectualizing. But it is very important, it seems to me, to note that the response required of us, in each instance, is a passionate, uncritical acceptance of a point of view.

I am not implying, by the way, that there is no legitimate function for propaganda. There are several semantic environments — advertising, for example — where it is quite reasonable for one person to ask another to believe what he is saying. In fact, much of our literature — especially, popular literature — amounts to a direct appeal to our emotions. To the extent that such appeals are cathartic or entertaining or, in some sense, a stimulus to self-discovery, they are invaluable. In other words, propaganda is not, by itself, a problem, if it comes dressed in its natural clothing. But when it presents itself as something else, regardless of the cause it represents, it is a form of stupid talk that can be, and has been, extremely dangerous. It is dangerous for two reasons. First, propaganda demands a way of responding which can become habitual. If we allow ourselves, too easily, to summon the emotions that our own causes require, we may be unable to hold them back when confronted with someone else's causes. And second, propaganda has a tendency to work best on groups rather than individuals. It has the effect of turning groups into crowds, which is what Huxley calls "herd poisoning." As he describes it, herd poisoning is "an active, extraverted drug. The crowd-intoxicated individual escapes from responsibility, intelligence, and morality into a kind of frantic, animal mindlessness."

Here, Huxley is talking about what happens when an individual has joined with other individuals in a semantic environment where propaganda, unchecked, is doing its work. Stupid talk is transformed into an orgy of crazy talk, the consequences of which can be found in graves stretching from Siberia to Mississippi to Weimar to Peking. (This last sentence is, of course, propaganda, pure and simple, but I like it, anyway.)

From the Summer 1979 Et cetera.

LANGUAGE CLUES FOR THE RHETORICAL CRITIC

Dan F. Hahn

IF WE WERE TO ASK the average person why it is important to pay attention to the language of politicians, I suspect we would be told that it is necessary because politicians lie.

While there may be nothing inherently wrong with that answer, I want to suggest that there are several more significant reasons to watch their language closely — one which stems from the nature of language and one which is necessitated by the assumptions of most social science research.

The most important of the reasons is that a person's language structures his perceptions. "Students of language, following Whorf and Sapir, are coming more and more to assert the intimate interaction between language, perception, and action, and even going so far, as Whorf does, to argue that once particular 'ways of analyzing and reporting experience . . . have become fixed in the language as integrated fashions of speaking; they tend to influence the ways in which the personality not only communicates, but also analyzes nature, notices or neglects types of relationships and phenomena, channels . . . reasoning, and builds the house of . . . consciousness.' "[1]

The Sapir-Whorf hypothesis is most easily demonstrated in cross-cultural studies. Francisco Moreno offers this illustration: ". . . if a child is taught Spanish as his mother tongue . . . he would also be taught by implication to develop an essentially fatalistic attitude toward life . . . the inevitability of what hap-

---

Dan Hahn is an Associate Professor in the Department of Communication Arts and Sciences at Queens College, New York.

pens to him will seldom be questioned. A very simple English statement as 'I lost my keys' is impossible to reproduce in Spanish comparable psycholinguistic form. In Spanish you would have to say 'Se me han perdido las llaves' which literally translated means 'The keys have gotten lost from me.' " Moreno concludes that cultural and linguistic conditioning further cause one to judge the attitudes implicit in the language. For example, the native English speaker would be "probably horrified at the Spanish lack of willingness to accept responsibility for the loss of the keys"; while the native speaker of Spanish "would be equally horrified at the claim to have control over things he is sure you cannot control."[2]

Another cross-cultural example comes from an analysis of how Blacks and Whites are cued by their different dialects to perceive time. White English features a tripartite verb structure of past, present and future (I was, I am, I will be), while Black English features the continuous form (I be: past, present *and* future).

Each system has advantages and disadvantages. The White version tends artificially to break up the universal elements of time in terms of personal position, thus leading its practitioners to overlook the causal relationship between yesterday, today and tomorrow. One contemporary result is the obsession with an unsophisticated poster enblazoned with the drivel: "Today is the first day of the rest of my life." In a sense, of course, the poster is true — but it obscures much more than it reveals.

The problem with Black English is just the opposite. That is, it posits the impossibility of change. Thus, in Black English the phrase "I be working" means "I was working yesterday, I am working today and I will be working tomorrow." It is a language that accepts the status quo — which might be acceptable if the Black status quo were good — but given the present conditions of Blacks in our society the language is defeatist in effect.

Obviously, these different languages provide us with differing perceptions — and that is an important *political* fact. The continuous verb form is conservative — it says that tomorrow will be like today so there's no sense in voting, running for office, or otherwise trying to bring about a change.

The important thing to remember, then, is that our actions are determined by our perceptions, which are determined by our language. If, for instance, we were to ask why we have poverty in this rich country, we would likely get one of two answers. Some people would point to the inadequacies of poor people, while others would assert that poverty is caused by the way our economic system functions. Note here that the language in which the problem is described will cue us to quite different solutions. If the problem is described as stemming from personal inadequacies, that leads us to direct our attempts at individuals, while the systemic description may guide us toward an overhaul of the system. Unfortunately, however, the practical result of either description is to lead to inaction — the "human nature" description runs up against the belief that "you can't change human nature," while the "economic law" perception makes poverty appear "either unconquerable or so hard to change that few will support the political effort."[3]

And when both descriptions are being bruited about in the political arena, with each political actor believing in his description, his perception, the changes of any significant action become even less. No wonder Nietzsche rejected what he called the "dogma of immaculate perception."

And no wonder we need to pay attention to the language of our politicians, because now we understand that when a politician describes Communism as cancer his solution is implied: surgical removal before it spreads. And when the local school board candidate suggests that some literature is poison we know he will want to lock it away where the kids can't get at it.

So language analysis can lead us to understand and even predict the actions of politicians. But it may be even more significant if we understand that their language may also explain the apathy and inactivity of the average citizen.

Thus, when the President describes a situation as a "crisis," our tendency is to quit complaining and line up in support of his policy. When he arouses our fears by telling of Russia's new weapons superiority we supinely allow an escalation of our military budget . . . and when he says that the exorbitant budget will solve the problem we sigh with relief and appreciation.

Surprisingly, however, it isn't just crisis that keeps us in line. So does the normal. So when a bureaucrat describes his action as "routine," we tend to go along. We shrug, perhaps with disgust — but without major objection — and conclude "that's the way things are."

But political analysts have tended to miss the significance of public quiescence because of the behavioral bias of most social science research. As Michael Lipsky has observed,

> . . . both protest and pluralist analysis direct attention to overt activity, when the more interesting and certainly more critical political observation is that most people generally neither protest nor participate to any great degree.
>
> Many students of American politics have been chronically unable to analyze the characteristically low levels of participation and dissent successfully because they have trained themselves to focus attention exclusively on what they call behavior, by which they mean readily observable actions. Thus survey research, roll calls, and various interviewing techniques have thrived as basis for analysis because they display actions . . . or provide insight into attitudes, the motivational background for actions. The difficulty with research of this kind is that there is a range of political developments to which the researcher is blind. This is the area of *caused inaction*, inaction best explained as induced by influences outside of the individual. The fawn, unmoving in the thicket, may be asleep, but it also may be paralyzed with fear of a predator. In the latter case, only the observer who is alert to the structure of power will provide a persuasive account of the fawn's behavior.[4]

Assuming, then, that you agree with me that the analysis of the language clues of our politicians is necessary, it remains to detail what those clues are. And that will, of necessity, lead us into much speculation. For this kind of analysis has hardly begun. But let's not let the lack of definitive studies deter us — rather, let's lay out some speculations and try to identify areas for subsequent research.

First, let's hypothesize about what might be learned from examining a politician's deployment of various parts of speech.

The nouns of a politician will tell you which portions of the world he sees as relevant. They will, in a sense, show you of what he is conscious and thus the arenas in which he will be active.

His verbs will explain his behavior patterns and his attitudes toward leadership. Is he active or passive? If he perceives life as controllable he will be more likely to use strong verbs.

In his adjectives will be found his opinion of the world — the judgments he makes about it. And if you examine his adjective clusters you should be able to discover the categories he utilizes to make judgments — moral, practical, aesthetic, etc.

His adverbs will suggest salience and intensity, and will tend to show you not only what is to be done, but how he plans to do it. Thus, those who expected Carter to be an active President in the FDR mold obviously overlooked his heavy campaign reliance upon adverbs like *gradually, modestly, accurately,* and *slowly.*

Connectives, of course, establish relationships, but they may also suggest dominance (and fear of being dominated). That is, one who utilizes an abnormally high number of connectives probably does so because he doesn't want to be interrupted.

Pronoun use can tell us a good deal about the speaker. For instance, Nixon's use of pronouns typed him as a benevolent dictator. The pronoun "I" tended to be followed by action verbs, while "we" and "us" tended to be used in the receiving position. The Nixonian formula, then, was "I, President Nixon, have acted . . . and we, the citizens, reap the benefits of the action." Pronoun frequency is also revealing. Consider, for example, the implications of the fact that Nixon used "I" ten times as often in foreign policy as in domestic policy speeches . . . or that in the White House tapes he was found to utilize "I" sixteen times as often as it is found in normal conversation.

But in this early stage of our study, I would suggest that the most promising avenue might be metaphor analysis. Does the politician describe human activities in mechanical terms — *input, output, feedback,* etc? If so, we might speculate that he would not be terribly concerned with what the rest of us might think of as the preciousness of human life, that he might try to manipulate humans as if they were some higher manifestation of IBM circuitry.

If he describes any aspect of society as *sick*, we should be alerted that treatment is on the way . . . and we ought to know whether he perceives himself as a chiropractor or surgeon before we cast our ballots.

If we find him utilizing a lot of water metaphors we should understand that he sees the situation as desperate—as we can discover if we abstract out the metaphors and string them together. Here, for instance, is the compilation from Goldwater's acceptance speech at the 1964 Republican convention: Due to "foggy thinking," "the tide has been running against freedom" and we are sinking in a "swampland of collectivism." Therefore, despite the detractors who say "don't rock the boat," the "campaign which we launch here" will "set the tide running again in the cause of freedom." "The past will be submerged" and we will travel democracy's "ocean highway" where freedom will accompany the "rising tide of prosperity." Clearly, Goldwater's liquid metaphors demonstrated that he perceived the situation of the country under Johnson as dangerous; but the American people did not see it quite that way. They did not feel that his analysis put him in the "mainstream" of contemporary thought, and they cast their ballots as though he were floundering in the backwash of Darwinianism.

Finally, I should mention form as an area in which we can get clues from political language. Take, for instance, the line from John Kennedy's Inaugural Address that so caught the imagination of Americans: "Ask not what your country can do for you, but what you can do for your country." But what *can* most of us do? Pay taxes. Die in a war. Work, and thereby avoid welfare. Be law-abiding. Clearly, all these behaviors are either sacrificial or pedestrian. So why did Americans react so positively to the line? Certainly part of the answer relates to the form of the line. As Murray Edelman points out, "Word orders like 'Ask not what . . .' are not used in ordinary conversation or even ordinary speechmaking. We associate the unusual deployment of verb, adverb, and accusative pronoun with biblical language and with eloquent oratory of the past, and we respond to the poetry of these associations."[5] That is, the form recalls other deployments of the same form and the audience reacts to the speaker as though he were of the other genre—a poet, or even a minor prophet—rather than a politician. The form deflects an audience's thought from the content of the line to the image of the speaker, and, simultaneously transforms the speaker from a mediocre politician to a poet or prophet.

In both capitalism and politics there is a form of address that argues honesty. In a capitalist society, all are familiar with the Latin *caveat emptor*, the notion that the buyer should beware. Yet we have all had the experience of having a salesperson tell us, conspiratorially, that "it's a good thing you came in today, because tomorrow the item you are interested in will be $10 more." The form of the dialogue is: "I'm on your side. I'll level with you and sell it to you today, even though my commission would be better if you delayed your purchase twenty-four hours." Maybe we believe the salesperson; maybe we buy the item; and maybe we end up in the store the next day shopping for another item. How do we act toward our salesperson? Yesterday his form told us, "today I'm looking out for you—tomorrow I'll be lining my own pockets." If we are smart, we will take him at his word. (Of course, if we were that smart we probably wouldn't have believed him yesterday, but that is another story.) The present point is that his manner of telling us yesterday of his trustworthiness makes him suspect today.

Politics has its own version of the personal *caveat emptor*. It is the Senator asking, "Can I speak frankly?", the President averring, "I'll be honest with you." This form may have temporary success, but it implicitly conveys to an audience that these times are exceptions to the non-frank, dishonest norm. Misused often enough, they can turn into liabilities—just as Nixon's phrase, "let me make one thing perfectly clear," came to signal his audience to watch for the obfuscation, the muddying phrase, the escape clause in what he was about to say.

Practically any piece of meta-communication (i.e., communication about the communication) underlines in about the same way. When a professor says, "Listen carefully, this point is important," he underlines that point but also, implicitly, says that what follows after that point in his presentation is not important.

Another form used in politics, as in the rest of life, is what is called "affirmation by denial." As Lucy Komisar notes, "If I say, 'I shall not compare thee to a summer's day, a rose, a running brook,' I have in spite of myself made those comparisons, and the day, rose, and brook have a positive existence in my speech."[6] When a politician says, "I wouldn't think of doing X," only one thing is clear—he *did* think of doing it; it did cross his mind. When Henry Kissinger, after the Mayaguez affair, said "We are not going around looking for opportunities to prove our manhood," one critic responded, "It was a curious comment for the question had never been asked, and it made it clear that at a level very close to his consciousness, Secretary Kissinger knew that this was precisely what America's reaction had been all about."[7]

Of course, you understand, I wouldn't dream of saying that the good Secretary lied.

NOTES AND REFERENCES

1. Annette Kolodny, *The Lay of the Land: Metaphor as Experience and History in American Life and Letters* (Chapel Hill: U. of North Carolina Press, 1975), p. 148.
2. Francisco Jose Moreno, "The Myth of Political Rationality," *International Journal of Social Psychiatry* (Winter/Spring, 1974-75), pp. 21-26.
3. Murray Edelman, *Political Language: Words That Succeed and Policies That Fail* (New York: Academic Press, 1977), pp. 7-8.
4. Michael Lipsky, in Edelman, *Political Language*, p. xix.
5. Murray Edelman, "Myths, Metaphors, and Political Conformity," *Psychiatry*, 30 (1967) p. 226.
6. J. Hillis Miller, "The Still Heart: Poetic Form in Wordsworth," *New Literary History*, 2 (Winter, 1971), p. 305.
7. Lucy Komisar, "You Won't Have Uncle Sam to Kick Around Any More," *The New York Times*, June 30, 1976, p. 29.

From the Spring 1978 Et cetera.

WHY POLITICS BORE US

Dan F. Hahn

AMONG THE MOST BORING things to listen to are reports of the achievements of neighbors' children, accounts of the sexual exploits of those of whom you're already jealous, the recounting of the dreams of those whose waking hours are also dull, and all accounts of politics.

Nonetheless, I not only intend to write about politics, but have taken as my responsibility the analysis of why politics strikes so many as dull.

I assume that I do not have to go to any great lengths to demonstrate that, indeed, most people find the political world boring. That would seem to be self-evident, if from nothing else, from the low level of voter turn-out in the United States.

But as another index, let's look at the figures for the Carter-Ford debates of 1976. Those three debates, it will be recalled, were ballyhooed as the greatest electoral events in modern times, sure to be crucial in deciding the next president, "historic" in the grandest meaning of that overworked word. And, befitting their status, they were carried on all three commercial networks as well as on public television; in short, if the TV was on at all it probably was tuned to the debates.

Given that saturation, how many watched? Neilsen ratings showed that 72.5% of the populace watched debate 1, declining to 65.3% for number 2, and 59.7% for the final debate.[1] These numbers, it must be remembered, are cumulative. For

---

Dan F. Hahn is an Associate Professor of Communication Arts and Sciences at Queens College in New York City. This paper was delivered at the 1980 International Conference on General Semantics in Toronto.

any given minute of any of the debates the actual audience was 20% less, or 52%, 45% and 39%.[2]

And what did this audience think of what they saw? Thirty-five percent found them "rather dull," as opposed to the 17% who thought them "very interesting"; 44% saw them as "not revealing," compared to 16% who found them "very revealing"; and 41% agreed that they were "uninformative," countered by 14% who perceived them to be "very informative."[3]

On a recent talk show Art Buchwald was asked whether he was concerned about the fact that 54% of the American population were reportedly disenchanted with the 1980 choice between Carter and Reagan. He replied, "No, but I am worried about the 46% who think the choice is okay." I feel the same way about the 17% who saw the 1976 debates as "very interesting." I suspect they're the same people I see at my local laundromat, mesmerized watching their clothes tumble toward cleanliness.

As an inveterate politician-watcher, I *had* to view the debates. And, my God, were they dull! Yet, I must also admit that they were the most exciting part of the campaign. Modern political campaigns are boring. Let's see why.

To do so we will have to turn our attention to another often-boring subject: history. To avoid dullness as much as possible, I will rely heavily on a marvelous new book by Paul Corcoran, *Political Language and Rhetoric.*

In the pre-literate age, according to Corcoran, rhetoric functioned not only as persuasion but also for the storage and preservation of information. But the development of literacy took care of the problems of information access and retrieval, so rhetoric was shorn of those duties and, in fact, no longer needed to concern itself with information. "Speaking became, especially in official capacities, reportorial in nature. The speech was no longer the final object. Books, official texts, data, and other records were always 'back there,' somehow being referred to. Speech, then, became a sign of something else — a report or reflexive reference to something outside itself. By virtue of this condition, speech tended to the ceremonial, the public display of something understood to be far more complex than what could be presented in the utterance of 'mere' speech. The speech was therefore perfunctory, prefatory, a distillate of the 'body of information' that could be found elsewhere."[5]

Meanwhile, the assumption that rhetoricians ought to be involved in argumentation about matters of public concern increasingly evaporated, starting in the sixteenth century, when rhetoric "underwent a transformation in the school curriculum and in philosophical circles that separated it from dialectical logic (and hence the substance of arguments); separated it from grammar (and hence the structure of speech), and relegated it to the status of an 'art' of elegant and mannered speaking. At the same time, the elevated status of logic, resulting from educational methods which assigned to logic all responsibility for the accumulation and disposition of knowledge, was gradually lost when the influence of scientific experimentation promised a method of inquiry and discovery as compared with logic's association with disputation and deduction."[6]

Then, as the amount and complexity of information increased, and the methods of storage and retrieval became more complicated with modern computers and video storage units, requiring special languages and techniques for retrieval, even the *possibility* of a linkage between rhetoric and information disappeared.

Contemporary political rhetoric, then, has nothing to rely upon but commonplaces — received wisdom. But audiences do not need to be persuaded of the truth of that wisdom . . . rather, they need to be persuaded that the speaker is identified with the right truths. Thus, we have "image" campaigns, where the function is not to argue about policy or value but to demonstrate that the speaker is identified with the right policies and values.

"Replacing persuasion as a rhetorical aim is the process of identification. Here the speaker invokes symbolic commonplaces by which he endeavors to associate himself (especially) and his proposals (if any) with images, ideas, and values which are far from new or specialized in character — uncontroversial within the dominant culture. These conventional items, as might be expected, are little more than platitudes such as order, brotherhood, peaceableness, the new and the good (progress), the old and the familiar (tradition), and synonyms for the common will of 'the people.'

"It will be readily observed that speeches based upon conventional identification have little need of persuasion or the livelier devices of gesture to win a point or the acceptance of a new body of information. Nor will such speeches require a logical method to convince the audience of the truth of conventional values. Of course, identification is a form of persuasion aimed at gaining a desired response from an audience, even if its use does not require the resolution of controversial propositions or the mastery of new subject matter. The objective is the acceptance in the listener's mind of the coincidence between conventional values and the speaker, or, conversely, the lack of confidence between those values and the speaker's opponent.

"The status of a speaker becomes a matter of special importance when his function is no longer associated with expertise or valued information, and when he identifies himself with merely conventional ideas. Consequently, the status, or more broadly, the 'image' of the speaker must become the centre of focus of any rhetorical performance."[7]

While it would be possible for the politicians to hire specialists to retrieve the needed information and, because of the visual capacities of television, to project the information to the audience, they will not do so because the audience is incapable of processing such information.

Besides, such an information-packed presentation would upset the audience expectations, an obviously unpersuasive step that any rhetorician would avoid if possible. The audience, far from expecting information, looks upon political speeches as performances. "The audience focuses upon the manner of delivery of an oration, not because it has no interest in the literal contents, but precisely because of the tacit assumption that any speech, however well or poorly delivered, can only be reportorial and referential, that is, merely a symbolic schema of the speech's 'real' contents. The audience thus assumes that the most important thing about the speech is the very fact that it is a speech, that is, an oral performance."[8]

We have, then, arrived at a point where speakers don't try

to say anything, and the audience doesn't expect them to—indeed, perhaps doesn't even want them to.

Even the supposedly "exciting" new medium, television, contributes to the boredom in at least three additional ways, namely, by establishing distance, by the ease of reproduction, and by setting unobtainable standards.

The distance established by television is enormous. I can remember my father telling of the excitement of traveling sixty miles by buckboard to hear William Jennings Bryan speak. By comparison, "broadcast rhetoric, even a 'live telecast,' cannot avoid impersonality and isolation—a type of total privacy—for both speaker and listener. The speaker faces an unresponsive microphone, the listener hears a disembodied voice, or a voice appearing to accompany a telescreen image . . ."[9] Impersonal and isolated—can one come up with a better recipe for boredom?

Television also leads to boredom by repetition. Any produced political production (advertisement clip, edited speech, sound track overlays, etc.) "can be repeated indefinitely in reproducing identical facsimiles."[10] It will be noted that in these reproductions the speaker doesn't change, while events do—from day to day. Thus, not only may we find the candidate dull from repetition, we also may find him uninformed for not keeping up with events, or untrustworthy because he is more interested in himself than events.

We should also realize that television creates boredom by setting unobtainable standards. Politics cannot be as funny as "Mork" or as gripping as a horror story. Additionally, the production components available for candidate manipulation in 30-second ads undermine more traditional approaches by becoming "the standard[s] for rhetorical performance in contemporary electoral politics."[11] That is, the produced appearance can be "perfect." Thus, when we see the politicians in unproduced appearances they appear dull and bland by comparison, leading us to boredom.

And that boredom is reinforced by the fact that most of us know nothing of politics. Why does that matter? Haven't you ever been to a cocktail party where all the conversations were about topics you knew nothing about. Well, politics is that way for most people, because most of us are so preoccupied with our own lives—making a living, tending our front lawns, and washing our cars—that we don't have, or take, time to understand politics. Thus, in a recent Gallup poll of 17- and 18-year-olds, "Eighty-one percent of those polled did not know that party conventions make the final choice of presidential nominees, 41 percent were unaware that China is the most populous nation in the world, and only 18 percent understood the meaning of 'detente' . . . only 50 percent of the young people surveyed knew that each state has two U.S. Senators, that the number of Representatives is based on population, and that the President cannot appoint members of Congress."[12]

And television does little to counteract this ignorance. In network evening news coverage of the 1976 campaign, fully 60% was devoted to such "Horserace" concerns as winning, losing, strategy, logistics, support, appearances, crowds, and hoopla, while only 28% was given to the substance of the campaign.[13]

Unfortunately, the generalized language of politicians doesn't help either. In the United States, the two-party system requires generalizations. Unlike most countries, our political parties are not narrowly ideological, easy to identify as to position on issues. Rather, they are broad, non-ideological. Each party tries to appeal to practically everybody in the electorate. In order to do so they state their positions in broad generalizations. Unfortunately, this generalization process is often self-defeating for the official once in office because the legislation or executive decision, once adopted, will be much more specific in application than the rhetoric implied.

Take, as an example, Nixon's 1968 "Plan for Peace" in Vietnam. The "Plan" had no content. Those who wanted to bomb the North back to the Stone Age could assume that that was Nixon's plan. Those who wanted an immediate withdrawal could hope that Nixon planned to do exactly that. But once elected, Nixon had to select specific policies, and those specifics could not please as many people as had his rhetorical generalizations. Thus, the generalization which had helped Nixon gain the office made it difficult for him to govern once in office. It is always thus. The generalization is required by the necessity of appealing to a diverse audience. The disillusionment is required by the necessity of implementing a specific policy. And continual disillusionment, we should understand, leads to boredom and apathy. It should be noted that much of the potential excitement of the 1980 Democratic Convention was defused by language. On the second day of the Convention Jody Powell announced that the Carter and Kennedy forces were getting together to find language acceptable to both sides (not acceptable *substance*, but acceptable *language*!).

Generalizations are flat, boring, whereas individuals are colorful and interesting. To take all of the poor and lump them together into the "culturally disadvantaged" is to generalize away their individual differences. Some people *are* poor because they are culturally disadvantaged. But, some have had home lives that denied the values of the culture. Some are lazy. Some are frozen out by the racism of the society. Some are stupid. Some are the victims of unethical or illegal business practices. Etc. but we take one attribute of their lives, poverty, assume a generalized cause, cultural disadvantagement, and use that generalization to define them.

And it strikes us as perfectly natural to do so. Our whole technology supports the tendency toward sameness. In an earlier, more natural existence, we were struck by the differentiations in nature and took individual ideosyncrasies as positive values. As technology took over we came to value sameness. As we wander rootless through our country we find security in the identical blandness of Howard Johnson motels, we feel at home under the golden arches of McDonalds. A friend of mine recently wanted to give her daughter a birthday she would remember. She wanted to take her to the Bolshoi Ballet, then to the Russian Tea Room for dinner. The kid? She wanted to go to the circus and dine at Burger King. Assembly line food, bad as it is, has the value of predictability. The hamburgers not only taste alike, they also taste like the Colonel's chicken, college cafeteria tuna salad sandwiches, and, for that matter, pretty much like any piece of mass-produced cardboard. "More mass production of more things will step up the race toward total abstraction;

one rose can be different from another, but washing machines and refrigerators are not all that strong on individuality."[14]

Neither are the Nixons, Fords, Carters, and Reagans of the world. Those who do dare to be different—the John Kennedys, the Malcolm X's, the Martin Luther Kings—are shown how much we appreciate their individualism. With their eclipse, the rest of us have pretty well settled down into the generalized, undifferentiated mass—cardboard caricatures of humans, enjoying our TV dinners while erstwhile Walter summarizes all of the significant ideosynratic activities of today's world in 30 minutes (well, 21 plus commercials, but why quibble?).

Speaking of Walter's reports leads me to my next point, that generalizations allow our leaders to engage in a drama of suspense and solution that ensures our allegiance as it befuddles our minds. "Every regime both encourages public anxiety and placates it through rhetoric and reassuring gestures. We are constantly told that the Russians are ahead of us in this or that weapons system or that some trouble spot threatens peace or American interests. At the same time we are reassured that American military power is massive and that leaders are acting with maximal effectiveness. The cycle of anxiety and reassurance provides a supportive following."[15]

The threat is generalized, beyond our individual power to ascertain. The reassurance is generalized, hidden behind walls of secrecy. Lacking the knowledge to challenge either the extent of the threats or the efficacy of the reassuring counter-measures, we are dangled on generalized rhetorical strings manipulated by our leaders. Betrayed by generalizations, we hang there helplessly—washing our cars, mowing our lawns, and supinely re-electing our leaders.

But why don't we see through them? Why do we vote for them and vote for them and vote for them, *ad nauseam*?

In order to understand that we first have to realize that most Americans are wedded to the status quo. They don't want change—and if they do contemplate change, they want it on their own terms. The language of politics "works" because it is not threatening. The code words reassure. The politician's language is calculated to demonstrate that "he is conforming and presents no risk of doing anything that will upset the established order or question its basic value premises. Through his stylized language form he is broadcasting the message that just as his words are banal, so his ideas are banal."[16] In short, the politician who says nothing is not a threat; if he mouths language with which his audience is comfortable he can be assumed to be safe, to favor the right things and oppose the wrong ones. He is properly middle-of-the-road. His mediocre-ness recommends him.

When the populace does contemplate change, which isn't often, they want that change to be on their own terms. Thus, political language functions to allow them to perceive the politician as recommending what they themselves prefer. "Ambiguities are useful . . . because they leave the auditors free to supply their own content for the ambiguities and thus persuade themselves."[17] Take this line from Nixon's Second Inaugural: "Let us resolve that this era will be what it can become: a time of great responsibilities, greatly borne, in which we renew the spirit and the promise of America as we enter our third century as a nation." Beautiful! The lines could have been spoken by any politician from Abbie Hoffman on the left to Robert Welch on the right. The sentence has absolutely no content; the auditors are completely free to envision whatever future they desire.

Political language, then, keeps us from "catching on" to the political windbags in two ways: first, it soothes us by talking our language; second, it is structured so as to allow us to persuade ourselves. No wonder it is effective. And no wonder we are bored. So we complain about a lack of leadership, and search for a hero, not remembering that Ralph Waldo Emerson told us that "Every hero becomes a bore at last."[18] But, judging from our election-day activities, we must have a vestigial memory of these lines of G.K. Chesterton:

> They spoke of progress spiring round,
>   Of Light and Mrs. Humphry Ward—
> It is not true to say I frowned,
>   Or ran about the room and roared;
> I might have simply sat and snored—

> I rose politely in the club
> And said, 'I feel a little bored;
> Will someone take me to a pub?'[19]

NOTES AND REFERENCES

1. John P. Robinson, "The Polls," in Sidney Kraus (Ed.). *The Great Debates: Carter vs. Ford, 1976.* (Bloomington: Indiana University Press, 1979), p. 263.
2. *Ibid.*, p. 262.
3. *Ibid.*, p. 263.
4. Paul Corcoran. *Political Language and Rhetoric* (Austin: University of Texas Press, 1979).
5. *Ibid.*, p. 125.
6. *Ibid.*, p. 75.
7. *Ibid.*, p. 169.
8. *Ibid.*, pp. 129-130.
9. *Ibid.*, p. 157.
10. *Ibid.*, p. 141.
11. *Ibid.*, p. 143.
12. "Uninformed Voters," *The Wilson Quarterly*, 3 (Summer, 1979), p. 29.
13. Thomas E. Patterson, "The 1976 Horserace," *The Wilson Quarterly*, 1 (Spring, 1977), p. 75.
14. Anthony Burgess, "The Future of Anglo-American," *Harper's Magazine*, 236 (February, 1968), p. 56.
15. Murray Edelman, "On Policies that Fail," *The Progressive*, May, 1975), p. 22.
16. Murray Edelman, "Myths, Metaphors, and Political Conformity," *Psychiatry*, 30 (1967), p. 221.
17. Dan F. Hahn, "Nixon's Second (Hortatory) Inaugural," *Speaker and Gavel*, 10 (May, 1973), p. 113.
18. Quoted in *The Oxford Dictionary of Quotations*, Third Edition (Oxford: Oxford University Press, 1979), p. 208.
19. *Ibid.*, p. 146.

From the Winter 1980 Et cetera.

METAPHOR AND SOCIAL BELIEF

Weller Embler

GRAMMARIANS HAVE OFTEN busied themselves defining what a metaphor *is*. But it is more meaningful in our day to find out what a metaphor *does*. The little words 'like' and 'as' exert an enormous influence over our thoughts and our behavior; and there is vastly more to figurative language than the customary pedagogical distinctions between similes and metaphors. Our behavior is a function of the words we use. More often than not, our thoughts do not select the words we use; instead, words determine the thoughts we have. We can say with some assurance that language develops out of social conditions and in turn influences social behavior.

Modern rhetorics and grammar books insist that written and spoken English shall avoid the hackneyed figure of speech. Triteness, they say, is 'evidence of a failure to attain animation and originality in expression.' But the trite figure is worn-out not because it has been used often before, but because it cannot bear the burden of new attitudes. Consider the following extended figure of speech from the novel *Young Man with a Horn* by Dorothy Baker.

> Fortune, in its workings, has something in common with a slot-machine. There are those who can bait it forever and never get more than an odd assortment of lemons for their pains; but once in a while there will come a man for whom all the grooves line up, and when that happens there's no end to the showering down.

Weller Embler was head of the department of humanities, Cooper Union for the Advancement of Science and Art, New York City.

Fortune (or the more common 'Fate') is a concept for which the only referent in the external world is a series of observable events without an assignable cause, and creative writers in all ages have sought analogies which will force the concept of fate, for the time being, at least, to accept a local habitation and a name. For instance, to the Elizabethans, it was quite believable that the capricious order of happenings should be governed by malicious creatures who looked like very old women. When the fantastical Witches appear before Macbeth and Banquo announcing Macbeth's ascendancy from Glamis to Cawdor to King, it appeared to Shakespeare's audience that the course of Macbeth's life was chargeable to the whims of the horrid sisters. What is important is not the originality of the metaphors 'invented' by Dorothy Baker and William Shakespeare but the relationship which their figures of speech bear to their times. If we think of events of our lives as controlled by witches or even controlled by some force known only to witches, we shall behave in one way; if we think that the course of our experience is a matter of statistical probabilities, we shall behave in quite another way.

A whole philosophy of life is often implicit in the metaphors of creative writers, the philosophy of an entire generation, indeed, even of an entire civilization. In the great tradition of the western world, it has been common to liken (in some essential respects) men to gods. Classical man so loved the gods he had created that he wished to emulate them and to be like them. Ulysses was not a god, but he had many things in common with the classical divinities, and it was fair to call him god-like. In other words, it was important to the social attitudes of Homer's Greece to believe that some men at least were 'like' gods; and it is common knowledge that this belief in the divinity of man was responsible for much that was fairest and best in the classical civilization. The statues of Phidias are metaphors inspired by this ideal; the temples and the great dramas and the noble philosophies all testify to the comparison.

By way of contrast to the Greek, consider the figurative language of a modern novelist. In one of John Steinbeck's short stories, 'The Leader of the People,' the old grandfather of the story had at one time been a man of the frontier world of Indians and buffalo. But it wasn't Indians that were important, he tells his grandson, Jody, 'nor adventures, nor even getting out here. It was a whole bunch of people made into one big crawling beast. . . . Every man wanted something for himself, but the big beast that was all of them wanted only westering.' And while Jody thinks of 'the wide plains and of the wagons moving across like centipedes,' his grandfather continues, saying 'We carried life out here and set it down the way those ants carry eggs. And I was the leader.'

We must remember that Steinbeck matured as a writer during the depression era and that his social philosophy grew out of the social problems of the 1930s. In his search for a social philosophy which could meet the problems of his day, he turned for assistance to the biological sciences. In these he found sound method, tested hypotheses, and, if it could be translated into language descriptive of human behavior, a body of usable information about subhuman life. Steinbeck was one of the first American novelists to think consistently and seriously, but not always clearly, and mostly with a political purpose in mind, of men as something other than men. And it became Steinbeck's habit to compare human beings with marine animals, with land animals, and with insects. It may be fairly said that Steinbeck's dramatic similarities between mice and men, between fish and men (*Sea of Cortez*), between centipedes and men, whether drawn from observation or embedded within the firm system of ecology, have changed the social thinking of many readers.

To future generations, an age may be known by the metaphors it chose to express its ideals. Between 1798 and 1859 a good deal happened to change men's minds about the world they lived in. Among other revolutions in thought not the least effective was the change in attitude toward nature. Wordsworth had said that nature was full of consolation, of joy, and of wisdom. Presently, however, as a result of geological and biological investigations, nature ceased to be regarded as 'Wordsworthian' and came to be thought of as 'Darwinian.' The theory of natural selection brought about a new attitude toward nature that had perforce to be expressed and communicated in new figures of speech. Tennyson was not simply striving to attain animation and originality in expression when he described nature as 'red in tooth and claw.' The association of abstract nature with tigers was striking, but for the Victorians it was also to become 'true.' *In Memoriam* anticipated the *Origin of Species* by nearly a decade, but its representation of nature as a tiger was subsequently to assist in the firm entrenchment of the Darwinian hypothesis; in fact, I suspect that it did more to consolidate the philosophy of struggle than did the *Origin of Species* itself.

As a force behind nineteenth-century socialism, Edward Bellamy's famous stagecoach metaphor in his *Looking Backward* had an effect that was immense. Its pertinence to the social conditions of the time, and the 'rightness' of its phrasing gave verbal form to many an inarticulated thought. The analogy of the watch in eighteenth-century Deism was so befitting the ideas of the scientists, poets, and philosophers of the age that the analogy became a 'truth' and God a cosmic clock-maker. When an age abandons its attitudes, it will exile its figures to the limbo for clichés, and new metaphors will take the place of the old. T.S. Eliot inspired a whole generation with the image of the wasteland; and in 1935 Horace Gregory's poetic picture of a chorus of men joining hands to make a new world supplanted, for a time, the figure of the wasteland.

Metaphor as Statement of Fact

But it is here that we must observe an important linguistic and social phenomenon. It will be noted that Homer does not say that men *are* gods but only that in certain respects they resemble gods. Wordsworth does not say that nature *is* a teacher, but only that nature is like a teacher. Yet when metaphor is new, those who find their attitudes implicit in the metaphor construe the metaphor to be a statement of identity, that is, a statement of fact. Figures of speech, when they are fitting and felicitous, and especially when they occur in print, give poetic sanction, as it were, to hitherto dimly felt, inarticulated beliefs. When metaphor is new, and when the reader does not enjoy the perspective vouchsafed by time, the metaphor is taken literally, and its function is not that of rhetorical device, but of statement of fact, *prescribing* certain kinds of behavior. *Indeed, it may be said that the habit which sees the germane metaphor as a statement of identity is a habit which changes the character of civilizations.*

Iago is a villain, but a clever one, and he says many things which were pleasing to an Elizabethan ear. For instance:

> 'Tis in ourselves that we are thus or thus. Our bodies are our gardens, to which our will are gardeners; so that if we will plant nettles, or sow lettuce, set hyssop and weed up thyme, supply it with one gender of herbs, or district it with many, either to have it sterile with idleness, or manured with industry, why, the power and corrigible authority of this lies in our wills.

We may find Shakespeare's figure entertainingly turned, and we may even agree with the sentiment expressed, but in the twentieth century we shall hardly be aware of more than a casual similarity between ourselves and gardens. But when my friend explains to me that life is like a pin-ball machine — that we are little balls shot out through an alley, kicked around from place to place, sometimes ringing a bell or flashing a light, and eventually falling into a trough and rolling out of sight — when he says this, I inquire whether his figure is not perhaps the perfect analogy. His figure has a lively meaning for us today because we believe in the laws of probability, and half suspect the aimlessness of our existence. For all practical purposes, I am well prepared to think of life and pin-ball machines as identities, of taking my friend's metaphor as a statement of fact about human experience.

When we read in Friedrich von Schelling that 'architecture is frozen music,' we are charmed with the originality and neatness of the analogy. But when James Johnson Sweeney in describing Piet Mondrian's painting *Victory Boogie-Woogie* says that 'The eye is led from one group of color notes to another at varying speeds; at the same time contrasted with this endless change in the minor motives we have a constant repetition of the right angle theme like a persistent bass chord sounding through a sprinkle of running arpeggios and grace notes from the treble,' we are convinced for the moment that the canvas *is* music.

The figure of Socrates as a gadfly is interesting but seldom taken literally. Yet when the villain in the cinema is called a 'rat' and shot thrice in the abdomen forthwith, it is a nice question whether the villain was a man or a rat. We know that Grieg's music is not pink bonbons stuffed with snow, although we rather admire the aptness of the similarity and the sensuousness of the image. Yet when someone says of the music of Shostakovich that it is the 'cacophonous scream of a communist manifesto,' we wonder if that is not perhaps 'true.' We are delighted with the little girl who said that carbonated water tastes 'like my foot's asleep,' but when we say a dish we don't like is 'garbage,' it is indeed! When Byron says of poetry that it is the lava of the imagination which prevents an eruption, the metaphor strikes us as an amusing romantic definition of poetry; but when a contemporary writer (I have forgotten who) says that a poem is the sublimation of the social irritant which troubled the poet, just as a pearl is the 'higher order' of the speck which irritated the oyster, we accept the metaphor as a statement of fact about all poetry.

The intricate and highly complex network making up the human nervous system has often been likened to a telephonic organization in which messages are sent out from central offices over the 'wires' of the system to all areas of the organism. The analogy is a picturesque explanation of the way the human nervous system 'seems to work.' At the moment, the telephone metaphor is being supplanted by an electronic metaphor in a new system of efficiency called Cybernetics. In this system the mind is likened to a communication system which has its own 'feedback,' making possible automatic adjustments between what it imagines to be 'out there' and what is really out there. But what the human nervous system will be likened to a century from now is unpredictable. New analogies will depend on future neurological theories and on future social, moral, and technological developments.

Most figurative language is not dangerous in its effects. It is when we take political and social metaphors literally, as statements of identities, that we must proceed with caution. Far more than we are aware, the way we use language determines what the social philosophy of our society will be. When we take figurative language literally, we are in danger of behaving as if something were true which is manifestly not true *unless we proceed to make it so.* Orators disturbed with social conditions will see new relationships and will express them with vigor. The figure of the 'brotherhood of man' arose out of the way the Age of Reason chose to look at its political situation; the figure was unusually far-reaching in its political effect.

Effect of Metaphor on Modern Behavior

Let us examine several current metaphors, stated or felt, which express 'truths' of modern social beliefs and which, because they are often taken as identities, are in many ways responsible for modern social behavior.

1. Murray Schumach's extended figure of speech which appeared on the front page of The New York *Times* for February 26, 1946, is, to be sure, innocuous enough; moreover, it is an analogy which occurs to us as rather common, one which would seem to most people living in New York City to bear itself out in many exact ways:

> Complete shutdown of the city's subways would be almost as disastrous to the city as a serious circulatory ailment to a human being. For New York's subways are her main veins and arteries, distributing her human corpuscles throughout the municipal body twenty-four hours a day.

Mr. Schumach had no ulterior motive, I am sure, in describing New York City in this fashion. I do not want to be misunderstood in what follows as saying that the authors of social metaphors are each and all conspirators against the public morale. Nor do I suggest that Mr. Schumach has caused the inhabitants of New York City to think of themselves as corpuscles. The idea had probably occurred to some people before. But I do suggest that the author of this figure has himself seen New York City in this way and that henceforth some of his readers will unconsciously identify *other* people in New York City as corpuscles. The effect of such metaphors is subtle. If the city is personified as a monstrous human being, and its inhabitants think of themselves as red and white corpuscles, presently, from their understanding of what red and white corpuscles do, they may be inclined to act as if they were, and that might or might not be a good thing; but if carried to extremes, the habit of behaving like a red corpuscle within a monstrous body will change the culture patterns of a society.

2. If it were not for the fact that a colleague of mine brought the following parallel to my attention, as a parallel that came spontaneously to his mind, I should consider it rather too far-fetched for inclusion in this essay. In the December 28, 1942 issue of *Life*, there is printed an extraordinary picture of Field Marshal Rommel's army retreating westward along the Mediterranean coast. The picture was photographed from a British plane, and it strongly resembles a slide of bacteria as seen under a microscope. New instruments, new inventions cause us to 'see' things differently. In the *Life* picture we see thousands of men who look 'exactly' *like* bacteria. The resemblance is so striking that for a moment we suspect an identity. If we say enough times that men are like or look like bacteria, and if we see enough pictures showing the resemblance, we shall soon begin to behave toward men as we behave toward bacteria. (One is reminded here, for example, of the rather widespread use of the phrase 'to be immunized against totalitarian philosophies.') Most important of all, from the social point of view, is the fact that our world is prepared in a great variety of ways to think of men as bacteria. Was it Robert Louis Stevenson who referred to humanity as a disease on the face of the earth? In any event, more than one sensitive person has taken Stevenson's metaphor literally and despaired.

3. I have often heard large cities referred to as jungles. The main characteristics of a jungle in darkest Africa, as I have read, are an amoral attitude toward all creatures outside the family, the need for alertness in order to survive, the constant feeling of insecurity, and the value of certain traits such as strength, cunning, and agility. Now it is quite possible that these are characteristics of modern city life, and in these respects,

therefore, life in a city is like life in a jungle. This is, if true, and we suspect it is, unfortunate, for no one whom I know wants to live in a jungle. It is perfectly natural to think of a city as a jungle, perhaps, but the more we think of it in that way and the more we extend the analogy, the more likely it is that the city will *be* a jungle. At the moment, at any rate, a large city is not a 'jungle,' it is only in some respects like a jungle, and presumably the differences can be pointed out. When, therefore, we insist that the city *is* a jungle, we are no longer speaking figuratively, we are making a statement of moral fact; indeed, we are issuing (as did Upton Sinclair) a moral ultimatum.

4. Oswald Spengler was a master of intellectual analogy, perhaps the greatest of all time, certainly second to none in the modern world. *The Decline of the West* foretells the eventual demise of the western world, but the entire structure of Spengler's thesis rests on a metaphor. The organic theory of history is a figure of speech, which, simply put, says that a civilization is *like* a living creature—it is born, it grows, and it decays. But Spengler's book is no cause for pessimism, for a civilization is not identical with a living being, as will be seen when Spengler is as old as Homer. A civilization seems to be in some (pertinent, we admit) respects like a living being. But it should have occurred to someone long ago, and perhaps it did, that to take Spengler literally is to put all one's faith in the logic of 'if.' If one believes that the western world has entered upon a stage of decline, then what Spengler says about the western world is 'true.' If there were to take place an historical experience such as a 'decline,' it would perhaps happen as Spengler has described it. In fact, so long as we understand Spengler's analogies to be identities, so long shall we believe in, *and perhaps assist in*, the inevitable decline of the western world.[1]

5. One of the most pertinent of modern metaphors, one that seems to many young people to be an accurate description of our modern world is the analogy of the myth of Sisyphus with contemporary experience. Sisyphus was the mortal condemned

by the gods for his sins to roll a stone to the top of a mountain from which the stone falls back down the mountain of its own weight, and Sisyphus must again roll it to the top. The labor of Sisyphus goes on endlessly forever. Albert Camus, contemporary French novelist, and expositor of the 'philosophy of the absurd,' has written a philosophical work entitled *The Myth of Sisyphus*, and in this work he says, 'The gods thought with some reason that there was no punishment more awful than useless and hopeless labor.' Although Camus thinks of Sisyphus as a tragic hero, noble in his scorn of the gods, he also thinks of him as the absurd hero, and he likens the worker of today to Sisyphus. 'The worker of today labors every day of his life at the same tasks and his destiny is no less absurd.'

But the myth of Sisyphus is a story, as a moving picture is a story, as a ballad is a story as an epic is a novel is a story. We often think of ourselves as 'like' a character out of a novel or story. In fact, a whole nation of people (generally speaking) thought of themselves as 'like' the Siegfried or Brunhild of Teutonic mythology. It is pleasant to some people to suspect that they have something in common with Siegfried, but if we say we *are* Siegfried, unless the whole world agrees with us, we are in trouble. We are not less in error if we take the myth of Sisyphus literally and say that we are Sisyphus, that we are absurd heroes engaged in 'useless and hopeless labor.' It is only too patently true that our world seems to be 'like' the Hell of Sisyphus. But that our world *is* the Hell of Sisyphus and that we *are* doomed to hopeless labor is a fiction evolving out of an inferred identity which simply does not exist. Camus has used his parallel as a device for illuminating and criticizing the social world of today. If we take his figure literally, and especially if we take it without an understanding of its 'tragic' implications, we are likely to be very unhappy if nothing more.

6. A good deal of theoretical discourse is diagrammatic in character. The Ptolemaic cosmology in the form of a diagram says only that as far as can be observed and inferred, the universe is 'like' the diagram. Diagrammatic representations which are the results of inference and imaginative picturing forth of an

idea cannot be tested empirically, and we must beware of seeing identities where they do not exist.[2]

To take the most illustrious modern example, I turn to the popularized psychology of Sigmund Freud. (But first I should like to point out that I have the greatest respect for Freud, and I should be the last to choose to discredit psychoanalysis. Only provincial prejudice finds Freud ridiculous and offensive.) Freud was a poet and a philosopher. Freud's work is one long extended figure of speech, as is the *Divine Comedy* of Dante. Both Dante and Freud have written allegories of the spiritual life. If there were a Hell, it might be 'like' Dante's. I think it was Waldo Frank who said somewhere that if you believe in Hell, it makes a great deal of difference to you how many circles there 'really are.' If you take Freud literally, the true nature and character of 'complexes' makes a great deal of difference; but what the analyst says in effect is that we act 'as if' we had an Oedipus complex, supposing there were such a thing as an Oedipus complex, just as a physician might have said in the seventeenth century that his patient behaved as if he were a witch, supposing that there were such things as witches. But the 'cure' for witches was different.

Freud was a philosopher whom many people have taken literally, assuming that the subconscious as Freud describes it is *identical* with some 'part' of our 'self.' Freud's diagram of the Id, the Ego, and the Super-Ego is a schema which is metaphor useful merely in discussion. In *An Autobiographical Study* Freud warned against taking his schematic representations literally. 'The subdivision of the unconscious is part of an attempt to picture the apparatus of the mind as being built up of a number of *functional systems* whose interrelations may be expressed in spatial terms, without reference, of course, to the actual anatomy of the brain.' But many readers will take the image of the subconscious literally. We imagine the Id as a murky 'depth' of turbulence somewhere at the bottom of the 'mind,' its poisonous fumes rising up from deep upon deep of mystery through the trap door of the censor at night when the censor is 'asleep.' The Ego, our every-day consciousness, lives on the first-floor of the mind, looks out of its windows, and conforms to the customs of the every-day world—the bewildered little man of the cartoon who always stands between two opposing forces. Above, at the 'top' of our mind, is the Super-Ego, a kind of stern father who looks down upon our conscious behavior and issues commands.

Even professional analysts sometimes 'think' in this manner; and amateur psychologists, as I have discovered, almost invariably do. It is impossible to know how much such a 'metaphor' has affected the common reader in his attitudes toward life, but it is fairly certain that many have taken the figure of the subconscious literally, saying that this is the way the mind works. On the contrary, we should say that our inner life seems only in some respects to be *like* the Freudian description.

7. Drawing analogies between the subject-matter of zoology and biology and the subject-matter of the social sciences has been very popular in recent years among some social thinkers. It has been fashionable to think of men as animals and even as insects. One of the most common parallels drawn by fascist theorizers is the parallel between men and ants. I recall magazine articles describing Nazi scientists observing ant societies in order to discover how human society may most easily be converted into a society similar to (or identical with) that of the white ant of Africa.

The propagandistic use of the ant metaphor has been most vividly described by a character in Arthur Koestler's novel *Arrival and Departure*. In the enthusiasm with which Koestler's Nazi speaks, we see among other things that the language he uses has convinced him beyond any doubt of the desirability of understanding that ants and men are, for political purposes, identical. When, as in Nazi Germany, men are likened to ants, then beyond question men will be treated as though they were ants. Whatever is thinkable is also possible in the world of today.

> Absolute conditioning must finally result in the creation of a collective consciousness in the full biological sense of the term. Nature has a perfect working model for it in the city-states of the African white ant. They each embrace several million members

of the race, they cover areas up to fifty square miles and function with absolute expediency. They have perfect division of labor; they control highly complicated technical devices including a system of heating by vegetable fermentation which keeps the temperature in their vaults constant through all seasons; they enforce a mathematically perfect birthrate policy. And yet they have no planning body, no blueprints, no governing administration, not even the means of written communication. How is this possible? The answer usually given is 'by instinct'; but such a highly differentiated instinct which is shared by, and limited to, members of one city-state amounts to nothing less than a collective brain-function of the state organism. In a similar way, and probably helped by artificially-produced biological mutations, the individuals in the supra-state will become mere cells in an organism of a higher order — a million-legged, million-armed cyclopean colossus. . . .

8. It is apparent from the illustrations I have used that our contemporary social similitudes are often drawn from the biological sciences. The master metaphor of the modern world, however, is drawn from technology and is the identification of men with machines.

In our thinking we often, nay almost invariably, make the distinguished blunder of supposing that the human body is a machine, that it works as a machine works, according to the laws of mechanics. *Why* we prefer to 'think' in this way about ourselves is open to speculation. In any event, that we should be unaware of the simple fact that men are only in a few unimportant respects like machines, but that machines are, *as far as they go*, in all respects like men is the supreme misunderstanding of our time and accounts almost exclusively for our lack, just when we need it most, of a real humanistic philosophy. The obvious fact is that machines are like men for the simple reason that man made the machine, as far as he could, *in his own image*. It would be unpleasing to some ears to have it said that man left out a soul when he made the machine, but that, or something very like that, is precisely what happened.

In recent years the machine has been perfected to perform uncanny tasks, the most striking being the calculation and solution of involved mathematical problems. The electronic brain has its place in the imaginations of men as the Most High.

Presently we shall wish that our nerve cells were as clever as electron tubes, quite forgetting that it was our nerve cells that had the wit to create electron tubes.

Make no mistake about it, we think more highly of our machines than we do of ourselves. We try to live up to the machine, to learn from the machine, to be more nearly machines, because we think they are better than we are.[3] It appears that our dearest wish is to *be* machines and to function wholly as they do. This wish will strike future ages as the dominating feature of a lost society, of a deluded people who worshipped their engines more than their gods, to say nothing of themselves.

But creative writers and some social philosophers have been saying all this for more than a hundred years. There is little excuse for me to labor the point. All I wish to insist upon is that the way we use language may account in part for our madness. The moment we say that the human being *is* a machine, at that moment we shall believe that the human being can be conditioned to behave in a perfectly predictable way with admirable regularity. Then it is that we shall have made of ourselves something less, ever so much less, than we are. But if we speak with caution to the effect that machines are *in some respects* like human beings, we can put the machine to its good use and still keep our self-respect and our humanity.

If ever we needed to think of man as man, as unique, identical with nothing else in the world, it is today. Contemporary imagery is blurred and confused. Our hardest intellectual task is to keep things apart, to separate out issues and ideas from one another. Our present efforts are to see all particulars as alike, and we tend to force identities where only similarities exist. No two things are identical, although we seem to want to think so. We have abandoned the exact and differentiated in favor of mingled associations and blurred relationships. The use of analogy in all branches of human thought is indispensable; but the making of nice distinctions is equally important and has ever been a leading characteristic of the human mind. The knowledge of subtle differences — as between people of different cultures, between one human being and another, or even between brands of coffee, kinds of perfumes, vintages of wines, spoiled food and edible food, poison and medicine, beauty and ugliness, justice and injustice—is a knowledge invaluable to mankind. What is more, the knowledge of differences leads to an understanding of relationships. We are more likely to be at home in our world not so much by striving to cut each particular to the same pattern, as by studying to understand the tenuous, the subtle, the often beautiful relationships which are the foundations of human society and to a great extent the joy of life. The knowledge of just and workable relationships among dissimilars is what every philosopher, every artist, and every statesman has longed to attain.

NOTES AND REFERENCES

1. Talking about a 'possible' future event will in itself tend to bring the event to pass. And the evidence selected to anticipate the event will direct the event to take the form foreseen. That people often behave according to the way they have expressed their expectations is brilliantly discussed by Robert K. Merton in his article 'The Self-Fulfilling Prophecy,' *Antioch Review*, 8:193ff (1948).
2. For an analysis of schematic, symbolic, and tropic 'fictions' see Hans Vaihinger, *The Philosophy of 'As if'* (London 1949), 24ff. In fact, Vaihinger's work is throughout a painstaking study of the consciously false assumptions which are implicit in most if not all metaphorical expressions. In many aspects, my 'Metaphor and Social Belief' is a kind of extended footnote to *The Philosophy of 'As if.'*
3. While preparing this article for publication, the writer was introduced to *Dianetics* by L. Ronald Hubbard (New York 1950). In this 'modern science of mental health' would appear to be the most appalling example yet of the identification of men with machines. Constructed in the name of efficiency, the central theme of *Dianetics* depends on the fiction that a human being is a calculating machine capable of functioning in a 100 per cent mechanical fashion.

From the Winter 1951 Et cetera.

WHORF'S HYPOTHESIS:
The Case of Dutch and English

C. Weggelaar

WHORF'S HYPOTHESIS, ALSO known as the theory of linguistic relativity, is the view that language does not only serve to express our thoughts, but also shapes and molds them to a considerable extent. Every language contains a number of assumptions about the nature of reality, and our world view depends on the language we use. This determinism is not absolute, however. If we are conscious of the limitations our language imposes, we may transcend them to some extent. Hence, the prime importance of studying different languages.

In the United States, this theory is generally connected with the names of Edward Sapir and Benjamin Lee Whorf. Related views have been voiced in Europe from time to time, e.g. by Karl Wilhelm von Humboldt. But even though Whorf's hypothesis has roused considerable interest in some circles (among general semanticists, for instance), empirical research has been rather slow in appearing, and, to opponents of linguistic relativity, it has not been particularly convincing. As I see it, there are two main reasons for this.

1. We are dealing with abstractions of a very high order. When we are talking about metaphysical assumptions hidden in the structure of language, we may, in a general way, feel what we are trying to say, but it is very difficult to relate our words to observable facts. Furthermore, in modern linguistics

---

C. **Weggelaar** is from Elspeet, Holland. With this article, he made his first appearance in *Et cetera*.

the term "structure of language" tends to be limited to the formal aspects of language: the sound system, the classes of meaningful elements, and the ways in which they may be combined. This is not what Whorf had in mind:

> In my study of the Hopi language, what I now see as an opportunity to work on this problem was first thrust upon me before I was clearly aware of the problem. The seemingly endless task of describing the morphology did finally end. Yet it was evident, especially in the light of Sapir's lectures on Navaho, that the description of the *language* was far from complete. I knew for example the morphological formation of plurals, but not how to use plurals. It was evident that the category of plural in Hopi was not the same thing as in English, French or German. Certain things that were plural in these languages were singular in Hopi. The phase of investigation which now began consumed nearly two more years.[1]

For Whorf, the study of a language evidently includes the way in which words and grammatical forms are used, in other words, their meanings. Following Leonard Bloomfield, American linguists have tended to exclude meaning as a legitimate object of linguistics, however. What goes on in the speaker or hearer of a sentence belongs to psychology or neurology: "In the division of scientific labor, the linguist deals only with the speech signal, . . . he is not competent to deal with problems of physiology and psychology."[2] This attitude has been changed during the last ten or twenty years, but its influence can still be felt.

2. Whorf's own work on linguistic relativity centers on comparisons between Hopi, an American Indian language, and Standard Average European (SAE). According to Whorf, all European languages are essentially similar ("with the *possible*, (but doubtful,) exception of Balto-Slavic and non-Indo-European"[3]). This eliminates all easily accessible languages and cultures from our field of observation. In order to study the influence of linguistic structure on thought and action, we must turn to the really exotic languages, like American Indian, African, etc. Obviously, the number of people qualified for this kind of work is very small.

In this paper, I will take the position that Standard Average European is not the uniform entity which Whorf believed it to be. Dutch and English are closely related languages. They both developed from a common western Germanic stock. They both underwent some influence from Celtic, and, more recently, a rather massive influence from French. Yet, there is quite a number of differences between both languages. I will try to show that at least some of these differences may be related to differences in outlook and world view between the peoples involved.

Sources of Data

A practical problem in this kind of study is the collecting of source data. Traditional grammars need not contain all relevant facts, and inclusion of some particular fact about a language does not tell us much about its practical importance, e.g., its text frequency. Therefore, I started comparing texts of a number of English books with the texts of their respective translations in Dutch. Differences were noted on filing cards. A translator generally tries to follow the text of his original as closely as possible. At the same time, his translation has to be as natural and idiomatic as possible. Any divergence from the wording of the original text, therefore, may point to some "structural" difference between the languages in question.

The present paper is based on data from the following three texts: Richard Adams, *Watership Down*, Chapter Three[4] and the Dutch translation by Max Schuchart.[5]
Rudyard Kipling, *The Jungle Book: Rikki Tikki Tavi*[6] and the Dutch translation by J. and M. Duyvewaert.[7]
Roger Zelazny, *Nine Princes in Amber*,[8] and the excellent Dutch translation by J.A. Schalekamp.[9]
These texts will be referred to as A, K, and Z, respectively. Individual quotations will be indicated by their page numbers in the English and Dutch versions, in that order.

A difference between original and translation was judged to be present whenever a word in English was not matched exactly with a corresponding word in Dutch, i.e., when a word was added, left out, or translated by a word of slightly different meaning. This includes those cases in which a singular noun is translated by a plural noun and vice versa, differences in the use of tenses, and idiomatic expressions rendered by a different idiom. Differences in this sense of the word were much more numerous than I had expected originally. For instance, the Dutch version of A contains 1096 words, 327 (about 30%) of which do not correspond exactly to words in the English version. In all cases, the change in wording seems justified: a more literal translation would have resulted in unnatural Dutch. Translation, obviously, is not a matter of simple word substitution.

In many cases, differences were due to the use of different idiomatic expressions. Furthermore, English tends to use participles and abstract nouns in cases where Dutch uses subordinate clauses and infinitive constructions. Among the remaining cases a number of recurrent patterns could be distinguished, the most important of which will be discussed in the following sections.

Reflexive Constructions

Dutch frequently uses reflexive pronouns, i.e., the words corresponding to "myself," "yourself," "himself," etc. in expressions like "he shot himself." In many cases, a verb used intransitively in English corresponds to a reflexive expression in Dutch. For instance, the verb *bewegen* means "to move," in the sense of moving something. "To move," in the sense of making a movement, is *zich bewegen*, literally, "to move oneself." In the same way, we distinguish between *omdraaien*, "to turn (something) around," and *zich omdraaien*, "to turn around" (intransitively), or *herinneren*, "to remind," and *zich herinneren*, "to remember" ("remind oneself of something").

In some cases, the reflexive pronoun is used to mark intentional actions of living beings. *Bewegen*, "to move," may be used intransitively to refer to movements of inanimate objects, or perhaps to movements a person makes in his sleep. Intentional movement of persons and animals is always *zich bewegen*. In other cases, the use of the reflexive pronoun is obligatory, and the verb or expression is never used without it. For instance, "to feel . . . (happy, sad, ill, etc.)" is always reflexive in Dutch: one feels oneself being happy, sad, ill, etc.

Consequently, a single verb in English often corresponds to a reflexive expression in Dutch. I found fifty-four instances in my data: five in A, twenty-four in K, and twenty-five in Z. The opposite occurs but three times, all instances in K.

This use of reflexive constructions is quite common in most continental European languages. Compared to continental European, English almost seems to avoid the use of reflexives. Judging from the grammars I consulted, the same may be true of the Celtic languages. Perhaps we must divide Whorf's SAE into Standard Continental European and Standard Insular European.

Continental European languages constantly force their speakers to talk as if they are making themselves move, making themselves do something, reminding themselves of something, feeling or observing themselves, etc. Each one of us must use reflexive expressions many hundreds of times every day. I cannot help feeling that this must influence our attitude towards ourselves, towards self-observation and introspection, and perhaps towards consciously playing a role. After all, Emile Coué, one of the pioneers of autosuggestive psychotherapy, obtained remarkable results by having his patients repeat a set formula twenty times every morning and every evening for the duration of some weeks. Grammatical habits last all our life.

In English, the word "self-conscious" has definitely negative overtones: "Marked by undue or morbid preoccupation with one's own personality; so far self-centered as to suppose one is the object of observation by others" (OED). The literal translation of "self-conscious" into Dutch has almost exactly the opposite meaning. *Zelfbewust* = being conscious of one's own worth, feeling one's own importance. The German word *selbstbewusst* has the same implications. In English, self-observation does not feel quite natural, not quite healthy. Observing oneself = feeling uneasy. In continental European, being conscious of yourself is more likely feeling that *you* are the origin of your own actions. You are, to some extent and in some sense, creating your own existence.

Continental European languages show considerable differences as to the scope and frequency of relative constructions.

They are most frequent in southern European languages (French, Italian, Spanish, etc.). Here they may refer to all kinds of actions: movement in space, body position, vocal communication, social role, thinking, feeling, etc.[10] These are, to the speaker of these languages, not things one just happens to do: they are the aspects of yourself you are consciously creating and working with. Hence people from southern Europe tend to set much value on "outer" aspects of the self, on matters like clothing, personal ornaments, good manners, etc. They are expressive in speech and movement up to the point of appearing (to us) theatrical. Living up to one's social role is a form of art, generally practiced with style and enthusiasm.[11]

In English, playing a role most often has the sense of being phony. In a number of American books on psychotherapy I have read, the word "role" was almost invariably preceded by the adjective "artificial." There is a wide gap between a person's role and his real self. This may to some extent be pop psychology, but popular psychology is often more sensitive to cultural differences than the more scientific variants. From the southern European point of view, social roles are an essential and integral part of a person's self. Without them, he would not be able to survive in a civilized society or in any society at all. So one chooses one's role and has fun.

In Dutch, reflexive pronouns are less frequent than they are in French or Italian, and they tend to be restricted to a few specific areas of meaning. Many verbs of thinking and feeling are reflexive expressions. Besides *zich voelen*, "to feel," I noted *zich afvragen*, "to wonder" (to ask oneself), *zich bewust zijn van*, "to realize" (be conscious to oneself of something), *zich zorgen maken*, "to worry" (to make worries for oneself). A smaller group refers to general movement in space: *zich bewegen*, "to move," and *zich omdraaien*, "to turn around." In K, I also noted the archaic *zich neerzetten*, "to sit down" (to put oneself down in a sitting position). German is much like Dutch in this respect, but it tends to use more reflexive expressions referring to external actions.

According to the point of view of Dutch grammar, thinking and feeling are a very special kind of action. They are the things which you are making yourself do, and for which you are responsible. External behavior, outer appearance, and good manners are not parts of the self in the same way. They are things you just happen to have. Correspondingly, the Dutch tend to be introspective, conscientious, and serious-minded. We tend to approach all problems in life from a moral angle. Differences in opinion are taken very seriously, and both our churches and our political system have been plagued by scores and scores of small groups differing on ever finer points of doctrine. The Dutch word for this attitude is *principieel*, an adjective derived from *principe*, "principle," but only in the sense of moral or religious precept. Being *principieel* involves moral integrity, striving for internal consistency and standing for your own opinions, even if it defies your own ends. In fact, this is what we are often doing.

On the other hand, the Dutch are prepared to tolerate all kinds of divergent opinions if (and only if) some moral principle is involved. Conscience to us is always a matter of individual choice and internal consistency. Conscientious objectors are allowed some substitute for military service if they can prove that their objections are really *principieel*. If any inconsistency is found in their opinion, they will have to serve their time in prison. Parents who on religious grounds refuse to have their children inoculated are suffered to endanger public health — since it is a matter of *principe*. So if you ever have an argument with a Dutchman, try to involve some religious or ethical principle. You are not likely to convince him, but if you are *principieel* enough, he will at least respect you.[12, 13]

On a more philosophical level, the continental European use of reflexive pronouns would seem to be reflected in Cartesian dualism. According to Descartes, there is an absolute distinction between body (extended substance) and soul (thinking substance). The body is essentially a kind of machine, and the soul is steering and directing it. "I move" is *je me mouve* in French, "I move myself," which is very close to "my soul moves my body." This same construction occurs in many continental European languages, and Descartes' philosophy had a profound influence all over the continent. In England, it never gained much acceptance, and David Hume explicitly contradicted the notion that there exists something like a self in the sense of the Cartesian soul:

> For my part, when I enter most intimately into what I call *myself*, I always stumble on some particular perception or other, of heat or cold, light or shade, love or hatred, pain or pleasure. I never can catch *myself* at any time without a perception, and never can observe any thing but the perception. . . . If any one upon serious and unprejudic'd reflection thinks he has a different notion of *himself*, I must confess I can reason no longer with him. All I can allow him is, that he may be in the right as well as I, and that we are essentially different in this particular. He may, perhaps, perceive something simple and continu'd, which he calls *himself*; tho' I am certain there is no such principle in me.[14]

The same pattern recurs in the history of psychology. Wilhelm Wundt, the founder of experimental psychology, wrote that all psychology begins with introspection, and uses experiment and natural history as subsidiary means of research.[15] In continental European psychology, introspection always remained an acceptable and sometimes even an important method. In England, on the other hand, the emphasis was on statistical analysis since the days of Spearman and Galton. The first American psychologists more or less followed the continental European lead, but since the turn of the century the emphasis shifted toward behaviorism:

> The working of the nervous system is not accessible to observation from without, and the person himself has no sense-organs (such as he has, for instance, for the muscles of his hands) with which he himself could observe what goes on in his nerves. Therefore, the psychologist must resort to indirect methods of approach.[16]

To speakers of continental European languages, the observation of the self is felt to be an easy and natural act. To speakers of English, it would seem either extremely stressful, or scientifically impossible. The similarity between these attitudes and our respective grammatical habits is striking.

Temporal Perspective

At first sight, the differences between the Dutch and the English tense systems are rather insignificant. Both languages distinguish past and present tenses; the future and perfect tenses are formed by means of auxiliary verbs that are partly identical. The English future uses "shall" and "will," the Dutch future has *zal* (plural *zullen*). The English perfect tenses use "to have," whereas Dutch uses both *hebben*, "to have," and *zijn*, "to be." The chief difference seems to be that Dutch has no regular progressive form. *Ik schrijf* is both "I write" and "I am writing." Yet in my data there are some curious shifts in the use of some tenses. They are not particularly numerous, but they all tend to follow the same pattern.

Firstly, I noted some cases in which an English past or perfect tense corresponds to a Dutch present (one case in A, two in K, and five in Z). For instance: "I never had spirit enough . . ." = *Nooit heb ik moed genoeg* . . . (K 106/113), or, "That shows you weren't so smart" = *Dat bewijst dat je niet zo slim bent*. In Dutch, both the past and perfect tense indicates an action or state concluded in the past. The past tense is used in continuous narrative, the perfect tense in mentioning isolated facts from the past. Parenthetically, this causes some shifts from past tense in English to perfect tense in Dutch (five cases in A, two in K, five in Z). States and actions continuing into the present are expressed in the present tense. To have used the past or (more likely) the perfect tense in translating the above quotations into Dutch would imply something like, "But now I've got the guts to do it," or "But now you are really clever."

Secondly, the English future tense may correspond to a Dutch present (two cases in A, one in K, six in Z). The Dutch future tense is not much of a temporal form, really. Future events which are felt to be normal and natural results of present conditions are expressed by means of the present tense. Dutch shares this trait with German, the Scandinavian languages, and Finnish (and, presumably, Esthonian). The future auxiliary *zal*, *zullen* is used only when the future is not the natural outcome of the present, e.g., in emphatic promises. It also may denote uncertainty, especially when accompanied by the adverb *wel*, and in that case it may even refer to the present time.[17]

The Dutch present, therefore, includes parts of the English past and future. From the Dutch point of view, the English present refers to a very small slice of time. The Dutch present generally implies a sense of duration. Therefore, in some cases the English present must be translated by means of the verb *beginnen*, "to begin, to start," especially if the main verb refers to a sudden action. The verb "to be"in these cases is usually translated *worden*, "to become." Other expressions stressing the sudden onset of action also may be used (eight cases in K, ten in Z). Essentially the same thing happens in translating the word "time." The normal Dutch word for "time" is *tijd*, but *tijd* implies duration. The English word "time" may refer to some dimensionless point in time, or it may be used in counting repetitions ("this time," "six times," etc.). In these cases, Dutch must use words like *ogenblik* (moment, literally "an eye's wink") or *keer, maal,* "turn," "repetition."

This view of time would seem to make for a quiet and conservative attitude. The past merges into the present, the present merges into the future. Indeed, it has been said that in Holland everything happens fifty years later. Yet there have been a number of very fast and far-reaching changes in our country over the past twenty or thirty years. "Scarcely any other country in western Europe has made so many fundamental alterations in its attitudes, its economy, its way of life, with such outstanding success and, relatively, so little friction and violence."[18] This apparent paradox is easily solved. For a Dutchman there is no break between the present and the future. We cannot shrug it off by saying "mañana," or "tomorrow is another day." Much of the future is already present to us, and has to be dealt with here and now.

The Dutch are generally happiest when they are able to work on some long-range project, either individually or collectively.[19] I might mention the great *Dictionary of the Dutch Language*, started by M. de Vries and L.A. te Winkel in 1864, which covers its field so exhaustively that it took more than one hundred years to reach the letter V. In a more commercial sphere, we have some of the largest multinationals outside the United States: Philips, Royal Dutch/Shell, and Unilever. An even better example may be our land reclamation projects.[20] On a small scale, land reclamation has been going on since the Middle Ages. At this moment, we have two large projects going, the Delta works and the Zuyder Zee works. The Delta project started after the flood of 1953 and will not be completed before 1985. The Zuyder Zee works started in 1920, but the first plans were made in 1849. Of course, to some extent we have been pressed to this kind of work by our environment. But there are other parts of Europe that might have profited from this kind of treatment and where nobody ever got the idea.

In his study on Hopi, Whorf[21] stressed the "timeless" character of the verb in this language. He connected this trait with the Hopi emphasis on concentrated continuous action and preparation. The Dutch verb is not as timeless as the verb in Hopi, but it is certainly more timeless than the verb in French or English. It is interesting that this linguistic trait in both cases is paralleled by substantially the same attitude: a preference for long-range projects requiring earnest and continuous effort. Preparing for future eventualities (future in your view, that is, not necessarily in ours) is a Dutch characteristic, too. We are said to have one of the best social security systems in the world. The same is true of Denmark and Sweden, countries in whose languages also a present tense may be used to refer to future time. Sometimes I wonder if people in other countries eventually would be better off if they were to abolish the future tense.

Detailed Description

An exercise sometimes recommended in general semantics is writing in E-Prime, or E'.[22] This is an artificial language consisting of all words and grammatical patterns of natural English minus the forms of the verb "to be." The aim is to stay closer to observational facts, and to avoid unwarranted generalizations. According to my data, Dutch is fairly close to E-Prime. In quite a number of cases, I found norms of "to be" translated by a more specific verb in Dutch (nine cases in A, twelve in K, and twenty in Z). For instance: "(He told me) not to be impulsive" = . . . *dat ik niet impulsief moest handelen* (". . . that I should not act impulsively") (A 26/19). "He was very stiff" = *Hij voelde zich erg stijf* ("He felt himself very stiff," with the reflexive construction mentioned previously (K 108/116). "I was certain" = *Ik wist zeker* ("I knew for certain") (Z 28/30).

In a number of cases, "to be" is translated by one of the "positional" verbs: *staan* = "to stand," *zitten* = "to sit," *liggen* = "to lie, be lying down," or *lopen* = "to walk." Dutch has a frequent sentence pattern in which these verbs are construed with the infinitive of another verb: *Ik zit te schrijven* = "I am sitting and writing," or *Hij loopt te fluiten* = "He is walking and whistling." A literal translation in English is not possible. German likewise lacks this construction. Some American Indian languages seem to use positional verbs in a comparable way. The meaning of the Dutch construction is often close to the English progressive tenses, but it also may translate the simple present or past tense (five cases in K, one in Z). Its chief aim is just to add some perceptual detail.

From the Dutch point of view, these details are important. People or things do not just exist, they are standing, sitting, lying down, walking, etc. Verbs like "put" or "replace" must be translated by different words, according to the position the object is put in. This habit of careful observation and description is a pervasive trait of our culture. In Dutch painting, every detail is rendered with the same loving care, every part of the picture tells its own story, every landscape is alive as far as the eye can reach. In our literature, the same tendency occurs, but often with less fortunate results. The emphasis is on description, on "painting a situation by means of words"; the plot of the story is less important. The best part of our literature is lyrical poetry, where description of reality mirrors inner feeling.[23]

In daily life, we likewise tend to pay much attention to details. As soon as you cross the Dutch-German border, you will notice that the brickwork in Germany is jointed less carefully. Over the centuries, visitors have commented on the cleanliness, neatness, and orderliness of the Dutch. "The attention to detail is continued and repeated inside the houses. On the window sill, there is a row of potted plants interspersed with knickknacks—strangely-shaped shells, paperweights, a piece of coral, miniature vases—small, but to the Dutch, strangely significant things. The Dutch have always loved small objects."[24]

This love of details and small things is reinforced by another trait of our language, the use of diminutive nouns. Every noun in Dutch has a special diminutive form (generally ending in -*tje*, -*kje*, -*pje*) expressing both smallness and affection. The use of these forms is rather idiomatic, and also subject to individual habit, but they enable us to express fine shades of attitude towards the object spoken about. In my data, diminutives are used most freely in K (seventy-one instances). They are typically used to refer to Rikki-Tikki the mongoose himself, or to the boy, or to the birds, or their respective body parts or actions. They are never used to refer to the cobras or their young, the principal "bad guys" of the story. In other words, diminutives are used to draw a line between "good" and "bad," and "good" is automatically equated with "small." (I counted twenty diminutives in Z, generally nouns that are used only in their diminutive form. A has three diminutive nouns, and the name "Fiver" is always rendered by a diminutive.)

Our habit of closely observing and describing details has yet another consequence. The Dutch tend to stay close to empirical facts, and to avoid abstraction at all costs. In this respect, there is a world of difference between Dutch and German thought. Dutch scientists tend to be keen observers, not theorists. We have no great philosophers—Spinoza did live in Holland, to be sure, but Dutch was not his native language. We even have no great theologians, though religion has been a matter of continuous interest in the Netherlands.[25] Due to this avoidance of theoretical issues, new developments may go unnoticed abroad. The first clinic for psychotherapy in the world was founded in Amsterdam, in 1887, for instance. Perhaps this is not amazing, in view of our particular way of using reflexive pronouns. The first grand theories on psychotherapy were formulated in German-speaking countries, and the work of the Amsterdam clinic is all but forgotten.

There are a few other patterns of differences in my data, but they occur less frequently. I think the patterns I described are sufficient to show that there are a number of structural differences between Dutch and English ("structural" in Whorf's sense of the word), and that these differences may be related to differences in life-style or world-view. Furthermore, I hope to have shown that European languages may offer a fruitful field for further research on Whorf's hypothesis.

NOTES AND REFERENCES

1. Whorf, B.L., "The Relation of Habitual Thought and Behavior to Language," *Language, Thought and Reality, Selected Writings of Benjamin Lee Whorf*, John B. Carroll, (ed.) (Cambridge, Mass.: MIT Press, 1956), p. 138.
2. Bloomfield, L., *Language* (New York: Holt, 1933), p. 32.
3. Whorf, B.L., *op. cit.*
4. Adams, R., *Watership Down* (Penguin Books, 1974), pp. 25-28.
5. Adams, R., *Waterschapsheuvel* (Utrecht/Antwerpen: Prisma Boeken, 1978), pp. 18-21.
6. Kipling, R., *The Jungle Book* (London: Pan Books, 1967), (original edition 1894) pp. 99-114.
7. Kipling, R., *Het Djungelboek* (Amsterdam: Wereld-Bibliotheek), pp. 106-123.
8. Zelazny, R., *Nine Princes in Amber* (New York: Avon Books, 1972), pp. 25-37.
9. Zelazny, R., *Prinsen van Amber* (Utrecht/Antwerpen: Prisma Boeken, 1974), pp. 27-40.
10. To quote some examples from French: *se passer* = to happen, *s'altérer, se modifier, se transformer* = to change, *se servir de* = to use, *se conduire* = to behave, *s'en aller* = to go away, *s'approcher de* = to approach, *s'asseoir* = to sit down, *s'informer de* = to inquire after, *s'écrier* = to exclaim, *se décider à* = to resolve to . . ., *se plaire à* = to like, *se tromper* = to make a mistake, *se méfier de* = to distrust. The reflexive pronoun is *se, s'* = oneself. This list could be continued almost indefinitely.
11. Chorus, Prof. dr. A., *De Nederlander uiterlijk en innerlijk* (Sijthoff, Leiden, 1964), pp. 28-29.
12. Chorus, A., *op. cit.*, pp. 46-50.
13. Huggett, F.E., *The Dutch Today* (The Hague: Government Publishing Office, 1978), especially pp. 56-66.
14. Cited after Reeves, J.W., *Body and Mind in Western Thought* (Penguin Books, 1958), pp. 340; 341.
15. Boring, E.G., *A History of Experimental Psychology* (New York: Appleton-Century-Crofts, 1957), p. 320.

16. Bloomfield, L., *op. cit.*, p. 34.
17. These tendencies would probably have been more evident if I had been able to include natural dialogue in my data. Books are predominantly written in the past tense, both in Dutch and in English.
18. Huggett, F.E., *op. cit.*, p. 5.
19. Chorus, A., *op. cit.*, p. 52.
20. Huggett, F.E., *op. cit.*, pp. 32-42.
21. Whorf, B.L., *op. cit.*, pp .148-152.
22. Bois, J.S., *The Art of Awareness* (Dubuque: Wm. C. Brown, 1966), pp. 192-193.
23. Chorus, A., *op. cit.*, pp. 82-107.
24. Huggett, F.E., *op. cit.*, p. 23.
25. Chorus, A., *op. cit.*, pp. 107-112.

From the Winter 1982 Et cetera.

SEMANTIC DIFFICULTIES IN INTERNATIONAL COMMUNICATION

Edmund S. Glenn

IT IS TOO OFTEN ASSUMED that the problem of transmitting the ideas of one national or cultural group to members of another national or cultural group is principally a problem of language. It is likewise assumed that that problem can always be solved by the use of appropriate linguistic techniques—translation and interpretation. A constant and professional preoccupation with the problem of international communication has convinced me of the fallacy of this point of view.

Patterns of Thought

Both an eminent professional philosopher, Professor Max Otto, and a very prominent layman, President Eisenhower, have recently stated that each man has a philosophy, whether or not he is aware of that fact. This means of course that people think in accordance with definite methods or patterns of thought. The methods may vary from individual to individual and even more from nation to nation.

Philosophical controversy is a historical fact. It is a mistake to believe that philosophical differences of opinion exist only at the level of conscious and deliberate controversies waged by professional philosophers. Ideas originated by philosophers permeate entire cultural groups; they are in fact what distinguishes one cultural group from another. The individuality of,

---

Edmund S. Glenn was Chief of the Interpreting Branch of the Division of Language Services, Department of State.

for instance, Western culture, or Chinese culture, cannot be denied. The fact that when speaking of the English, the Americans, the French, or the Spanish, we tend to use expressions such as "national character" should not blind us to the fact that what is meant by "character" is in reality the embodiment of a philosophy or the habitual use of a method of judging and thinking. Thus the French describe themselves as Cartesian; the English and the Americans seldom describe themselves, but still they act consistently in such a manner as to be described by others as pragmatic or empirical. Professor Karl Pribram writes,

> Mutual understanding and peaceful relations among the peoples of the earth have been impeded not only by the multiplicity of languages but to an even greater degree by differences in patterns of thought — that is, by differences in the methods adopted for defining the sources of knowledge, and for organizing coherent thinking.
>
> No mind can function to its own satisfaction without certain assumptions regarding the origin of its basic concepts and its ability to relate these concepts to each other. These assumptions have undergone significant changes in the course of time and have varied more or less among nations and among social groups at any given time. These differences in methods of reasoning have generated tension, ill-feeling, and even hatred.

The determination of the relationship between the patterns of thought of the cultural or national group whose ideas are to be communicated, to the patterns of thought of the cultural or national group which is to receive the communication, is an integral part of international communication. Failure to determine such relationships, and to act in accordance with such determinations, will almost unavoidably lead to misunderstandings.

Soviet diplomats often qualify the position taken by their Western counterparts as "incorrect" (nepravilnoe). In doing so, they do not accuse their opponents of falsifying facts, but merely of not interpreting them "correctly." This attitude is explicable only if viewed in the context of the Marxist-Hegelian pattern of thought, according to which historical situations evolve in a unique and predetermined manner. Thus an attitude not in accordance with theory is not in accordance with truth either;

it is as incorrect as the false solution of a mathematical problem. Conversely, representatives of our side tend to propose compromise or transactional solutions. Margaret Mead *et al* write that this attitude merely bewilders many representatives of the other side, and leads them to accuse us of hypocrisy, because it does not embody any ideological position recognizable to them. The idea that there are "two sides to every question" is an embodiment of nominalistic philosophy, and is hard to understand for those unfamiliar with this philosophy or with its influence.

Or again, on a slightly different plane: a simple English "No" tends to be interpreted by members of the Arabic culture as meaning "Yes." A real "No" would need to be emphasized; the simple "No" indicates merely a desire for further negotiation. Likewise a non-emphasized "Yes" will often be interpreted as a polite refusal. (E. Shuby)

Not all patterns of thought, or rather not everything in patterns of thought, is due to the influence of well-defined methodologies. Association of ideas plays a great part in thought; thus, clearly, each man's thought is to a large extent a function of this man's past.

Thus for instance, the word "colonialism" carries particularly irritating connotations to most Americans whereas it carries no such connotations to most Englishmen, Frenchmen, or Dutchmen. The reason for it is obviously anchored in history. It may not necessarily be, on the part of the Americans, the effect of a fully thought out political theory, but may be a simple association of ideas based on verbal habits which describe the American revolution as the rising of "colonies" against an "empire."

Denotation and Connotation

Problems of this type appear in a much more complicated form whenever two words in two different languages have the same denotation but different connotations.

Thus for instance, the French word "contribuable" and the English word "taxpayer" denote the same thing, but their connotations are not identical. "Taxpayer" is a word descriptive of physical action, of something which might have been seen with the eyes. It evokes the image of a man paying money at, for instance, a teller's window. "Contribuable," on the contrary, embodies an abstract principle. It evokes not an image but a thought, the thought that all citizens must contribute to the welfare of the nation of which they are a part.

Let us consider for a moment the connotations of these two words in the context of the North Atlantic Treaty Organization. A normal reaction on the American side will be: Does the man who pays get a fair return on his money? Or, in other words, is the Mutual Assistance Program really the best way of getting the most security for the least cost? A typical reaction on the French side will be quite different: Does everyone contribute equally to the common cause? Are the Americans as deeply and personally involved as the French? I would not be surprised if some of the differences of opinion which arose at various moments within NATO between the United States and France were not due to a large extent to this particular semantic difficulty.

The Role of Language

The preceding paragraph showed how patterns of thought may influence language and in turn be influenced by it. Both "taxpayer" and "contribuable" are comparative neologisms. If a certain method of word formation — by intension — was chosen by the French, it is because it corresponded to the pattern of thought prevalent in France. If another method of word formation — by extension — was chosen by the English, it is because it corresponded to their most general pattern of thought. Thus, peculiarities of language may constitute good indications of the prevalent manner of thinking.

However, once created, words and expressions assume an active role and contribute to the fashioning of thought. Thus two types of situations arise:

1. Cases where a given language is capable of expressing various shades of meaning and where the pattern of expression selected by given individuals provides a clue for the determination of their pattern of thought.

2. Cases where a certain combination of denotation and con-

notation can not be obtained in a simple manner in a given language.

An example of the first case may be found in the following expressions: "What should we do under the circumstances?" and "What does the situation require?" Although the denotations of these two questions are just about identical, the answers, influenced in part by connotations, may tend to be different. The point is that although one of these two forms will appear more natural than the other, the English language is capable of using both.

The following occurrence may be presented as an example of the second case: At an international conference which took place a few years ago and in which both the United States and the Soviet Union participated, it became rapidly apparent that the Soviet Union would not sign the agreement in preparation. The reason for it was a disagreement in substance, which could not be overcome. The Russians, however, continued to participate in the work of the various committees, and in particular of the drafting committee, mainly it seemed in order to preserve diplomatic niceties. Their representatives were seldom heard from.

Thus, considerable surprise was created when a seemingly unimportant proposal by the U.S. delegate resulted in an outburst of violent Soviet opposition. Even more surprising was the attitude of most Europeans and in particular of the French who publicly supported the United States but privately stated that it was a mistake to have backed the Soviets against the wall by an attitude which they described as rigid and overbearing. The proposal of the U.S. delegate consisted in inserting in the preamble to the proposed agreement a clause taken from another instrument and containing the expression "expanding economy."

I would suggest the following explanation for this incident: the expression "expanding economy" is neutral with respect to the Aristotelian categories of accident and essence. An "expanding economy" may be an economy which happens to be expanding because of various outside influences, or else an economy which is expanding because of characteristics inherent to its nature.

In Russian "expanding economy" becomes "rasshiryayushchiyasya ekonomiya" in which the reflexive form is used. Although it would be incorrect to say that "rasshiryayushchiyasya" has the denotation of the English expression "self-expanding" it unquestionably carries a connotation which will lead a Russian-speaking listener to conclude that "expanding economy" means an economy expanding for reasons inherent to its nature.

Thus in this case language itself directed the attention of the listener away from one possible explanation and in the direction of another. To compound the felony the difference between accident and essence is much more important to a person whose mind follows the Marxist-Hegelian pattern than to a person whose mind folows an empirical or pragmatic bent. The fact that an economy is expanding may warrant a certain type of action in the eyes of the empiricist, whichever be the cause of the expansion of the economy. To a Hegelian an economy expanding for accidental causes is bound to reverse itself unavoidably and rapidly.

Now it so happens that Marxist theory rules that the economy of the Western world must contract and cannot expand. Thus the recognition of an inherently expanding character in this economy, and this in an official document, could not fail to appear completely unacceptable to a Soviet delegate.

Classification of Patterns of Thought

The problem of defining, describing and analyzing patterns of thought is not the only one which needs to be faced in the field of international communications. Questions such as translation *proprio motu*, choice of media and levels of approach, etc., also deserve attention. However, as they have been less neglected than were the problems of basic philosophical, ethnical, anthropological and linguistic determinations, they will be considered outside the scope of this paper.

I will deal here only with the analysis of pronouncements made by persons belonging to the Western cultural world and using one of the European languages. I do not feel competent at the present moment to do any work which would extend beyond the boundary defined above. In consequence, the classifications suggested below will be such as to help in analyzing a field limited to one culture, albeit an important one. Three basic groups of criteria will be used in the sample analysis at the end of this paper.

1. PATTERNS OF REASONING. Professor Karl Pribram, who has pointed out the importance of linguistically determined assumptions in the formation of concepts, distinguishes, in his book *Conflicting Patterns of Thought*, the following four patterns of reasoning.

a. *Universalistic reasoning.* Universalistic reasoning is based on the premise that the human mind is able to grasp directly the order of the universe. Reason is credited with the power to know the truth with the aid of given general concepts and to establish absolutely valid rules for the organization of human relationships in accordance with these concepts. Universalistic reasoning proceeds from the general to the particular; it believes that general concepts, or universals, possess a reality independent from those of their components or constituents. The best way to determine what will happen in a given case is to know what happens in a more general category and then to determine what particular modifiers make the case in question a slight exception to the general rule.

b. *Nominalistic, or hypothetical, reasoning.* Nominalistic philosophy rejects the belief that general concepts have a reality of their own; instead it considers them merely as names, as convenient categories, more or less arbitrarily established by human minds. Reasoning proceeds from the particular to the general. Any exercise in pure reason establishes merely a hypothesis which must be verified by concrete experience.

Although these description of patterns of thought may give the impression of dealing with abstract and complex reasonings, the influence of the patterns of thought described above may be found also at very concrete levels. Thus, for example, French visitors to New York are in general highly critical of the New York subway. What repels them is not the dirt or the crowding, but the evident lack of comprehensive planning in the geographical distribution of lines. For instance, there is no subway line which would take one from the business district around Wall Street to the new business district around Rockefeller Center, or from the Cloisters to the Metropolitan Museum of Art. The argument that the New York subway is the one which carries the greatest number of persons the most rapidly over the greatest distances from home to work and from work home does not impress the French visitors overly much.

On the contrary, the Paris Métro covers all of Paris like a spider web. Convenient change-over stations make it possible to go from any monument to any other. At the same time the Métro strikes the American visitor as almost unbelievably slow. It does not reach very far into the suburbs, where many people live, and its routes do not necessarily follow the pattern of home to work and work to home connections.

I will put it that the Paris Métro is based on the universalistic concept of a means of transit designed to provide for the needs of a city, considered as such, or as a universal, a collective noun. Lines run from one point of interest to another, no part of the city being deprived of a means of communication with all of the other parts; at the same time considerations such as the density of traffic are almost completely disregarded. On the contrary the New York subway is nominalistic; there is no network planned to cover a collective entity, the city; on the contrary, lines are built in such a way as to do the most possible good to the greatest possible number of individuals considered as such. It is not much help to those who want to go from one residential area to another — but then people go fairly seldom from one residential area to another. On the contrary, it is every day that people go from home to work and from work home, and the New York subway is planned according to this consideration.

The names selected in each case by popular usage express the same preoccupation as the planning. "Métro" is an abbreviation of "métropolitain" or "metropolitan." The French language has resources which would have enabled Parisians to have selected a name such as "subway," but they did not choose to do so. Likewise English has the word "metropolitan," and the official titles of the various subway organizations in New York include words such as "transfer," "transit," and "system," yet the names chosen by the public are "subway," "el," or in Britain, "underground" or "tube."

It might be noted that "chemin de fer" is etymologically as well as factually similar to "railroad." But then, French railroads have the same characteristics from the point of view of planning as does the New York subway. Rail lines follow lines of probable maximum density which in France means that they radiate from Paris to the provinces. At the same time the network is not completed by transversal roads; the shortest way of getting from one provincial town to another may very often be the long way through Paris. This state of affairs was always considered illogical by the French and was violently criticized by them. As a result of this criticism it has been corrected to a large extent. The same criticism might have been leveled against American railroads. I remember being told that the best way to get from Sheridan, Wyoming to San Francisco was through Seattle. Yet the criticism which might have been leveled at the American roads are in fact never heard. The American public understands that it is not economical to provide trains for occasional travel along low-demand routes.

Now it so happens that the French railroads were started by English capital and planned under English inspiration: they even run on the left whereas everything else in France runs on the right. Thus even this exception seems to confirm the rule: the fact that France is by and large a universalistic country does not mean that nominalism is entirely without influence there.

c. *Intuitional or organismic reasoning.* This type of reasoning stresses intuition rather than systematic cogitation. It is thus in a position to ignore some of the basic opposition between nominalism and universalism. It considers that the relationship between a collectivity and its members may be compared to the relationship between a biological organism and its component cells. Organismic reasoning opposes intuitive to discursive consciousness and claims that reliance on one's intuition enables man to be "independent yet subject to one's duties" (Joel). It is often associated with extreme nationalism and prevalent in Germanic and Slavic Central Europe.

d. *Dialectic reasoning.* Hegelian dialectics are derived from universalism and, like universalism, believe in the possibility of a full understanding of the universe through reason. "But, according to the principles of dialectics, comprehension of the ever-changing nature of the phenomena and the flux of events can not be achieved with the aid of rigid concepts, alleged to be implanted in the human mind. The course of events is believed to be determined by the operation of antagonistic forces and must be understood with the aid of concepts adjusted to the contradictions logically represented by these forces." (Pribram).

Marxist dialectic materialism follows the Hegelian pattern which it modifies by the dogma of the predominance of materialistic factors.

2. THE VERB TO BE AND THE VERB TO DO. The classification described above has been used very successfully by Professor Pribram in the analysis of a broad historical evolution of the patterns of thought. Other types of classification may be useful in supplementing it in cases of a more concrete nature.

One such method of classification may be found in the difference which separates the logic of the verb "to do" from the logic of the verb "to be."

The logic of the verb "to be" is basically two-valued: things are either thus or not thus. Propositions are either true or false. Meaningless propositions may generally be eliminated and reasoning presented in such a way that a two-valued logic applies.

On the contrary the logic of the verb "to do" is essentially multi-valued: one does not do things truly or untruly, one does them more or less well.

All men are confronted with situations in which they tend to reason in terms of the verb "to be" and with other situations in which they tend to reason in terms of the verb "to do." There are, however, still other situations which may be studied by either of the methods correlated with these two verbs. Choices made by various individuals are indicative of the patterns of thought followed by them.

Quite obviously a prevalence of reasoning in terms of the logic of the verb "to do" ties in with nominalism, while a prevalence of reasoning in terms of the logic of the verb "to be" ties in with universalism. Thus an analysis undertaken in terms of these two verbs will be helpful in detecting patterns of thought which might fall within the scope of the classification under 1. More than that, such an analysis will also show why it is that in some cases nominalists and universalists reach different conclusions even when starting from identical premises.

Let us take as examples the two concepts of compromise and intervention. If A wishes to paint the wall black and B wishes to paint it white, they may reach an honorable compromise by painting it grey. If A now states that the wall is black, and B states that the wall is white, they may not compromise by calling it grey, as this would make liars of both of them. They may try to convince one another, they may try to fight it out, or they may drop the subject.

I believe that the instability of the French cabinets is due to the fact that, when faced with an issue, the French tend to ask themselves, "What is right?" That is why there are so many issues which often come up for debate and seldom reach the stage of solution. That is also why action can be undertaken only at the expense of excluding from the cabinet for the time being those who do not agree with the majority and who can compromise only by being absent, even temporarily.

It may be noted that the verb "to compromise" has a dual meaning both in French and in English, as for instance in "compromise the difference" and "compromise one's integrity." The first of these two meanings is by far the more frequent in English, the second one by far the more frequent in French.

Let us turn now to the concept of intervention. A and B intend to have lunch together but have not agreed on the choice of a restaurant. They discuss the question in terms of their likes and dislikes, one saying that he would like to go one place and the other that he would like to go to another. C, who has not been invited, overhears the conversation, steps in and tells them what to do. C's attitude would be unanimously considered extremely rude: the action taken by a group to which he doesn't belong, in a case when this action does not affect him, is none of his business.

Once more A and B intend to have lunch but are not in agreement on the choice of a restaurant. This time, however, they conduct their discussion in terms of the verb "to be,' A saying that food is better at one place and B that it is better at another. C, who still has not been invited, again overhears their conversation, again steps in offering some factual information about either or both of the two places. This time C's attitude will probably be quite acceptable.

Yet in fact there is no difference between the two situations. If a person wants to have lunch at a certain restaurant, it is probably because the person in question believes that the food is good there. Conversely, to say that food is good at a place means simply that one likes what is served there. As for factual information, one might do well to remember Goethe's saying: that which we call facts are nothing but our own pet theories. Thus again the difference is not in the situation, but in the patterns of thought.

It may be noted that French has several words which more or less mean intervention, for instance "intervention," "immixion," "ingérence." The two latter have a pejorative meaning. If now we pass from the nouns to the verbs, we see that the verbs corresponding to the pejorative nouns take the reflexive form, thus: "s'immiscer," "s'ingérer," but "intervenir." Thus clearly what brings in the pejorative meaning is an insistence on the intervener, the doer, as opposed to an insistence on the situation.

Let us now consider the hypothetical case of the country A which wishes another Country B to take a certain step of a very controversial nature. Country A is basically nominalistic, Country B is basically universalistic. Country A will not try to influence public opinion in Country B; its government thinks of intervention in terms of the verb "to do" and considers it *a priori* as an unfriendly gesture. Country A will try to negotiate directly this issue at government level, offering perhaps some inducements in another field as basis for a compromise, which, being nominalistic, it considers honorable. Unfortunately Country B, being universalistic, cannot accept a bareface compromise. At the same time it would not necessarily have resented an intervention, even addressed directly to its own public opinion, if such intervention were made in sufficiently theoretical and impersonal terms.

3. DENOTATION AND CONNOTATION. Of the two methods of classification suggested above, only one may be qualified as linguistic. Yet language may influence thought or else be used as an indication of an existing pattern of thought correlated with a pattern of expression in many more ways than one. Unfortunately the field of the mutual influence of language and thought is as yet largely unexplored. In consequence purely linguistic manners of classification will need to be developed slowly, through experience.

It appears clear, nevertheless, that a search for connotation as distinct from denotation may clarify many concrete situations. Some examples of situations of this kind have been given previously, some others will be found below.

In seeking to systematize the influence of connotations particular attention will have to be paid to the formation of names of sets or classes, or of representatives of sets, either through extension or through intension. Extensive or descriptive formation will generally indicate the prevalence of nominalist patterns and of multi-valued logic. On the contrary, intensive formation will indicate the prevalence of universalistic patterns. Both types of word formation will be found in most languages. Areas in which words are formed by one or the other system will in general correspond to areas in which a corresponding type of reasoning is prevalent.

Analysis of connotations should go beyond simple words. It should also embrace sentence structure, set expressions made up of several words, current metaphors, proverbs and manners in which groups of words may be formed around the same root.

For instance an expression such as "faire faire," which can never be properly translated in to English — "to have something done" lacks both spontaneity and generality — is in itself an indication of a certain contempt towards action and at the same time is an expression of respect towards the thought which precedes action; in other words it is an expression of universalistic thinking.

The use of the verb "to do" as the principal auxiliary verb in English is also a program in itself.

The systems of classification suggested above are not intended to cover the entire field. They are, rather, examples of lines which can be followed. No analysis should neglect the possibility of finding other explanations such as the ones which may be derived from the implications of history, even where those implications cannot be expressed in terms of semantic or philosophical categorization.

Thus, for instance, of all the great democracies the United States is the one which shows the greatest intolerance of domestic communism. I believe that an explanation of this fact may be found in the very tradition of the beginnings of an American nationality. Most European countries are founded on a tradition of indigenous ancestry. There are naturalized Frenchmen and Britons, and other Frenchmen and Britons who are descendants of immigrants, but people of these descriptions constitute very small minorities of the citizens of their respective countries. In consequence it is difficult for European countries to consider unwelcome the exponent of any political ideology as long as he can point out a long line of indigenous ancestry. On the contrary, the United States as a nation was created by men and women who had come to a new continent in order to establish a society based on certain definite ideals. It may be interesting to note in that connection how much more important is for American tradition the settlement of the Pilgrims in 1620 than is the settlement of the gentlemen adventurers of Virginia in 1607. The United States thus bases its tradition on the establishment of an ideology on virgin soil. It is thus quite normal for Americans to think that those who wish to establish some other ideology should go and do it somewhere else.

From the Spring 1954 Et cetera.

NEMAWASHI: A Japanese Form of Interpersonal Communication

Mitsuko Saito

Introduction

THIS IS A PRELIMINARY study on *nemawashi*, a word which cannot be translated into the English language because it contains an aspect of meaning peculiar to Japanese culture. Japanese people seem to use *nemawashi* frequently as a technique of interpersonal communication to build up or maintain felicitous relationships through transactions now and in the future. In foreign countries, there seem to be similar words used in situations of such interpersonal communication at the time of decision-making or consensus-building. In the Philippines, *barangay* seems to be used in the rural communities, and *musyawara* in Indonesia also seems to have connotations similar to *nemawashi*.[1] In this paper, the writer does not make any reference to *barangay* and *musyawara*, but it is commonly understood in Japan that these words are used to solve conflicts in intragroup situations and are analogous to *nemawashi* in some respect. In English, *prearrangement* comes closest to the meaning of *nemawashi*.[2] But *prearrangement* seems to have the connotation of conspiracy and this is inappropriate for *nemawashi*. In Japan, conspiracy appears when nemawashi fails, for nemawashi is a mechanism designed to promote group harmony (wa) and conspiracy destroys such harmony.

Mistuko Saito is a Professor at the International Christian University in Tokyo and a Director of the International Society for General Semantics. This paper was delivered at the 32nd Conference of the International Communication Association, Boston, 1982.

Studies have been conducted on nemawashi in the fields of domestic and international relations, government organizations, business management, etc. But the study of nemawashi has not been taken up from an interpersonal communication perspective, and in this paper it is treated as a behavioral mechanism[3] which is peculiar to Japanese culture in interpersonal communication situations. *Nemawashi* has both positive and negative connotations. It seems to the writer that Americans seem to pick up the negative connotations more often than the Japanese do, and confuse it with *prearrangement*. Then what are the negative and positive connotations? How are they used, and how do they function in interpersonal communication situations? Why is nemawashi necessary, and why is it peculiar to the Japanese national character? Why do Japanese people say nemawashi is a type of behavior particularly suited to the sentiments of the Japanese people? Presumably, the answer has to do with the value system which exists in Japanese culture, and the particular emphasis on group solidarity.[4]

The Origin and Meaning of Nemawashi

Nemawashi originally was and still is a professional term used by *Uekiya*,[5] an expert on trees who is not exactly a gardener nor a landscaper in the ordinary sense. An Uekiya does nemawashi when he transplants trees or handles trees individually and carefully. To make transplanting successful, the Uekiya cuts fine roots around the main root deeply and smoothes the ends of the roots in a round shape, one or two years before transplanting.[6] The tree, with the fine roots cut off around the main trunk in a nice, round shape, is left alone for a couple of years, during which period new fine roots sprout and strengthen the main root.[7] The secret of good nemawashi and successful transplanting lies in this shaping of rough ends in a good round form. Thus, the meaning of nemawashi originates from the act of rounding out the branch roots and allowing for a period of growth in which the main root is strengthened. Then the tree is transplanted to a new environment, having been fully prepared for its adjustment. An Uekiya believes a tree is like a man; both can adapt to new environments successfully if they are properly prepared. Thus, the word *nemawashi* is applied to the human context. In a decision-making process in Japanese culture, the horizontal relationships between people have to be made smooth, rounded out. This is the task of nemawashi. Through careful personal interaction, one can improve empathy and cooperation in attaining a common goal. Efforts in daily interpersonal communication to maintain smooth relationships and empathic communication are indispensable: discussion or debate is not enough. Empathy serves a crucial role for the Japanese in interpersonal communication as they believe this empathy rounds out the interactive process.[8] The Japanese custom of going out for a drink with others after work is a necessary part of their unconscious development of empathic interaction with one another. Exchanging *oseibo*[9] and *ochugen*[10] also contributes to maintaining this interaction. The American custom of showers (gift-giving: bridal, baby, etc.) has some similarities but does not seem a part of a larger integrated network of non-verbal interaction.

Nemawashi is used to deal with horizontal rather than vertical relationships in interpersonal communication situations. In Japan, the vertical relationships are obvious but horizontal relationships have not been articulated, although they are essential in human group relationships. *Nakama ishiki*[11] is the word used to describe horizontal group relationships. Thus, at the time of decision-making or problem-solving before a meeting, nemawashi has to be conducted. A person who engages in nemawashi has to select members of the group who are important or those who are of a type to criticize quickly and loudly and to have a good talk together with them on the topic in detail before the meeting. This procedure is analogous to the way an Uekiya rounds out the fine roots carefully before transplanting.

Nemawashi as an Interpersonal Interactive Mechanism

Nemawashi seems to have a bilevel structure. The lower level consists of human relationships and the concept of *wa*,[12] which is the philosophical foundation of nemawashi, refers to the maintaining of harmonious human relations by giving full and empathic consideration to others in family or working situations of every kind. This lower level serves as the base of interpersonal communication for the Japanese, reinforcing the sense of loyalty to the group to which they belong.[13]

As interpersonal interaction is ever-changing, the Japanese people cement the base structure very firmly with conscious effort. The upper structure of nemawashi has to do with the task, the purpose to be achieved, and decision-making. The full structure of nemawashi cannot be divided, for the levels function in a holistic way. Daisetsu Suzuki, the noted Buddhist philosopher, says that feeling and emotion play a very strong role in the Japanese thinking process. Suzuki points out that the Japanese way of thinking also can be classified as a holistic way of thinking,[14] as is illustrated in the dual structure of interpersonal communication among the Japanese people. Holistic thinking, as included in the formulation *nonelementalism*, is a basic general semantics principle.

Nemawashi requires the proper *kuuki*, a term which refers to the human atmosphere or "vibrations" necessary in the situation to accomplish a particular purpose.[15] Therefore, nemawashi has first to create the proper kuuki of the situation, because kuuki influences and dominates the decision-making.[16] The Japanese people are often influenced by kuuki at conferences or meetings. Nemawashi and kuuki are inseparable since nemawashi tries to create a human atmosphere to round out human relationships. According to Hichihei Yamamoto, the writer and philosopher, kuuki controls people and directs them in a certain direction, so that one could say that the decision-making is usually made by the kuuki itself.[17] So, Japanese people at a meeting have to be kuuki-oriented as well as issue-oriented in making decisions.[18]

The Japanese have a tendency to avoid confrontation in public,[19] sounding out the situation and the various opinions of people first. There is a saying which explains the reason why the Japanese avoid open confrontation: *Zen Aku wo ogande toore, Yo no naka wa, Nani ga zen yara, Nani ga aku yara.*[20] (In life, it is difficult to determine what is good and what is evil, so don't be too sure about your own value judgments.) This reveals the philosophy of the Japanese people towards interpersonal communication. For a Japanese, it is most important to establish harmonious relationships among people and to avoid adversary relationships. Nemawashi is a necessary technique to maintain good human relationships among people, especially when controversial issues arise. It is out of this philosophy that the Japanese pay a great deal of attention to nemawashi as an interpersonal communication mechanism.

The function of nemawashi is to make the above-mentioned interpersonal interactive mechanism workable in Japanese society and to create the proper kind of human atmosphere to feel out a situation and to elicit an honest, frank exchange of ideas, and, very importantly, all off the record.[21] *Hara wo watte hanasu*, which means to have a "heart-to-heart talk," is the ultimate goal of the nemawashi technique. Of course, without a definite purpose or objective, nemawashi can move in an ethically negative direction.[22] It is said that Japanese society is built on the network of personal connections. If a person knows a good number of people with whom he sustains friendly relations, he can use his own personal connections to get work done when he cannot do it alone. His friends put themselves out to help him out of his predicament, but he himself feels an obligation to return the favor to them later. So the friendship is carefully maintained through the practice of *Oseibo* and *Ochugen* (end-of-the-year and midsummer gift giving) and seasonal greetings all of which are important means of preserving harmony in social relationships. In the same vein, a Japanese often goes to parties and gatherings just to make an appearance to be in touch with the people he knows. These seem to be the nonverbal aspects of nemawashi as they are the means of maintaining interpersonal interaction among people.

The process of nemawashi follows an order which is an integral part of the nemawashi technique. Without this order, nemawashi would not be successful in terms of attaining its objective. Nemawashi has to start from the very bottom of its dual structure to build up a transactional relationship. A nemawashi transaction starts with a one-to-one personal interaction. The object of this is to establish individual trust in one another without regard to personal interests.[23] Thus, it requires perseverance, patience, and generosity. Nemawashi at this stage needs to be personal and private rather than open and public and has to be cultivated with the long-range perspective of the Uekiya. A happy type of person who thinks good of people and does things for others seems to be the most competent and effective in doing nemawashi.[24]

Nemawashi requires a careful selection of people, for a careless selection ends up in an unsuccessful result. The people to be objects for nemawashi should not be too high in rank but should be in a position to influence the decision-makers.[25] The person conducting nemawashi also should not be too high-ranking, but should be someone in an advisory or assisting position.[26] Such people can carry out nemawashi for the group because they know the desires of both top level and rank and file as well as the issue at hand. In other words, these people can be both wa-oriented and task-oriented at the same time. Nemawashi works like a drama behind the scene in communication situations, and a person who is doing nemawashi must sell himself first tactfully, since human relations are more important than the content of the issue itself. At this point, even the smallest things in rhetorical situations cannot be overlooked. For instance, how to carry on a telephone conversation or the appropriate place for a meeting or the language which is used. By observing and sensing small things in rhetorical situations, the person who carries out nemawashi should be able to discriminate the true feelings of the other. Fumihiko Kohno, a leading industrialist with Mitsubishi, once said in his book, "The best technique of nemawashi is not to create enemies and nemawashi means everything when it comes to the promotion of personnel matters."[27] This indicates that nemawashi is not an easy task to perform. The person has to be competent in every aspect of human relations.

The next stage of nemawashi begins with exploration. People are sounded out for ideas and the person executing nemawashi becomes an empathic communicator.[28] An empathic communicator begins with listening, since by being a good listener he collects crucial information. Exploration starts out with "small talk," and progresses on to more substantial matters.

Throughout the process, interaction is of supreme importance because a clear understanding of what others think about the problem makes it possible to find out whether consensus can be achieved or not.

The upper structure of nemawashi is the task-oriented aspect. When a task is presented, an exchange of opinions, ideas, and desires will take place, but unless a solid base structure has firmly been established, empathic communication will not occur and consensus will not be achieved. The base structure is of primary importance and this lower foundation must be constructed first. Professor Okabe[29] mentions that the Japanese use a human-relations-oriented approach as a decision-making strategy instead of the specific task-oriented approaches common in the West.

In the course of nemawashi, if it is discovered that the majority does not fundamentally disagree with the objective, persuasion is the next step. The Japanese way of persuasion is a type of joint venture requiring both compromise and sensitivity to the group. This method of persuasion may be expressed in the following way: "We understand your point of view also, but the majority wishes this. Please consider the good of the whole group."[30] The appeal to maintain wa, to close eyes to small differences, is used. Nakama ishiki is used as a pressure mechanism, and empathy also can be used to maintain wa. After the consensus has been gained, repeated reconfirmations are made to remind the group of the decision. Here the ringi[31] system is used to formalize and reinforce the agreement made on the basis of nemawashi so that backsliding does not happen at a later date.

Strengths and Weaknesses

What are the strengths of nemawashi, in interpersonal communication situations? In the workplace, nemawashi creates kuuki, a human atmosphere conducive to cooperation in a natural fashion. As a result of nemawashi, warm, relaxing human relations are maintained. Thirdly, nemawashi promotes a spirit of considering others first, meeting each other half way, and not demonstrating egocentricism. The nemawashi type of interpersonal communication raises the morale of the working place and also gives individuals a sense of participation. Quick implementation of the task is made possible. People can easily be united into a task force to work on a specific problem since nemawashi cements the base structure of interpersonal communication and therefore produces a multiplying effect on the output of their work.

As a Japanese, the writer is aware that the negative aspects of nemawashi frequently outweigh its strengths. For example in order to do nemawashi, one has to allow for a great deal of time; in other words, it is extremely time-consuming for the individual. Furthermore, it is a painstaking and difficult procedure. Thus in the process of transmitting the messages, information gets distorted, omitted, or arbitrarily added. In these ways, it has a tendency to become inaccurate. Especially if the base structure is not firm, nemawashi invites misunderstanding of the issue rather than clarification. The ideal solution may not be reflected in the consensus after nemawashi is conducted.

However, what the consensus does achieve when nemawashi is effective is the best possible or most realistic solution given the time, place, and circumstances of the issue. Therefore, if another person thinks of a better solution to the issue, he must start nemawashi anew vertically and horizontally in order to achieve a new consensus without destroying the solidarity upon which the previous one depended. At any rate, interpersonal communication takes place to build up transactional relationships.

At this point, it has to be emphasized that nemawashi has a definite purpose or objective, and a person who does nemawashi has to keep that goal in mind all of the time. Without a definite sense of purpose and a firm base structure nemawashi may fail, and, if it does, it may be taken as a kind of conspiracy and plot to undermine the solidarity of the group and the full participation of all members.

Ma-ma-ism[32] and *Kao wo tateru*[33] have to be dealt with very carefully in the interpersonal communication situation. Ma-ma-ism is the way to settle differences to keep harmonious relationships, and Kao wo tateru is also a device used to maintain harmonious interpersonal interaction, as it means to show deference. Both are very important elements of nemawashi as a technique of interpersonal communication.

To be successful, nemawashi must be used in accordance with an ethical standard which relates to the maintenance of group solidarity. This standard is not clearly set; it can only be said that nemawashi must be purpose-oriented, and directly connected to the purpose of the task intended to benefit the group as a whole.

Many young people now take a dim view of nemawashi, because they feel that the lack of open discussion and the group pressure prevent frank expression of individual opinion and frustrate attempts to deal directly with the issue. Group solidarity is for them often less important than the attempt to find an ideal solution.

Conclusion

In this preliminary study, the writer has tried to indicate why the Japanese people seem to think nemawashi is a peculiarly Japanese type of interpersonal communication. Nemawashi is group harmony, a wa-oriented behavior mechanism. Since the purpose is to establish transactional relationships among people, maintaining good human relationships becomes more important than achieving the task. Nemawashi as an interpersonal communication mechanism has a dual structure which functions holistically. The upper level is task-oriented and secondary while the base level is human relationship-oriented and primary in importance. The base structure is always given priority over the upper structure in all circumstances. The other important element of nemawashi is the order of procedure.

The appropriate people to be the objects for nemawashi must first be selected carefully. Proper attention must also be given to the selection of the person who will do nemawashi, because he will assume a covert leadership role in the group. He must be intelligent enough to know the issue and be able to socialize easily, as he has to create kuuki, which is needed to establish smooth interpersonal transactions. Thus nemawashi as an interpersonal communication technique requires that the one who does nemawashi be a consistent and effective empathic communicator.

Nemawashi is a device for exchanging human warmth in Japanese culture, to help Japanese to be empathic communicators. While it has many defects as the young people of Japan often point out, nevertheless it is deeply rooted in Japanese culture as a fundamental interpersonal communication technique. It also seems to be intimately related to the patterns of decision-making which have proved successful in Japanese business. Rather than outright rejection or defense of nemawashi, the proper approach would be to conduct detailed scientific research on nemawashi as a Japanese form of interpersonal communication. By doing this, we may be able to prevent misunderstandings and unfortunate frictions which might occur in intercultural communication.

NOTES AND REFERENCES

1. Kato, Eiichi, "Nemawashi to Nihon-teki Fudo." (Nemawashi and the Climate of Japan) *Jichi-kenshu*, 1977, 203, p. 19.
2. Hashiguchi, Osamu, Toranosuke Takeshita, et al., "Taiken-teki Nemawashi-ron." (Case Studies on Nemawashi) *ibid.*, p. 2.
3. "Behavior mechanism" and "technique" are interchangeably used in this paper.
4. Gaul, Richard, Gruenberg, Nina, and Jungblut, Michael, *Japan-Report*, translated by Watari Masao (Tokyo: Simul Press, 1982), p. 15.
5. Kato, Eiichi, *Nihon-jin no Gyosei: Uchi no Ruru*. (Japanese Administration: The In-Group Rules) Tokyo, Daiichi Hoki, 1980, pp. 111-112.
6. *Nihon Kokugo Daijiten*, (Dictionary of the Japanese Language) Tokyo, Jujikan, Vol. 15, p. 662.
7. *Ibid.*
8. Saito, Mitsuko, "A Nurse: Empathic Communicator," *Kango Tenbo*, Vol. 7, No. 4, p. 30.
9. The custom of gift-giving at the end of the year.
10. The custom of gift-giving in midsummer.
11. *Nakama ishiki* mans a strong sense of fellowship and group identity. See the study by Toshinoo Yoneyama, *Nihon-jim no Nakama Ishiki*, Kodansah Gendai Shinsho, Tokyo, 1976, for a discussion of its importance in Japanese social and psychological behavior.
12. *Wa* means harmonious interpersonal relationship. It has been a fundamental concept in Japanese social and political thought since Prince Shotoku emphasized it strongly in his Seventeen Article Constitution of 604 A.D. See *The Seventeen Article Constitution of Prince Shotoku II*, Takeshi Umehara, Shogaku-kan, Tokyo, 1981.

13. Clark, Gregory, *The Japanese Tribe: Origins of a Nation's Uniqueness*, translated by Masumi Muramatsu (Tokyo: Simul Press, 1977), p. 112.
14. Akizuki, Ryumin, *Suzuki Daisetsu no Kotoba to Shiso*. (Words and Thought) (Tokyo: Kodan-sha, 1967), p. 191.
15. Yamanoto, Hichihei, "Kuuki" no Kenkyu. (A Study of Human Atmosphere) (Tokyo: Bungei Shunju, 1977), pp. 12-13.
16. *Ibid.*, p. 54.
17. *Ibid.*, pp. 12-13.
18. *Ibid.*, p. 20.
19. Kato, 1980, p. 109.
20. Kurata, Hyakuzo, *Honen to Shinran nno Shinko* (Tokyo: Shunju-sha, 1960), p. 28.
21. Kato, 1977, p. 23.
22. Hashiguchi, Takeshita, *et al.*, p. 13.
23. Kato, 1977, p. 22.
24. *Ibid.*
25. *Ibid.*, pp. 22-23.
26. Hashiguchi, Takeshita, *et al.*, p. 12.
27. Kato, 1977, p. 24.
28. The writer is using the terminology created by William S. Howell, *The Empathetic Communicator* (Belmont, Calif.: Wadsworth, 1982).
29. Okabe, Roichi, "Cultural Assumptions of Communication Theory from Eastern and Western Perspectives: The Case of Japan and the United States." Paper presented at SCA, Anaheim, Calif., Nov. 12-15, 1981, pp. 23-25.
30. Kato, 1980, p. 109.
31. *Ringi* literally means a system of referential inquiry about the superior's intentions. Kiyoaki Tsuji, "Decision-Making in the Japanese Governments: A Study of Ringi-sei," in *Political Development in Modern Japan*, ed. Robert E. Ward (Princeton, N.J.: Princeton University Press, 1968), p. 457.
32. Ma-ma-ism means applying to a principle of: "Let's forget little differences for the sake of group harmony." Ma-ma is the term used to suggest this in ordinary conversations.
33. This means to publicly show deference to another, thus to give him an advantage.

From the Fall 1982 Et cetera.

MEXICAN ASSUMPTIONS ABOUT INTERPERSONAL RELATIONS

Rogelio Diaz-Guerrero, M.D.

IT IS AMAZING HOW often psychotherapists will say to their patients, "The main problem is that you do not face reality." This statement of the patient's problem would seem simple and self-evident. The unspoken assumption, however, is that there is a "reality" which everyone can get to know, and that the task of psychotherapy is to help the patient first to see, then to face, this "reality."

Underlying this assumption is the familiar Western concept of an objective, concrete reality "out there." Undoubtedly this reality is an important one for us all to recognize. But is there not another kind of "reality" which must be accounted for? I refer to the "reality" created by the interactions between two or more people in a social or communicative relationship — their attitudes toward each other, their expectations of each other, the many intangibles, conscious and unconscious, of their mutual feelings. This "interpersonal reality," as I should like to call it, may be more important in human relations than the external reality.

Let us distinguish then between two kinds of reality: the *external* physical reality — the reality of nature; and the *interpersonal* reality of a state of affairs between two or more persons.

Let me select some examples of this "interpersonal reality" drawn from comparisons between Mexican and North American

---

Dr. Rogelio Diaz-Guerrero practiced psychiatry in Mexico City and taught at the National University of Mexico.

cultures. There are some fundamental differences between the socio-cultural assumptions of the complex Spanish-Mestizo-Indian grouping that constitutes the Mexican nationality and those of the Anglo-Saxon, Western European-derived culture of the United States.

Americans tend to view external reality as something to be subjected to their will, and the success of American technology is evidence of this orientation. Latin Americans, however, take a more fatalistic attitude towards nature and feel subjugated by it. Traditionally Mexicans have done little to put external reality under their control.

However, Mexicans tend surprisingly to assume that interpersonal reality can be modified at will. Interpersonal reality is not just a given state of affairs, as it is so often to Americans ("The neighbors *are* unfriendly," "Mr. Jones *is* a snob," etc.). It is highly fluid, because *I* am there and am able to act upon it. The most important implication of this assumption is that people actually *create* salient qualities of this interpersonal reality.

Here is another basic Mexican assumption. An interpersonal reaction is evaluated on the basis of the immediate pleasure and satisfaction it brings. By this I do not mean getting bridges built or even getting a job, but providing human rapport for the people involved.

Ask a Mexican for street directions. He will often go into a complex series of explanations and gestures, frequently grinning; he will make you *feel* good. But you may get nowhere with his directions! Simply because he cannot answer your question, the Mexican would never let the *real thing*, the pleasant interpersonal encounter, go to waste. A definition of such a concept of interpersonal reality as found among Mexicans might go like this: "The degree of reality of an interpersonal situation lies in the frequency, quality, and warmth of the interpersonal reactions that can be achieved in a given period of time." Such reactions are spontaneous and are more like choices than conventional responses. Even when conventionally worded, these reactions are not stereotyped, but have varied and pleasing emotional content.

The market place of the Aztecs was far more a place to socialize than to trade. This tradition continues today. The Indian woman spread her pottery in the street: two dozen cups and plates. The tourist likes the price and asks for the whole lot. To the tourist's surprise, the woman says in horror, "No! If you take them all what will I have to sell?" The process, the ceremony, the socialization of selling are to her far more important than the sale — much as she and her children could use the money.

Mexicans have thus developed some exquisite ways of relating to one another: politeness, *buena educación*, friendliness, romanticism, etc. Although Mexican social gestures have been criticized as mere formalities, to me they seem to be as honest as anything a person can show. Perhaps Mexicans have gone too far in this way of thinking; they would rather lose an argument than lose a friend. Americans, of course, win the arguments. But Mexicans will lose not only arguments but time and money so as not to lose interpersonal fun.

This concept of interpersonal reality is extremely suggestive for marital relations. Here the degree of "truth" in statements made between man and wife should not be measured in terms of their correspondence to external reality, but in terms of how well they help the couple get along. The verbal interchanges in marriage are not to be evaluated in terms of map-territory relationships, as if they were statements made at a conference of physicists, but rather in terms of their utility in creating and re-creating the on-going relationship. This is not to advocate a complete break with external reality, but to say that there is something more important than being objectively "right" in domestic controversies.

Psychoanalytic schools in the United States consider their systems to be dynamic. Yet in practice, since they hold to the view that reality is something that must be "faced," and fail to distinguish interpersonal from external reality, they hold to an extremely static view of human relations. They often hold to an extremely elaborate but rigidly set view of what interpersonal relations *are*. That is, a boy "cannot" escape hating his father, "cannot" escape wanting to eliminate him, "cannot" escape desiring the mother libidinally, "cannot" escape being jealous of his brother or sister. Parents are helpless to modify the situation; the interpersonal relations are set. Even Harry Stack Sullivan, of the "interpersonal theory" of psychiatry, prefers — however more flexibly — to have interpersonal relations defined and done with on the basis of avoidance of anxiety.

Furthermore, in their demand upon patients to "face reality," American psychiatrists often assume that this must inevitably be an unpleasant task for the patient — that to see what's what is to see something grim, dark, forbidding. Mexicans will not readily concede that reality — especially interpersonal reality — is necessarily forbidding. Hence in the psychotherapeutic situation a Mexican would see no *a priori* reason why it should not include a good deal of levity, light-heartedness, and humor.

Psychotherapists have generally recognized *within* an individual the strong sense of one's own identity which is often called "the *to-me* feeling." There can be a similar feeling *between* individuals which might be called "the enjoying-each-other feeling." There is a deeper kind of "togetherness" than that now being exploited in some American advertising.

The "togetherness" of interpersonal reality is so important, especially in the psychotherapeutic situation, that other realities have no meaning or consequence until the persons or groups involved have developed a reasonably fluid and friendly relationship and created their own interpersonal reality. If, as here proposed, learning in interpersonal situations is dependent upon our ability to get along, we can see the need to explore further the "together feeling" so highly valued in Latin American cultures.

From the Winter 1959 Et cetera.

ON COMMUNICATING ACROSS CULTURAL LINES

Edmund S. Glenn

THERE IS A FOLK TALE that comes to us from the foothills of the Himalayas. A man was trying to explain to a blind friend what colors are. He began with the color white.

"Well," he said, "it is like snow on the hills."

"Oh," the blind man said, "then it must be a wet and dampish sort of color, isn't it?"

"No, no," the man said. "It is also the same color as cotton or wool."

"Oh yes, I understand. It must be a fluffy color."

"No, it is also like paper."

"Then it must be a crackling or fragile color," said the blind man.

"No, not at all. It is also like china."

"Oh, then it must be a hard, smooth color."

It is very difficult for people to understand one another if they do not share the same experiences. Of course, we all share the experience of being human, but there are many experiences which we do share and which are different for all of us. It is these different experiences which make up what is called "culture" in the social sciences — the habits of everyday life, the cues to which people respond, the automatic reactions they have to whatever they see and hear. These often differ, and the differences may introduce misunderstandings where we seek understanding.

At the very beginning of the cultural exchange program, a French visitor came to the United States under the technical assistance program of the agency for International Development.

He said to an American friend, "Why aren't you people more frank with us?"

The American said, "Why? What do you mean?"

The Frenchman said, "You tell us that you are for free enterprise, but I have been traveling throughout the United States and I have seen that practically all the production — all the plants and factories — are nationalized."

The Frenchman's assumption arose from the fact that in France only buildings belonging to the French government fly the French flag, but in the United States it is customary for factories, schools, and many other buildings to fly the American flag. What the Frenchman analyzed was not the immediate perception. He analyzed the economic system, and what he saw he evaluated in his own way.

Misinterpretations of this type can take place at a variety of levels. They can take place at the level of understanding, at the level of ideas or values, and sometimes at the level of feelings. The most serious, in my opinion, are those that take place at the level of feelings. Very often misunderstandings at this level come, not from ill will, but from good will. Sometimes we hurt another's feelings without wanting to do it and without knowing that we are doing it. Those misunderstandings which come from ill will can be left to the Council of Churches. I am here concerned only with those that are unintentional.

Here is an example. A young Japanese student came to the United States, and he was overwhelmed by the cordial reception he was given. He said, "The American people are wonderful. They are so warm, so friendly — much beyond my expectations."

Some time later I was told that while traveling in the West, this same young man had had dinner with an American family and had remarked that he greatly admired the country's efficiency, organization and accomplishment. But, he said, there was one thing he would never quite understand, and that was why Americans were so cold, so distant.

His host was deeply hurt and asked him, "How can you consider us cold and unfriendly when so much foreign aid was voted by American citizens and paid for by American taxpayers?"

"Yes," said the young man, "this is precisely what I cannot

understand—how people who are so generous can be so cold at the same time."

The visit ended on a bit of a sour note.

The point here is that both the first and last statements by the young man are typical. Very often, upon arrival in this country our foreign visitors are astonished by the warmth and friendliness of the American people. But often after a few months they begin to feel homesick and lonely, and they blame the Americans for causing these feelings by being cold. Now, why is this? I believe it is simply a question of different rhythms.

Americans have one rhythm in their personal and family relations, in their friendships and their charities. People from other cultures have different rhythms. The American rhythm is fast. It is characterized by a rapid acceptance of others. However, it is seldom that Americans engage themselves entirely in a friendship. Our friendships are warm, but they are casual—and they are specialized. By specialized I mean, for example, you have a neighbor who drops by in the morning for coffee. You see her frequently, but you never invite her for dinner—not because you don't think she could handle a fork and a knife, but because you have seen her that morning. Therefore, you reserve your more formal invitation to dinner for someone who lives in a more distant part of the city and whom you would not see unless you extended an invitation for a special occasion. Now, if the first friend moves away and the second one moves nearby, you are likely to reverse this—see the second friend in the mornings for informal coffee meetings, and the first one you will invite more formally to dinner.

We are, in other words, guided very often by our own convenience. We make friends easily, and we don't feel it necessary to go to a great amount of trouble to see friends often when it becomes inconvenient to do so. There is a family whom my family and I like very much, but we haven't seen them for years. It has become inconvenient. Most of us have had that experience, and usually no one is hurt by it. But in similar circumstances people from many other cultures would be hurt very deeply.

A friend of mine—a famous psychologist, an American of Greek descent—has some friends who came from Greece awhile back, and after visiting him on the West Coast they finally settled in Cleveland. Recently the psychologist had to make a trip to Washington, and when his friend learned that he was coming across the country, he said, "Of course you are going to stop over in Cleveland to see me." My friend did so because he realized that this was part of the rhythm of Greek friendships. He could not cross the country, flying over Cleveland, without making a special point to stop and spend a few days with his friend.

Here is another example of what I mean by a specialized relationship. In Washington an Urban Volunteer Corps was organized. This corps was made up of people who gave one or two days of their time to tutoring children who were retarded in their reading, thereby enabling them to stay in school. This was done in an organized way, with tutors assigned to specific schools. When did they see the children they taught? During the lesson. For the most part there was no further contact and no further obligation.

This question also leads to a point of values. We often assume that our values are the right values simply because, for us they are the obvious values. An African friend of mine, an ambassador in Washington, recently said, "One of the things which has caused misunderstandings between your people and mine is that you Americans always speak of individualism as being good. We do not consider individualism good. You always oppose government to individualism. What we oppose to individualism is not the government, but the family, the clan, the small community of natural primary relations. We feel that an individualist is a lonely man.

If you talk to a Frenchman, on the other hand, he will say, "You Americans are not individualistic at all. You have no sense of individualism." To us an individualist is someone who takes care of his own life, who sets a goal for himself and goes to it. If two young men decide that their goal in life is to make good in the hardware business, and if each of them does it independently, we would say that these are two individualists. The French call individualism something entirely different. They say an individualist is someone who is different from others. If there are two people in the hardware business there can be no individualism. There is one too many. Different understandings, different senses of value, but nevertheless both views are perfectly legitimate as long as we understand each other.

Another situation which often creates misunderstandings is that in our culture, silence is a negation. If you express an opinion and there is a little silence and then the subject is changed, you know you have said something with which the person you are talking to does not agree. In many other cultures, in contrast, silence is a sign of agreement. When the Russians, French, Portuguese, Spanish, or Italians express an opinion and you do not reject it explicitly, they assume you have accepted it. Later, when they find you haven't, they feel you are hypocritical.

Cultures also differ in their attitudes about the value of oral argument and of reasoning things out. In many cultures an articulate statement of principles and the defense of principles are the marks of a good man or woman. There is a great belief that by arguing, truth will emerge. Americans don't usually believe this. We believe that arguments can lead only to friction; and, rather than arguing and becoming unfriendly, we would rather not mention the subject. We believe in seeing and touching and doing. That is what shows us reality. By way of contrast, in many other cultures what we sense as reality is something we merely see, but do not necessarily understand in principle. It is something without value. This again is a different orientation in the search for truth.

Some time ago I took the minutes of the Security Council of the United Nations, a document in three languages the meaning of which was agreed upon. Such differences as there were to be found were differences in form, and I wished to find out whether these differences could reveal some of the subconscious patterns of thought of the people who spoke the various languages. There was between Russian and English a constant introversion of subject and predicate. Where in English it was said that A is B, in Russian it appeared as B is A. In English we may say: "The first point on the agenda was the political question." This would appear in Russian as "The political question was the first point on the agenda." This difference may seem insignificant. In either case, people knew they had to appear in a certain room at 10:30 in the morning on the East River Drive in New York even if they disagreed from then on.

Yet it was quite revealing that all the subjects of Russian sentences were more abstract and more general than the predicates. All the subjects of the English sentences were more concrete, more particular, than the predicates. The point of the agenda is something you can see—it is something that is limited in time and space and location. The political question is broader, more difficult to define. And yet the subject, the obvious part of the sentence, appeared to the Russians to call for the abstract. This was confirmed by another pattern—that of sentences constructed with a subordinate clause which could be eliminated. Again, the subordinate clauses which could be eliminated in a Russian sentence always dealt with questions which were concrete, practical, and immediate. In English what could be eliminated was the abstract, the general, and the distant.

This can be compared to the economics of the two countries. In the Soviet Union there is a general plan, and all the actions of individuals are guided by it, determined deductively from the plan. In America we have many choices by dollar spenders, the aggregate of which makes up statistically our national economy.

Most visitors are well informed about the United States, but the information—as is most information acquired when one is far away from the subject—is usually the sort that is found in books and not the sort one finds in life.

So there are many ways in which misunderstandings between people from different cultures can occur. I believe that the best way to avoid these misunderstandings is to encourage foreign visitors to talk about their countries and to describe their people's way of doing things—their customs. One can then contrast this with a description of our way of doing things. Cultural change often occurs in such a meeting. In short, I believe that the greatest hope for all humanity is to learn from one another.

From the Winter 1969 Et cetera.

PUBLIC AND INSTANT DIPLOMACY

Moshe Ben-Eliezer

WHAT IS DIPLOMACY? The Oxford English Dictionary defines diplomacy as ". . . the management of international relations by negotiations; the method by which these relations are adjusted and managed by ambassadors and envoys."[1] In essence, diplomacy is a practice by which political entities with conflicting interests attempt to arrive, through negotiations, at some accommodation and agreement. Since the times of Ancient Greece and the Roman Empire, diplomacy has served as one of the tools of foreign policy and as the only method for resolving international conflicts peacefully. As such, diplomacy long projected an image of lengthy and complicated negotiations, motivated by rational political considerations, and conducted by diplomatic professionals, far away from the public eye and knowledge.

In view of the fact that diplomacy constitutes such an integral and essential component of the conduct of international affairs, as well as occupying a special place within the academic disciplines of political science and international relations, it is surprising that only rarely do diplomats and academicians ask the following important questions: 1) Is our conception of diplomacy nostalgic, outdated and totally wrong? 2) Have there been some fundamental changes in the principles and processes of diplomacy? 3) Is there a New diplomacy?

Moshe Ben-Eliezer is a graduate of the Hebrew University in Jerusalem and is presently with the Israeli Consulate in New York.

The thesis of this article is that the answer is "yes" to each of these questions; that modern technology in general, and the mass media in particular, have altered almost completely the context, structure, content and functions of diplomacy. This modern, or New diplomacy, differs in its goals and capabilities from the Traditional diplomacy to which we have been accustomed.

Traditional Diplomacy

Traditional diplomacy was best characterized as being a secret, professional, and prolonged form of negotiation. There is little doubt that pre-electronic technologies of communication shaped to a great extent its form and functions.

Diplomacy used to be a back region activity consisting of secret negotiations and secret agreements:

> . . . foreign policy was decided by a handful of specialists in striped pants closeted in quiet rooms. Governments rose and fell on the scratch of a pen without the public's knowing or really caring . . . Diplomacy was a very private affair.[2]

Harold Nicolson, the British diplomat, attributes this state of affairs to the general backwardness of the communications media, coupled with a general public apathy and ignorance in foreign affairs.

Diplomacy was conducted by experienced negotiators who shared a common bond of understanding, respect, and professionalism. These diplomats constituted a diplomatic team with its own shared back region performance and a mutual code of ethics.[3] Diplomacy was conducted not only away from the public eye and interest, but it was also usually free of direct political intervention. Because of the difficult information relay and slow feedback from the home base, the diplomat remained virtually a sole decision-maker in diplomatic matters. Poor media of communication and transportation prevented both the active participation of political leaders and the effective exercise of supervision.

Furthermore, slow and poor communication between the diplomat and his government back home accounts for the prolonged duration of negotiations. One may speculate that since decisions were arrived at slowly, this introduced a patient approach to diplomacy, which in turn may have enhanced the values of accommodation and compromise.

New Diplomacy

New diplomacy can be defined as being immediate, unprofessional and public. The essential purpose of diplomacy remains the resolution of international conflicts by peaceful means. However, fundamental changes in the forms and functions of diplomacy, changes brought about largely by the development and introduction of new media of communication, place a serious question mark on diplomacy's continued ability to fulfill that purpose.

New electronic media of communication, such as the telegraph, telephone, computer and teleprinter altered the diplomatic environment. These media produced instant information relay and created immediate feedback. Furthermore, information increased in quantity and volume and became source diversified. With the diversity of knowledge, the diplomat's specialized knowledge and his information gathering ability became just one source among many and his importance declined. Furthermore, these electronic media of communication and transportation increased both the possibility of effective supervision and direct political intervention in diplomatic negotiations and destroyed almost entirely the splendid isolation formerly enjoyed by the professional diplomat. Diplomacy has ceased to be the estate of the professional in the "striped pants" and has become an arena for the personal aggrandizement of elected and nominated political leaders. The professional diplomat is now subject to direct and unceasing supervision by both public and government. This has limited his ability to employ the art of diplomacy and exhibit his individual skills and knowledge. In many cases, the diplomat is relegated to playing a subordinate role, one devoid of any real influence or significance. With the growing personal participation of politicians in diplomatic negotiations, the diplomat increasingly finds himself left out of the negotiations altogether. As an example, during the recent SALT talks between the U.S. and the U.S.S.R., the U.S. ambassador, Malcolm Toon, was totally ignored during the last and most crucial stages of the negotiations. His expertise, which may have been invaluable at those stages, was completely ignored by Secretary of State Vance, who chose to deal directly with the Soviet envoy to Washington, or with the Soviet leaders. Harold Nicolson, who frowns upon such practices of political intervention in diplomacy, explains why:

> Clearly there are moments when it is essential that the Prime Minister or the Foreign Minister should attend important conferences. Yet repeated personal visits on the part of the Foreign Secretary . . . should not be encouraged. Such visits arouse public expectation, lead to misunderstandings, and create confusion . . . diplomacy is not the art of conversation, it is the art of negotiating agreements . . . As such it is, on all ordinary occasions, far better left to the professional diplomatist.[4]

Growing public concern with foreign affairs, a concern constantly nourished by the mass media, has raised the demand for a more public diplomacy. There is an increasing public realization that we live in a "shrinking" world, a world made smaller, more interdependent and more familiar, by sophisticated media of communication and transportation. The growing power of public opinion and the greater direct and indirect participation of the public in domestic and foreign affairs, at least in the democracies, underline this concern.

The clamor for public diplomacy, coupled with the increasing involvement of political leaders, has led to the creation of new forms of diplomacy. While Traditional diplomacy was essentially a bilateral affair, New diplomacy encourages the creation of newer forms of communication such as international conferences, multilateral negotiations, and summit conferences. These forms are by nature more accessible to the mass media and as such are much more publicized. Hence, what used to be a back region activity is increasingly turned into a front region performance.

Political leaders, usually lacking in diplomatic experience, often misunderstand the importance of secrecy to various phases of diplomacy and treat this most delicate of political activities with the same elephantine clumsiness often manifested in domestic affairs. In reality, it now seems that diplomacy is no longer characterized by rational-political considerations, but is merely an extension of domestic partisan politics. As an example, one may take President Carter's last Middle East trip. Without questioning the value or the expected duration of the peace agreement between Egypt and Israel, one may inquire whether the urgency to produce an agreement during that particular trip stemmed from the objective political needs of Egypt, Israel or even the U.S., or from the personal needs of a weak president eyeing the upcoming presidential elections. As the secret essence of diplomacy disappears, its ability to play its traditional role decreases:

> Admittedly, in most cases it is difficult for governments to make concessions once positions are openly taken. Sounding-board diplomacy often stirs ill-feeling in the interested countries, and creates obstacles for a reasonable settlement by compromise. Prestige plays an important role in international politics, and serious arrangements even in the private business are not prepared by statements in the marketplace.[5]

Instant diplomacy, or the need to produce immediate results, came about because of the growing participation of political leaders in diplomatic negotiations, and the increasing involvement of the mass media and the public in these negotiations. The politician has to achieve quick results because unlike the diplomat, he cannot devote himself to a single issue for too long. To the diplomat, diplomacy is his sole occupation, while the politician must contend with a multitude of issues on many fronts. The mass media, which are increasingly involved in diplomacy, are ill-suited because of their structure and their functions for the analysis and explanation of complex and prolonged diplomatic processes. The mass media in general, and the electronic media in particular, crave sensation and easy and immediate solutions. The public, being relatively ignorant in foreign affairs, demands that its leaders "produce results, fast!" This combination of politicians, mass media and public pressure facilitated the evolution of such diplomatic "mutations" as "shuttle diplomacy" and the "Camp David Marathon." These new forms of diplomacy introduce novel elements of pressure and immediacy into a delicate process, which by definition demands patience and persistence. The mere knowledge that Kissinger's plane was in mid-shuttle sufficed to cause anxiety for the various negotiators — since they had to reach a decision before his plane landed.

The Special Problem of Democratic Diplomacy

Technological media of communication in general, and the mass media in particular, interact with the socio-political context within which they function. Hence one may safely assume that the mass media will have different effects upon the diplomatic practices of a democratic society such as the U.S., as compared with their influence on the diplomacy of a totalitarian society like the U.S.S.R.

The mass media in the U.S.S.R. constitute another branch of the government and the Communist Party. As such, their purpose and function is not to provide objective information as much as to provide the public with selective information which is preselected and prescribed by the government. Indeed, Soviet ideology views the role of the mass media not as an expressive, independent force, but rather as a tool for the dissemination of internal and external propaganda:

> News must be organized; Otherwise, it is news of mere events and happening . . . news . . . must pursue a definite purpose . . . News is agitation by facts.[6]

Furthermore, the government can ensure that this function is fulfilled, since the mass media are owned and operated by the government and the Party and subjected to total supervision and censorship:

> The will of the Party is that the newspapers, radio, television, movies and the arts help convey the Party line . . . The Party line is more important than the facts about any situation described. When the facts don't conform to the line, the line prevails.[7]

The mass media in the U.S. also function within constraints. These constraints are either economic or patriotic-nationalistic. Nevertheless, the mass media in the U.S. have a much greater freedom of expression and criticism than their Soviet counterparts. This is because the American mass media are not owned or operated by the government and therefore are almost entirely free of direct and pure political censorship. This is not to say that the American mass media, which serve as conduits for economic and political interests, are free of external or self-imposed constraints. However, these constraints are both more subtle and less frequent than the political censorship employed in the U.S.S.R. The American mass media, while traditionally supportive of the government in major foreign ventures, still reserve the right to question certain policies, advise and criticize as during the Vietnam War and the Watergate Affair. Bernard Cohen claims that elected and nominated officials turn to the mass media for ideas, interpretation of foreign events, information, reaction to policies, and to convey and shape public opinion. The mass media, in turn, see their role as representatives of the public, and often as policy-makers, whose role is to influence the opinions of the public and the officials.[8]

There is also a great disparity in the active and effective participation of the public in political affairs, in the U.S. and U.S.S.R. While no one would claim that every American is a political animal, or that the citizens of the U.S. can directly or effectively influence all national and international affairs, still there is an American tradition of public participation in politics, backed by a mechanism of free elections and accountability to the electorate, which enhances the value and importance of public opinion and public pressure.

No similar mechanism exists for the participation of the Soviet public in the affairs of their nation. The ruling oligarchy can formulate its political and diplomatic goals and act upon them with almost total disregard for Soviet public opinion. Soviet leaders owe no explanations for their diplomatic feats and failures. They do not owe these explanations to the public or the mass media, but rather to the ruling body which formulates and executes all political decisions in that nation — the Communist Party.

Public diplomacy runs contrary to the totalitarian nature, as indeed do real political participation by the public and the existence of free media of information. The Soviets, who do not understand the workings of a democratic government like the U.S., express the same bewilderment when confronted by public diplomacy. In an article entitled "Too Many Negotiators," a Soviet academician and foreign affairs specialist expresses this bewilderment and finally makes the ultimate statement, ". . . it is still not clear who exactly in the U.S. can speak in international relations on behalf of the United States."[9]

Democratic societies fall victim quite naturally to the pitfalls of public diplomacy, since everything about this form of diplomacy appeals to their democratic ideals and conforms to their democratic culture and institutions. The mass media in the U.S. have transformed diplomacy into a more "open" and "democratic" practice—in which the public is afforded the opportunity to view, follow and respond at almost any stage of the diplomatic process. The mass media, by nature, must produce "news." When there is no legitimate news, the mass media produce it. In effect, the mass media, especially the electronic media, produce artificial crises, manufacture imaginary solutions, and reduce intricate diplomatic problems such as the Middle East Peace Negotiations to arguments and personality conflicts between Begin and Sadat.

The American public gets its information from the mass media. The public builds its political expectations under the media's guidance. As a result, a public which is mostly naive in foreign affairs demands that its leaders fulfill unrealistic expectations. Their time and efforts are not being invested in the search for constructive and long-lasting diplomatic solutions, but rather in the maintenance of their present and future political image.

One point must be made absolutely clear. There is an inherent contradiction between two aspects of the New diplomacy — immediacy and publicity. In this age of instant information relay, immediate feedback, and the pressing expectations of the public and the mass media, a negotiator must indulge in instant policy-making and arrive at immediate decisions. This need or pressure for immediacy seems to be obstructed by the equally strong need for publicity. Public diplomacy means the laborious task of explaining policies and convincing public opinion at home and abroad of every diplomatic move, and of any change in policy. This is a slow and arduous process.

As a result, an intolerable situation is being created, in which the democratic negotiator is being subjected to unbearable and contradictory pressures. On the one hand he must contend with his legitimate opponent across the negotiating table. On the other hand he must grapple with the contradicting pressures of immediacy and publicity, pressures brought to bear by the public and the mass media. This strange situation leads to political and diplomatic schizophrenia, which may manifest itself in some cases in the inability to reach firm decisions, and in other cases, in the formulation of rash and fallible policies.

This is not to say that diplomacy has no value. One only wishes to warn that in the race to make diplomacy more "public" and "democratic," we might be eliminating its rational and practical basis, and in doing so, diminishing its importance as a tool for the resolution of international conflicts. The intent of this article is not to call for the political censorship of the mass media, or the exclusion of the public from foreign affairs. That would be foolhardy indeed. The purpose of this article is to suggest that even in the democracies, there should be a clear differentiation between secret negotiations and secret agreements. Agreements should — no — *must* be approved by the public. Negotiations should not. On occasions, it may be beneficial for the sake of a successful diplomatic outcome to eliminate the participation of the public and the mass media from the negotiations.

NOTES AND REFERENCES

1. H. Nicolson, *Diplomacy* (London: Oxford University Press, 1963), p. 15.
2. J. Lee, *The Diplomatic Persuaders* (New York: John Wiley & Sons, Inc., 1968) (Preface).
3. S.D. Kertesz, *The Quest for Peace Through Diplomacy* (Englewood Cliffs, N.J.: Prentice-Hall, Inc., 1967), p. 19.
4. Nicolson, p. 100.
5. Kertesz, pp. 27-28.

6. B.A. Hazan, *Soviet Propaganda — a Case Study of the Middle East Conflict* (Jerusalem: Keter Publishing House Jerusalem Ltd., 1976), p. 40.
7. R.G. Kaiser, *Russia — The People and the Power* (New York: Atheneum, 1976), p. 200.
8. B.C. Cohen, *The Press and Foreign Policy* (Princeton: Princeton University Press, 1970).
9. *The New York Times*, July 13, 1979.

From the Winter 1979 Et cetera.

SELF-INTEREST AND INTERNATIONAL COMMUNICATION

Robert E. Kingsley

IN A WORLD WHICH is not burdened by excessive altruism, we might assume that a frank, honest acknowledgement of self-interest would be essential to effective communication across national boundaries. Conventional wisdom admonishes us to talk to each other in honest, realistic terms; and honesty dictates that we acknowledge our actions — whether by individuals, institutions, or national states — to be motivated basically by selfish interests.

The pose of national self-interest is so fashionable that it is seldom questioned. It is difficult to find an article on foreign affairs that does not include the overt or implied dictum: "no policy, of course, can be based on anything but complete national interest. Anything else would be either treason or folly." Our business philosophers are not far behind. It is a sign of the businessman's honesty for him to observe that the principal goal of economic activity is profit, hardly an altruistic objective; one would scarcely expect him, however well motivated, to turn his factory into a school or charitable institution.

I am not especially concerned about the philosophical or psychological subtleties of this stance, which attempts to explain human motivations in terms as simplistic as a pleasure-pain

---

Robert E. Kingsley was Government Relations Advisor of Esso Inter-America Inc. at the time this article was written.

philosophy. In practical terms, it should be calculated to disarm both friends and foes by its honesty and so create, if not empathy, at least a basis for international understanding.

The trouble is that it doesn't work that way. One reason may be that protestations of exclusive self-interest are as suspect as those of unalloyed altruism. Experience would indicate that no person, no group, no institution is all one way or the other; each is rather a mixed bag of tricks. Another reason for skepticism is that, if our actions are by definition selfishly motivated, what have we added to our understanding by this statement? In operational terms, it is hard to see how individuals or groups would have to act if they were to be less than completely selfish. To be "disinterested" would, in effect, be a contradiction in terms and therefore meaningless.

Consequently, to talk incessantly about our mean motivations serve only to erect psychological barriers to international communication without contributing anything to our understanding. Thus what starts out as great good sense, a shedding of hypocrisy and cant, ends by becoming nonsense that obstructs the flow of ideas and the resolution of international conflict.

The insidiousness of this philosophy is that it tends to polarize thinking by inferring that there are only two diametrically opposed ways of looking at an issue: "ours" and "theirs." It would logically follow that, since we are selfishly motivated, what is good for one side, at least in great measure, can be achieved only to the detriment of the other. International dialogue, as a result, becomes less concerned with seeking solutions to problems than with manipulating language and communication to obtain an advantage at someone else's expense.

It should not be surprising, then, that most of our attempts at international communication are concerned with identifying and denouncing the *intentions* of others. This leads to a conspiratorial view of international affairs in which a series of black-and-white symbols is manipulated to explain the crass motivations of outsiders (the CIA, Wall Street, materialism) and to justify our own (national integrity, economic independence, self-determination). Each conflict of interest or ideas is discussed in terms of the motivations behind it, which are generally conceived as being reprehensible in others and justifiable, although selfish, in ourselves.

The results of this thinking are all too apparent in our international communication, as for example when we discuss the possibilities of multilateral national disarmament. An impasse is reached because we cannot agree on the terms of inspection: One side assumes that full inspection is opposed because the other intends to hide its true strength; the other concludes that "they" will use disarmament negotiations in order to gain military advantage.

A similar phenomenon occurs when private U.S. business discusses the terms of investment in underdeveloped areas which need both capital and technology. The host nation frequently takes it for granted that private industry's objective is to make as much money as is feasible in the shortest period of time and to leave the country as few benefits as it can. Therefore, perhaps unwittingly, the nation seeks to attract the investor but at the same time to frustrate in many ways his legitimate economic objectives. His contribution to the national economy, at best, is popularly regarded as a necessary evil, and the intention behind it is scorned in accordance with national mythology.

Over the years I have become convinced that fully ninety percent of our international communication is wasted on mutual recriminations regarding the intentions of others. We live in an either-or world in which distrust and suspicion are the molds that shape our thinking and hold it within rigid, unprofitable confines. Because the intentions of others can only be surmised, and since there is a predisposition to believe that these are less than laudable, no objective criteria can be devised for the resolution of conflict.

An international dialogue based on such assumptions may be likened to what mathematicians call "zero-sum" games. In card games with which we are familiar, what one person gains another loses, so that the total adds up to zero. That is, when someone gains it is at another's expense, because no new assets are created. If we look at international relations in game terms, however, this obviously is not true. In fact, it is easier to conceive of such relationships resulting in either a loss or a gain for *both* sides. Given a modicum of cooperation and intelligence, it is indeed difficult to visualize how an international dialogue carried out in reasonably extensional terms can wholly benefit one party and damage the other.

The insight of games theory is that in many social situations there can be a mutuality of interest (which is not inconsistent with the psychology of self-interest). One must conclude, moreover, that this supposition corresponds more often to the reality of social situations, at least those which are approached rationally. More importantly, a dialogue which is pursued on this assumption can be productive because mutuality of interest may be measured by results, whereas intensional thinking which concerns itself almost exclusively with personal or group motivations must forever rest on conjecture and idle speculation.

From the Spring 1969 Et cetera.

V.
RELIABLE RESEARCH

POPPER'S FALLIBILISM

Henry Perkinson

SIR KARL POPPER HAS WRITTEN no books on education. He did publish a few, long-forgotten articles in Austrian educational journals early in his career. But he neither thinks of himself, nor do others consider him, an educational theorist. Universally, his philosophic depth and breadth is acknowledged: as an epistemologist, a social and political philosopher, and, above all, as a philosopher of science. A recent biographer reports that he is "considered by many to be the greatest philosopher of science that has ever been." Popper's philosophy has influenced physical and biological scientists, statesmen, historians, psychologists, physiologists, anthropologists, economists . . . but no educationists. Yet, his philosophy does have profound implications for this field too. It offers the theoretical basis for a non-authoritarian approach to education — the first such approach since Socrates.[1]

I

Karl Popper grew up in the heady intellectual milieu of Vienna in the early twentieth century. He tells how, while still in his teens, he participated in discussions and arguments about the theories of Marx, of Freud, of Adler, and of Einstein. One problem that particularly fascinated young Popper was the question of the scientific validity of these different theories, or, as he phrased it, the problem of demarcation between science and non-science.[2]

Henry Perkinson is a Professor of Philosophy and History of Education at New York University, and Editor of *The Gadfly*, an irreverent journal of education criticism.

What are the criteria for a scientific theory? Popper noted that many of his friends who admired Marx, Freud, and Adler were impressed by the explanatory power of their theories. "These theories appeared to be able to explain practically anything that happened within the field to which they referred. The study of any of them seemed to have the effect of an intellectual conversion or revelation, opening your eyes to a new truth hidden from those not yet initiated. Once your eyes were thus opened, you saw confirming instances everywhere: the world was full of verifications of the theory. What happened always confirmed it. Thus, its truth appeared manifest; and unbelievers were clearly people who did not want to see the manifest truth; who refused to see it, either because it was against their class interest, or because of the repressions which were still 'unanalyzed' and crying aloud for treatment."

His Marxist friends, Popper reports, could not open a newspaper without finding a news story (or the *way* a news story was presented) that confirmed their theory; and Freudians, or Adlerians, found their theories confirmed by each and every clinical observation that came up. But all these endless confirmations, Popper argues, only meant that one can interpret phenomena in the light of those theories; and since every conceivable phenomena could be interpreted in light of these theories, then these confirming instances meant very little.

But with Einstein, Popper realized, the situation was quite different. Einstein's theory about the universe led to making predictions; predictions that, if they did not hold up, would prove his theory wrong. Einstein's gravitational theory, for example, led to a prediction about "shifts" in the position of stars. Careful, experimental observation corroborated these predictions. But it was not the fact that the prediction held up that made Einstein's theory a scientific one. It was the fact that it *could have been shown to be false*. The theory was falsifiable.

What made Einstein's theory scientific — and different from those of Marx, Freud, and Adler — was that it was incompatible with certain possible results of observation. In short, Popper concludes, the criterion of the scientific status of a theory is its falsifiability, or refutability, or testability.

II

With this criterion of falsifiability, Popper not only made it possible to demarcate science from non-science, he also solved a problem central to the philosophy of science. Science, most everyone agrees, consists of law-like, general descriptive statements; e.g., "All stars, except planets, move in circles"; "All swans are white." Prior to Popper, the traditional question that had troubled scientists and philosophers of science was how to make these general statements certain. (The problem John Stuart Mill had wrestled with in his *Logic*.)

The answer proposed ever since the time of Francis Bacon was, induction. That is, through careful observation of a number of individual cases, the scientist could "induce" a general (universal) statement about all cases. After careful observation of a number of white swans, for example, the scientist could induce, "All swans are white."

But induction was a totally unsatisfactory answer. It was, one philosopher noted, the skeleton in the closet. David Hume (1711-1766) had conclusively demonstrated that induction is not valid — empirically or logically. The empirical objection is that universal statements refer to the future as well as the past and present. But it is impossible to observe the future. Thus, "all swans are white" says that swans not yet born will be white. This is something we cannot observe, hence cannot claim for empirical reasons. The logical objection to induction is that one cannot infer a universal statement from a singular statement, nor from any number of singular statements. Thus, "this swan is white," and "this second swan is white," and "this third swan is white" . . . etc. can never, logically, lead to the conclusion "All swans are white."

Bertrand Russell succinctly summed up the difficulty confronting science: "Induction is an independent, logical principle, incapable of being inferred either from experiences or from other logical principles . . . (but) . . . without this principle science is impossible."[3]

The only way science was possible, it seemed, was the way pointed out by Hume, who, after demonstrating the logical and empirical invalidity of induction, suggested that induction was a psychological process. That is, repeated instances of a phenomenon (white swans, e.g.) induce us to *believe* that all future instances will be like those observed so far. (We are led to believe that "All swans are white.")

To accept this psychological basis for induction is to admit that a scientific theory can never be absolutely certain: a scientific theory is only tentatively held (believed) on the basis of past confirmations. Thus, we *believe* that all swans are white because all the swans we have observed so far have been white. One difficulty with this psychological conception of induction is that it reduces science to belief and commitment, making it impossible to demarcate science from non-science. For, according to this construction of a scientific theory, the theories of Freud, Marx, and Adler were no different from that of Einstein: so far past experience has confirmed them — as Popper's friends in Vienna had argued. But this also means that *all* these theories were on a par with those of astrology, phrenology and alchemy, since the validity of a theory was a simple matter of belief. Bertrand Russell dramatically stated this difficulty with Hume's widely accepted psychological interpretation of induction when he wrote, "It is, therefore, important to discover whether there is any answer to Hume within a philosophy that is wholly or mainly *empirical*. If not, *there is no intellectual difference between sanity and insanity.* The lunatic who believes that he is a poached egg is to be condemned solely on the ground that he is in a minority. . . ."

By introducing falsifiability as the criterion for demarcating science from non-science, Popper provided a solution to the problem of how to validate scientific theories.

According to Popper, science is still made up of general statements, or theories. And these theories are tentative, never certain. (Popper lumps scientific "hypotheses," scientific "theories," and scientific "laws" all together and terms them all "theories.") But the tentativeness of scientific theories lies, he says, in the fact that they have not yet been falsified or refuted. Scientists use tests or experiments to establish the worth of a theory. Yet, in spite of what many people think, a scientific experiment does *not* confirm a theory; it merely tests it, and determines how well the theory holds up. A worthwhile theory, Popper concludes, is one that has been well-tested and has survived, a theory that has not yet been falsified.

To sum up: scientific theories are not provable, but they are testable. For, whereas billions and billions of confirming instances will not prove a universal statement, one counter-instance will falsify or refute a universal statement. For example, the observation of billions of white swans will not prove the universal statement that all swans are white, but observing one black swan will refute it.

III

Popper's notion of falsifiability is surprisingly fruitful. Falsifiability not only allows us to demarcate science from nonscience and to weed out worthwhile theories from false ones, it also explains how scientific knowledge grows.

Prior to Popper, those who addressed themselves to the question of how science grows usually tried to explain it as the result of the accumulation of observations. That is, the story went, as scientists gathered more and more data that confirmed the theories we hold about the universe, our scientific knowledge expanded.

But the problem with this explanation, as Popper pointed out, is that we can always, if we are clever enough, find confirmations of our theories. But such observed confirmations do not advance knowledge. They simply reinforce our belief in our theories. Centuries of observation, for example, had at one time "confirmed" the theory that the world was flat. Our scientific knowledge of the world did not advance, however, until explorers like Columbus falsified that theory. Falsification, Popper argues, is the key to the growth of science. Scientific knowledge grows through "the repeated overthrow of scientific theories and their replacement by better or more satisfactory ones."[5]

A better theory is one that is not subject to the same refutations as the theory it replaces. It is closer to the truth, or as Popper sometimes puts it, a better theory has a greater degree of verisimilitude. Also, of course, a better theory must have greater content—it must tell us more than the theory it replaces. And the more a theory says, then the more it excludes or forbids, and the greater the opportunities for falsifying it.

One can see this relation between greater content and higher falsifiability by comparing the following two sentences:

(A) Friday it will rain.
(B) Friday and Saturday it will rain.
  (i) the content of (B) is greater than (A): it provides us with more information.
  (ii) But (B) excludes more than (A): it prohibits two consecutive days of sunshine.
  (iii) Hence, (B) is less likely than (A) to hold up: it has more opportunity to be falsified.

So, if the growth of science consists, as it must, of the continual replacement of theories with ones that tell us more, then, Popper argues, this process is one of replacing any given theory with a more risky theory—one less likely to hold up to experiments or tests.

Popper's explanation of how scientific knowledge grows has obvious dramatic implications for the method of science. Instead of looking for theories likely to be confirmed by tests and trying to verify them, scientists should take a bolder approach: look for theories of high content—i.e., risky theories, theories that forbid much, theories with greater opportunities for falsification, theories less likely to be confirmed—and subject those theories to severe tests and experiments. This is what scientists must do, Popper argues, if scientific knowledge is to advance, if we are to replace our present theories with ones that tell us more.

IV

Popper's contention that science grows through falsification of theories and their replacement by better ones is clearly borne out by the history of science, for surely we have better theories about the world than our ancestors. But if falsification does lead to their replacement by better ones, then the question arises: where, or how, do scientists discover these better theories?

The traditional answer to this question is a psychological one. That is, scientists discover new and better theories by observation — the observation of numerous instances of a given phenomenon leads them to discover a theory about that phenomenon. Now, this psychology of discovery is simply a rendition of logical "induction." But, induction, we saw above, is not valid. Observations, however repetitious, of white swans cannot logically or empirically allow us to come up with the general (universal) statement "All swans are white." Therefore, Popper concludes, theories do not emerge from observation, neither directly nor indirectly. Psychology cannot explain how new theories come into being. In place of a psychology of discovery (an area in which he himself worked many years), we must turn, Popper insists, to a logic of discovery.[6]

Although many people do believe that science begins with observations, this is, Popper insists, logically impossible. He has repeatedly demonstrated the point in articles and lectures by challenging people: "Observe!" No one, he maintains, starts to observe without first having a definite question in mind, a question which might be decided by observations. So when told to observe, most people respond by asking, "What do you want me to observe?" Observation, Popper argues, comes *after* expectations. But expectations themselves are, or are derived from, theories (or hypotheses). So theories must, logically, precede observation. Every observation we make is made in light of a theory.

And theories? Where do they come from? Theories, Popper says, come from us, from human beings; we create them as conjectures. These conjectures are triggered by problems. And the problem itself comes into being only because of logical prior expectations, which means that every problem is logically related to a prior theory. A problem logically implies a prior inadequate theory. Thus, if we have a practical problem, say, with our car, this logically indicates we have an inadequate theory about the car — about its maintenance, its operations, or whatever.

This practical problem with our car leads us to create or conjecture a new theory about its maintenance, its operation, or wherever the problem lies. When our conjectured theory solves the problem, this means we have improved the original theory — the theory that generated the problem to begin with. Popper has expressed all of this by saying all knowledge is theory-impregnated, including our observations. Accordingly, all improvements in knowledge consist of the modification, possibly the rejection, of previous knowledge. This means that we must begin our lives with inborn theories, which is precisely what Popper concludes:

> I assert that every animal is born with expectations or anticipations, which could be framed as hypotheses; a kind of hypothetical knowledge. And I assert that we have, in this sense, some degree of inborn knowledge from which we may begin, even though it may be quite unreliable. This inborn knowledge, these inborn expectations, will, if disappointed, create *our first* problems; and the ensuing growth of our knowledge may, therefore, be described as consisting throughout of corrections and modifications of previous knowledge.[7]

It is important to note that Popper comes to this conclusion about inborn knowledge because of the logical necessity for *theories* to exist before having problems, or observations.

V

If the advancement of knowledge consists of the modification of previous knowledge, then those who would advance knowledge, must, logically, begin with problems — problems inherent in the existing knowledge or theories. These problems trigger the creation of better theories, theories that are closer to the truth, theories that tell us more. Now, if the growth of science begins with problems, then it behooves those who want to contribute to its growth to search out and discover problems. To do this means to criticize the existing theories, to try to find what is wrong with them, to try to falsify them.

So, once again, Popper reveals the fantastic fruitfulness of his falsificationist approach. Earlier, we saw that he used falsifiability to demarcate science from non-science: only those theories that can be falsified are scientific ones. In addition, he used falsification to weed out worthwhile theories; a worthwhile theory is one that survives attempts to falsify it. He has also used falsification to explain how knowledge grows, describing this process as the replacement of falsified theories by better ones. We advance knowledge through the falsification of existing theories, by discovering problems inherent in them. This triggers the creation of new theories or conjectures, and we ascertain how much better the new theory is by seeing if it has a higher information content (which means that there will be more opportunities to falsify it) and by seeing if it can better withstand attempts to falsify it.

On this matter of growth of scientific knowledge, Popper makes one last important point. If growth is to be continued, then continual criticism is called for. That is, continual attempts to falsify our theories will yield new problems that will trigger new conjectures or theories. The growth of science, then, is one of continual trial and error elimination, of conjecture followed by refutation which leads to new conjecture followed by refutation . . . and so it goes . . . resulting in ever better theories. One must not forget, however, that criticism presupposes existing theories, accepted theories. These theories usually come to us from tradition. Without tradition, knowledge would be impossible. But every bit of traditional knowledge is open to critical examination. "Thus, we might say," Popper writes, "that the most lasting contribution to the growth of scientific knowledge that a theory can make are the new problems which it raises, so that we are led back to the view of science and of the growth of knowledge as always starting from, and always ending with, problems — problems of ever increasing depth, and an ever increasing fertility in suggesting new problems."

Popper has schematically presented this conception of the growth of scientific knowledge in the following diagram — where P is the problem, TT the tentative theory, and EE error elimination or criticism:[8]

$$P_1 \rightarrow TT \rightarrow EE \rightarrow P_2$$

VI

In placing the responsibility for the growth of science on man himself, the responsibility to be critical, we come to what I consider the heart of Popper's philosophy, his conception of human beings as fallible creatures.

As Popper construes him, man is like God, a Creator, but unlike God, what he creates, including his own knowledge, is never perfect. This means, however, that what he creates can always be improved. And the responsibility for improving it rests with man himself. He must assume what Popper calls a critical approach, or a critical attitude. Through a critical approach to his knowledge, man can uncover the problems inherent in it and trigger his own new, better conjectures.

It is this conception of man as a fallible creator that helps explain Popper's emphasis on falsification. Man creates his knowledge, so it is never perfect; hence, he can never justify it. But he can improve it; by approaching it critically, he can discover when and how it is false. So, *because* man is fallible, the knowledge he creates can grow — not by the accumulation of "justified" knowledge, but through falsification or error elimination. And *because* he is fallible, he can identify which of the knowledge he creates is worthwhile — not by trying to justify or prove it, but by trying to falsify it, trying to eliminate its errors. And *because* he is fallible, he can demarcate scientific knowledge from non-scientific — not by verification, but by seeing if it is falsifiable.

Popper has identified the critical approach as the basic theme in his philosophy and he has tried to use it to fashion a new concept of human rationality, called critical rationality, to replace what he calls justificatory rationality.

According to justificatory rationality, human rationality consists in accepting only that knowledge or those theories we have justified, i.e., proven. But, as we saw above, no number of confirmations can ever prove or justify a theory. Since induction is not valid, justification is not possible.

What is possible is critical rationality. This consists in accepting only those theories that have withstood severe criticisms. Here we must note an important distinction Popper makes between logic and methodology. Logically, a single counterexample refutes a theory. But in practice, or at the methodological level, complete falsification is not possible —

for one can always doubt a statement, or make a mistake in observation, or escape refutation by definition. In short, we can always refuse to accept a contradiction.

But what this means, methodologically, Popper insists, is that we should assume a critical approach toward our theories, trying neither to immunize them from all falsification, nor accept falsification too readily. Only such a comprehensively critical approach will provide vigorous and severe testing of our theories.

VII

It should now be clear how revolutionary Karl Popper's philosophy is. At the center of this intellectual revolution is his total repudiation of induction:

> I hold that neither animals nor men use any procedure like induction, or any argument based on the repetition of instances. The belief that we use induction is simply a mistake. It is a kind of optical illusion.[9]

So Popper goes beyond David Hume, who first pointed out the logical and empirical arguments against induction, but ended up interpreting induction psychologically. Popper maintains that induction does not ever occur. The method we — animals and human beings — do use, he claims, is the method of trial and error elimination. We are misled because this method looks like induction. But the logic of trial and error elimination is totally different, and avoids all the difficulties traditionally connected to induction.

Prior to Popper, people had unsuccessfully tried to use induction to solve the problems about scientific knowledge discussed above. That is, they had tried to use induction to demarcate science from non-science, to weed out worthwhile theories, and to explain the growth of scientific knowledge. In each case, the story went, the method of induction produced true, justified, and accumlative knowledge. But this is a myth: induction is not valid, not justified; it does not exist; hence it explains nothing.

Most people find it very difficult to accept this. Induction, they say, is part of common sense. Everyone knows that we learn from experience. If we see a number of white swans and never a non-white one, we are led to generalize, or to conclude (to induce) that all swans are white. This, so the story goes, is how learning takes place. Yet, Popper insists that this common sense notion of how we learn is mistaken, like an optical illusion. Popper bases his argument against the existence of induction on what he calls the principle of transference, or the principle of the primacy of the logical situation. That is, if induction cannot occur logically, then it cannot occur psychologically. What really takes place, he says, is that we make observations in light of our theories, and then modify these theories when they are falsified by experience. Now, this *looks like* induction. It looks as if we are learning, or *receiving*, knowledge from the outside world through our observations or experiences. But in reality, it is we who create our theories (and in the first instance are born with theories), which we then modify when we discover, through observations or experiences, that these theories do not hold up.

So, as Popper views learning, we can learn from experience, but for him this means that our experiences can, if we are sufficiently critical, and lucky, reveal to us the inadequacy or falsity of our theories, triggering us to create better ones.

VIII

In construing human beings as fallible creators, Popper credits us with creating more than knowledge. Human beings create society too. The society we create, like our knowledge, is never perfect, but, like our knowledge, it can be improved — through criticism.

Here, his model is Socrates, who sought to improve Athens through criticism. But to improve society through criticism, we must have what Socrates had not: an open society — a society wherein the policies, practices, rules, and laws are open to criticism and where critics are taken seriously, not squelched and censured, or killed. The creation of an open society is up to us. We have to fashion institutions that hold society's decision makers open and responsive to criticisms — institutions that hold them accountable to those affected by their decisions.

Instead of worrying about who should rule, or who should make decisions in our social and political institutions, our social and political scientists should try to help people protect themselves against incompetent rulers and decision makers, and against those who would abuse their powers. And the way to do this, Popper suggests, is to trace the actual consequences of the present social and political arrangements, uncovering the evils these arrangements generate. Social and political scientists thus take on the role of critics of society — the Socratic role, if you will. Such criticism, when taken seriously, leads to critical dialogue or discussion, and then the modification or refinement of the existing arrangements in light of the unrefuted criticism. This improves the society through the elimination or diminution of the specific evils uncovered.[10]

Popper's view of social improvement emerges directly from his epistemological theory. Knowledge grows through trial and error elimination, so the growth of scientific knowledge depends upon the deliberate adoption of a critical approach. Here, in his social and political philosophy, he extends the critical approach to society. Of course, the critical approach cannot give us a perfect society any more than the critical approach can give us a perfect science. Society will always be imperfect because it is created by fallible beings, and because there will always exist irreconcilable clashes of values. But society can always be improved. We can always reduce the existing suffering and pain.

IX

In recent years, Popper has characterized his theory of growth of knowledge as a Darwinian theory. According to Darwin's theory of natural selection, the environment eliminated those organisms that were unfit or inadequate. Evolution or growth occurred when those organisms that did survive produced offspring that varied slightly from themselves, organisms that also survived and had progeny of their own. The crucial factor in evolution is the action of the environment as a critic — a critic that eliminates inadequate or unfit progeny.

So also, Popper says, in the evolution of our knowledge. It

grows and evolves through criticism—the elimination of recognized errors from our theories. Confronted with these discovered inadequacies or problems, we create new, and better, theories.

This Darwinian explanation of the growth of knowledge is meant to explain how knowledge really grows. It is not meant metaphorically: "The theory of knowledge which I wish to propose is a largely Darwinian theory of the growth of knowledge. From the amoeba to Einstein, the growth of knowledge is always the same: we try to solve our problems, and to obtain by a process of elimination something approaching adequacy in our tentative solutions."[11]

X

The Popper-Darwinian construction of improvement is directly applicable to the process of education, and provides what has been missing since Socrates: a non-authoritarian conception of that process. (Here, I must repeat that Karl Popper has not applied his theories to education. What follows is my own extrapolation, or adaptation, of his work.)

Most contemporary educators actually do construe the process of education as the process of promoting student growth: intellectual or cognitive growth, as well as moral, aesthetic, social, and—perhaps—emotional growth. Teachers try to improve or advance their students' theories, skills, dispositions. Yet, few educators employ a Darwinian approach to the task. In fact, it is not unjust to characterize the approach commonly used by most teachers as Lamarckian.

Lamarck, a predecessor of Darwin, thought evolution took place through the transmission of acquired characteristics. He would explain the giraffe's long neck, for example, as an instance of the transmission of acquired characteristics. In order to adapt to changing environmental conditions, Lamarck's giraffe had to grow a long neck so as to eat the leaves off the topmost branches. This newly acquired characteristic was then transmitted to the giraffe's progeny.

As with Lamarckian giraffes, so with Lamarckian teachers. They transmit knowledge, or learning (acquired characteristics of the human species) to each generation of students. But such Lamarckian transmission never occurs, neither in biology nor in education. Of course, teachers—some teachers, at any rate—can point to what they take to be successful transmission of skills or theories, or dispositions. The students—some students, at any rate—learned what was transmitted, didn't they? The answer to this, if the Popper-Darwinian theory of growth is correct, is that, yes, these students did grow, or learn, but this did not come about through transmission—any more than did the long neck of the giraffe. What really takes place is growth through selection.

All learning, all growth of knowledge, according to the Popper-Darwinian theory, consists of the modification or rejection of some form of knowledge that was there previously. And such modification results from the observed inadequacies of the previously held knowledge. So, anyone who learns something new—whether it is Boyle's law, or how to kick a football, or how to save money—is simply modifying a theory, a skill, or a disposition he already had, even if in some gross, vague, or unarticulated form. And he modified this knowledge in light of its observed inadequacies.

Now, what deceives us is that this process of learning through selection (i.e., through the elimination of inadequacies in our existing knowledge), *looks* like a process of transmission. For what we see is a teacher telling students, say, how to spell the word "cat"; and later we see the students correctly spelling the word "cat." This looks like transmission. But what is really happening is that the learner is going through the process of trial and error elimination. The learner already can speak, perhaps write as well, has seen cats, understands the sound "cat," and has some understanding of the relation of letters to sounds, letters to words, etc. So, invited to demonstrate what he knows, the learner goes through a process of trial and error elimination, sometimes correctly, sometimes with the help of the teacher, or the help of models. No transmission takes place. The learner has just modified the knowledge he already possesses through trial and error elimination.

The trouble with the transmission conception of the educational process, which has reigned since Aristotle, is not simply that it is wrong, but that it results in an authoritarian construction of education.

Construing education as a process of transmission converts it into imposition. The teacher's task is to impose knowledge, or learning, on the students. The knowledge transmitted is the acquired (justified? proven?) wisdom of society. Teachers who try to transmit usually employ many different tactics and stratagems to pull this off in a benign way. They try to "motivate" students to want to learn what they are supposed to learn. They try to match the materials to be learned to the learner — to his "needs," "interests," "abilities," "aptitude," and "capabilities." But the process is still one of imposition.

The argument against imposition is that it prevents growth. Here is the argument. If the Popper-Darwinian theory of growth is correct, then in all cases the student learns through trial and error elimination. So when teachers and schools try to impose learning, they are simply coercing students to adopt *their* criteria for identifying errors. They are saying, in effect, "All knowledge that is contrary to this knowledge we present to you is false." This prevents growth.

Here is another argument. Suppose teachers completely succeeded in imposing knowledge on the young and completely succeeded in "proving" that this knowledge was true. It is patently clear that for those students so taught (indoctrinated?) that the advancement of that knowledge would cease. Because, you see, these students would "know" the truth. So we are led to conclude that the growth of knowledge has occurred and will continue to occur *only* because teachers *failed* to impose knowledge on the young.

To sum up: construing the process of education as one of transmission is logically incompatible with the aim of promoting the growth of knowledge.

One reason why educators have not confronted the fact that the transmission conception of the educational process is inimical to growth is that there seemed to be no other way for education to take place except through transmission. But the Popper-Darwinian theory of growth does offer an alternative conception to the educational process, and thus an alternative conception of the functions of the teacher and the school.

XI

In adapting the Popper-Darwinian construction of growth, a teacher assumes that the student already possesses knowledge, and assumes, secondly, that the student is the source of growth. Rather than an imposer of knowledge, the teacher tries to create a critical environment, an environment responsive to the knowledge the student has, an environment that will help the student discover the inadequacy of that knowledge and encourages him to modify it. (It is important to note that such a critical environment presupposes that the student does have knowledge. As Popper has put it: "There can be no critical phase without a preceding dogmatic phase, a phase in which something—an expectation, a regularity of behavior—is formed, so that error elimination can begin to work on it.") The teacher, of course, is a central part of that critical environment, trying, like Socrates, to take seriously the student's knowledge and to help him become critical of it. The subject matter here becomes the material with which to elicit the student's knowledge and something against which he can test his knowledge. The teacher does not ask the student to accept the subject matter, but rather to encounter it—critically.

Now, much of this is not new, of course. One finds it adumbrated in twentieth century educational theorists such as Maria Montessori, A.S. Neill, Jean Piaget, and Carl Rogers. All these theorists in one way or another advise educators to create a supportive, responsive environment, an environment that permits students to interact freely with one another, with the teacher, with the subject matter. They all insist that given this kind of an environment, children will need no extensive rewards or punishments—they will learn naturally, through their own activity. Learners, these theorists all claim, do not require teachers.

In Popper's philosophy, we find a rigorous philosophical defense of this twentieth century theory of education. He provides a theory that explains why the educational practices of Montessori, of Neill, of Rogers, and yes, of Piaget, work. All these pedagogical geniuses were groping toward a non-authoritarian construction of education—a construction in keeping with human fallibility.

Karl Popper was himself a teacher in the Vienna schools for seven years before migrating to New Zealand when Hitler came to power. In his "Autobiography," he tells how as a college student he had dreamed of creating the kind of school that those twentieth century educational theorists later prescribed: "I dreamt of one day founding a school in which young people could learn without boredom, and would be stimulated to pose problems and discuss them; a school in which no unwanted answers to unasked questions would have to be listened to; in which one did not study for the sake of passing examinations."

Karl Popper never carried out that dream, never founded a school . . . but, he did create the philosophy for the founding of such a school of his dreams.

NOTES AND REFERENCES

1. Bryan Magee, *Karl Popper* (Modern Masters Series edited by Frank Kermode) (New York: The Viking Press, 1973), Introduction.
2. Karl Popper, "Science: Conjectures and Refutations" in *Conjectures and Refutations* (London: Routledge and Kegan Paul, 1963).
3. Bertrand Russell, *A History of Western Philosophy*, (New York: Simon and Schuster, 1964, 14th edition), p. 674.
4. Karl Popper, *The Logic of Scientific Discovery* (New York: Science Editions, 1961), English Translation of *Logik der Forschung* (1935).
5. "Truth, Rationality and the Growth of Scientific Knowledge," in *Conjectures and Refutations*.
6. Karl Popper, "Autobiography," in *The Philosophy of Karl Popper*, edited by Paul A. Schlipp (LaSalle, Ill.: Open Court, 1974), Section 12.
7. Karl Popper, "Evolution and the Tree of Knowledge," in *Objective Knowledge* (Oxford: Oxford University Press, 1972), p. 258.
8. Karl Popper, "On the Sources of Knowledge and Ignorance" and "Truth, Rationality and the Growth of Scientific Knowledge," in *Conjectures and Refutations*; and "Epistemology without a Knowing Subject," *Objective Knowledge*.
9. Karl Popper, "Replies to my Critics," Section 13, in *The Philosophy of Karl Popper*.
10. Karl Popper, *The Open Society and its Enemies* (London: Routledge and Kegan Paul, 1962, 4th edition), esp. Vol. I, Chapter 10.
11. "Evolution and the Tree of Knowledge," p. 261.

From the Spring 1978 Et cetera.

BIASING EFFECTS
OF EXPERIMENTERS

Robert Rosenthal

PSYCHOLOGISTS ARE SAID to be such a scientifically self-conscious group that there may one day be a psychology of those psychologists who study psychologists. That, for the most part, is in the future, but in the present there is a clearly developing psychology of the psychologist as he conducts his research with human and animal subjects.

The social situation which comes into being when an experimenter encounters his research subject is a situation of both general and unique importance to psychology and the other behavioral sciences. Its general importance derives from the fact that the interaction of experimenter and subject, like other two-person interactions, may be investigated empirically with a view to teaching us more about dyadic interaction in general. Its unique importance derives from the fact that the interaction of experimenter and subject, *un*like other dyadic interactions, is a major source of our knowledge in the behavioral sciences.

To the extent that we hope for dependable knowledge in psychology and the behavioral sciences generally, we must have dependable knowledge about the experimenter-subject interaction specifically. We can no more hope to acquire accurate information for our disciplines without an understanding of the data collection situation than astronomers and zoologists could hope to acquire accurate information for their disciplines without their understanding the effects of their telescopes and microscopes. It is for these reasons that increasing interest has been

---

Robert Rosenthal is a Professor of Social Psychology at Harvard University.

shown in the investigation of the experimenter-subject interaction system. And the outlook is anything but bleak. It does seem that we can profitably learn about those effects which experimenters unwittingly may have on the results of their research.

Experimenter Effects

It is useful to think of two major types of effects, usually unintentional, which psychologists can have upon the results of their research. The first type operates, so to speak, in the mind, in the eye, or in the hand of the psychologist. It operates without affecting the actual response of the human or animal subjects of the experiment. It is not interactional. The second type of experimenter effect is interactional. It operates by affecting the actual response of the subject of the experiment. It is a sub-type of this latter type of effect, the effects of the psychologist's expectancy or hypothesis on the results of the research, which will occupy most of this discussion. First, however, some examples of other effects of psychologists on their research will be mentioned.

Observer Effects. In any science, the experimenter must make provision for the careful observation and recording of the events under study. It is not always so easy to be sure that one has, in fact, made an accurate observation. That lesson was learned by the psychologists, who needed to know it, but it was not the psychologists who focused our attention on it originally. It was the astronomers.

Near the end of the eighteenth century, the royal astronomer at the Greenwich Observatory, a man named Maskelyne, discovered that his assistant, Kinnebrook, was consistently "too slow" in his observations of the movement of stars across the sky. Maskelyne cautioned Kinnebrook about his "errors," but the errors continued for months. Kinnebrook was fired.

The man who might have saved that job was Bessel, the astronomer at Königsberg, but he was twenty years too late. It was not until then that he arrived at the conclusion that Kinnebrook's "error" was probably not willful. Bessel studied the observations of stellar transits made by a number of senior astronomers. Differences in observation, he discovered, were the rule, not the exception.[1]

That early observation of the effects of the scientist on the observations of science made Bessel perhaps the first student of the psychology of scientists. More contemporary research on the psychology of scientists has shown that, while observer errors are not necessarily serious, they tend to occur in a biased manner. That is, more often than we would expect by chance, when errors of observation do occur, they tend to produce results more in the direction of the psychologist's hypothesis.[2]

To make the matter more concrete and to illustrate the probable rate at which observer or recording errors are made in the behavioral sciences, Table 1 has been prepared. On the basis of five studies involving 112 observers recording a total of 20,517 observations, we find that about 1% of the observations are in error. The last column of Table 1 shows that, more than two-thirds of the time, errors are in the direction of the observer's hypothesis.[3]

TABLE 1. RECORDING ERRORS IN FIVE EXPERIMENTS

STUDY	OBSERVERS	RECORDINGS	ERRORS	ERRORS %	BIAS %
1	28	11,125	126	1.13%	68%
2	30	3,000	20	0.67	75
3	11	828	6	0.72	67
4	34	1,770	30	1.69	85
5	9	3,794	36	0.95	— —
Sum	112	20,517	218	1.06%	71%
Median	28	3,000	30	0.95%	72%

Interpreter Effects. The interpretation of the data collected is part of the research process, and a glance at any of the technical journals of contemporary psychology will suggest strongly that while psychologists only rarely debate the observations made by one another, they often debate the interpretation of those observations. It is as difficult to state the rules for accurate interpretation of data as it is for accurate observation of data, but the variety of interpretations offered in explanation of the same data imply that many of us must turn out to be wrong. The history of science generally, and the history of psychology more specifically, suggest that more of us are wrong longer than we need to be because we hold our theories not quite lightly enough. The common practice of theory monogamy has its advantages, however. It does keep us motivated to make more crucial observations. In any case, interpreter effects seem less serious than observer effects. The reason is that the former are public while the latter are private. Given a set of observations, their interpretations become generally available to the scientific community. We are free to agree or disagree with any specific interpretation. Not so with the case of the observations themselves. Often these are made by a single investigator, so that we are not free to agree or disagree. We can only hope that no observer errors occurred and we can, and should, repeat the observations.

Intentional Effects. It happens sometimes in undergraduate laboratory science courses that students "collect" and report data too beautiful to be true. (That probably happens most often when students are taught to be scientists by being told what results they must get to do well in the course, rather than being taught the logic of scientific inquiry and the value of being quite open-eyed and open-minded.) Unfortunately, the history of science tells us that not only undergraduates have been dishonest in science. Fortunately, such instances are rare; nevertheless, intentional effects must be regarded as part of the inventory of the effects of investigators themselves. Three recent reports on important cases of scientific error that were very likely to have been intentional have been authored by Hixson,[4] Koestler,[5] and Wade.[6] The last of these, of greatest relevance to the present discussion, describes the case of the late Cyril Burt who, in three separate reports of more than twenty, more than thirty, and more than fifty pairs of twins, reported a correlation coefficient between IQ scores of these twins, who had been raised apart, of exactly .771 for all three studies! Such consistency of correlation would bespeak a statistical miracle if it were real, and Wade credits Leon Kamin for having made this discovery on what must surely have been the first careful reading of Burt.

Intentional effects, interpreter effects, and observer effects all operate without the experimenter's affecting his subject's response to the experimental task. In those effects of the experimenter himself, to be described next, we shall see that the subject's response to the experimental task is affected.

Biosocial Effects. The sex, age, and race of the investigator have all been found to affect the results of research. What we do not know and what we need to learn is whether subjects respond differently simply to the presence of experimenters varying in these biosocial attributes, or whether experimenters varying in these attributes behave differently toward their subjects and, therefore, obtain different responses from them because they have, in effect, altered the experimental situation for their subjects. So far, the evidence suggests that male and female experimenters, for example, conduct the "same" experiment quite differently, so that the different results they obtain may well be due to the fact that they unintentionally conducted different experiments. Male experimenters, for example, were found in two experiments to be more friendly to their subjects.

Biosocial attributes of the subject can also affect the experimenter's behavior, which, in turn, affects the subject's responses. In one study, for example, the interactions between experimenters and their subjects were recorded on sound films. The study found that only 12% of the experimenters ever smiled at their male subjects, while 70% of the experimenters smiled at their female subjects. Smiling by the experimenters, it was found, affected the results of the experiment. The moral is clear. Before claiming a sex difference in the results of behavioral research, we must first be sure that males and females were treated identically by the experimenter. If they were not, then sex differences may be due not to genic, constitutional, enculturational, or other factors but simply to the fact that males and females did not even participate in the same experiment.

Psychosocial Effects. The personality of the experimenter has also been found to affect the results of research. Experimenters who differ in anxiety, need for approval, hostility, authoritarianism, status, and warmth tend to obtain different responses from their experimental subjects. Experimenters higher in status, for example, tend to obtain more conforming responses from their subjects, and experimenters who are warmer in their interaction with their subjects tend to obtain more pleasant responses from their subjects. Warmer examiners administering standardized tests of intelligence are likely to obtain better intellectual performance than are cooler examiners or examiners who are more threatening or more strange to their examinees.

Situational Effects. Experimenters who are more experienced at conducting a given experiment obtain different responses from their subjects than do their less experienced colleagues. Experimenters who are acquainted with their subjects obtain different responses than do their colleagues who have never met their subjects before. The things that happen to experimenters during the course of their experiments, including the responses they obtain from their first few subjects, can all influence their behavior, and changes in their behavior can lead to changes in their subjects' responses. When the first few subjects of their experiments tend to respond as they are expected to respond, the behavior of the experimenters changes in such a way as to influence their subsequent subjects to respond too often in the direction of their hypotheses.

Modeling Effects. It sometimes happens that before experimenters conduct their studies, they try out the tasks they will later have their research subjects perform. Though the evidence on this point is not all that clear, it would seem that at least sometimes, the investigator's own performance becomes a factor in the subjects' performance. When the experimental stimuli are ambiguous, for example, subjects' interpretations of their meaning may too often agree with the investigator's own interpretations of the stimuli.

Expectancy Effects. Some expectation of how the research will turn out is virtually a constant in science. Psychologists, like other scientists generally, conduct research specifically to test hypotheses or expectations about the nature of things. In the behavioral sciences, the hypotheses held by investigators can lead them unintentionally to alter their behavior toward their subjects in such a way as to increase the likelihood that their subjects will respond so as to confirm their hypotheses or expectations. We are speaking then, of the investigator's hypothesis as a self-fulfilling prophecy. One prophesies an event, and the expectation of the event then changes the behavior of the prophet in such a way as to make the prophesied event more likely. The history of science documents the occurrence of this phenomenon with the case of Clever Hans as prime example.

Hans was the horse of Mr. von Osten, a German mathematics instructor. By tapping his foot, Hans was able to perform difficult mathematical calculations and he could spell, read, and solve problems of musical harmony. A distinguished panel of scientists and experts on animals ruled that no fraud was involved. There were no cues given to Hans to tell him when to start and when to stop the tapping of his foot. But of course there were such cues, though it remained for Oskar Pfungst to demonstrate the fact. Pfungst, in a series of brilliant experiments, showed that Hans could answer questions only when the questioner or experimenter himself knew the answer and was within Hans's view. Finally, Pfungst learned that a tiny forward movement of the experimenter's head was the signal for Hans to start tapping. A tiny upward movement of the head of the questioner or a raising of the eyebrows was the signal to Hans to stop his tapping. Hans's questioners expected Hans to give correct answers, and this expectation was reflected in their unwitting signal to Hans that the time had come for him to stop his tapping. Thus the questioner's expectation became the reason for Hans's amazing abilities. We turn now to a consideration of more recent experiments which show that an investigator's expectation can come to serve as self-fulfilling prophecy.

Recent Studies of Expectancy Effects

To demonstrate the effects of investigators' expectancy on the results of their research, at least two groups of experimenters are needed, each group with a different hypothesis or expectancy as to the outcome of its research. One approach might be to conduct a kind of census or poll of actual or potential experimenters in a given area of research in which opinions as to relationships between variables were divided. Some experimenters expecting one type of result and some experimenters expecting the opposite type of result might then be asked to conduct a standard experiment. If each group of experimenters obtained the results expected — results opposite to those expected by the other group of experimenters — we could conclude that the expectation of the experimenter does indeed affect the results of the research. Or could we? Perhaps not. The problem would be that experimenters who differ in their theories, hypotheses, or expectations might very well differ in a number of important related ways as well. The differences in the data they obtained from their subjects might be due, then, not to the differences in expectations about the results but to other variables correlated with expectancies.

A better strategy, therefore, than trying to find two groups of experimenters differing in their hypotheses would be to "create" two groups of experimenters differing only in the hypotheses or expectations they held about the results of a particular experiment. That was the plan employed in the following research.

Twelve experimenters were each given five rats which were to be taught to run a maze with the aid of visual cues. Half the experimenters were told their rats had been specially bred for maze-brightness; half the experimenters were told their rats had been bred for maze-dullness. Actually, of course, there were no differences between the rats assigned to each of the two groups. At the end of the experiment the results were clear. Rats which had been run by experimenters expecting brighter behavior showed significantly superior learning compared to rats run by experimenters expecting dull behavior.[8] The experiment was repeated, this time employing a series of learning experiments, each conducted in Skinner boxes. Half the experimenters were led to believe their rats were "Skinner box bright" and half were led to believe their animals were "Skinner box dull." Once again there were not really any differences in the two groups of rats, at least not until the end of the experiment. Then the allegedly brigher animals really were brighter, and the alleged dullards really duller.[9]

If rats became more bright when expected to by their experimenter, it seemed possible that children might become more bright when expected to by their teacher. Educational theorists had, after all, been saying for a long time that culturally disadvantaged children were unable to learn because their teachers expected them to be unable to learn. True, there was no experimental evidence for that theory, but the two studies employing rats suggested that these theorists might be correct. The following experiment was therefore conducted.[10]

The Pygmalion Experiment. All the children in an elementary school were administered a nonverbal test of intelligence, which was disguised as a test that would predict intellectual "blooming." There were eighteen classrooms in the school, three at each of the six grade levels. Within each grade level, the three classrooms were composed of children with above average ability, average ability, and below average ability, respectively. Within each of the eighteen classrooms, approximately 20% of the children were chosen at random to form the experimental group. Each teacher was given the names of the children from her class who were in the experimental condition. The teacher was told that these children had scored on the "test for intellectual blooming" such that they would show remarkable gains in intellectual competence during the next eight months of school. The only difference between the experimental group and the control group children, then, was in the mind of the teacher.

At the end of the school year, eight months later, all the children were retested with the same IQ test. Considering the school as a whole, those children from whom the teachers had been led to expect greater intellectual gain showed a significantly greater gain in IQ than did the children of the control group.

An Unexpected Finding in Pygmalion. At the time the Pygmalion experiment was conducted, there was already considerable evidence that interpersonal self-fulfulling prophecies

341

could occur, at least in laboratory settings. As the mathematical statisticians might put it, there were already some more than gentle prior probabilities that self-fulfilling prophecies could occur in the classroom.[11] It should not then have come as such a great surprise that teachers' expectations might affect pupils' intellectual development. For those well-acquainted with the prior research, the surprise value was, in fact, not all so great. There was, however, a surprise in the Pygmalion research. For this surprise there was no great prior probability, at least not in terms of many formal research studies.

At the end of the school year of the Pygmalion study, all teachers were asked to describe the classroom behavior of their pupils. Those children in whom intellectual growth was expected were described as having a significantly better chance of becoming successful in the future, as significantly more interesting, curious, and happy. There was a tendency, too, for these children to be seen as more appealing, adjusted, and affectionate, and as less in need of social approval. In short, the children in whom intellectual growth was expected became more intellectually alive and autonomous, or at least were so perceived by their teachers.

But we already know that the children of the experimental group gained more intellectually, so that perhaps it was the fact of such gaining that accounted for the more favorable ratings of these children's behavior and aptitude. But a great many of the control group children also gained in IQ during the course of the year. We might expect that those who gained more intellectually among these undesignated children would also be rated more favorably by their teachers. Such was not the case. The more the control group children gained in IQ, the more they were regarded as *less* well-adjusted, as *less* interesting, and as *less* affectionate. From these results it would seem that when children who are expected to grow intellectually do so, they are benefited in other ways as well. When children who are not specifically expected to develop intellectually do so, they seem either to show accompanying undesirable behavior or at least are perceived by their teachers as showing such undesirable behavior. If a child is to show intellectual gain, it seems to be better for his real or perceived intellectual vitality and for his real or perceived mental health if his teacher has been expecting him to grow intellectually. It appears worthwhile to investigate further the proposition that there may be hazards to unpredicted intellectual growth.[12]

The Generality of Interpersonal Expectancy Effects

In this brief paper there has been space to describe only a few experiments designed to test the hypothesis that one person's expectation can come to serve as a self-fulfilling prophecy for the behavior of another person. However, the basic issue is no longer in doubt. There are now well over 300 experiments investigating this phenomenon, and the cumulative results of all show an essentially zero probability that these results could have been obtained if there were no such phenomenon as interpersonal expectancy effects.[13]

The first column of Table 2 lists eight areas of behavioral research that have been investigated for the operation of interpersonal expectancy effects. The second column of Table 2 shows the number of studies that were conducted in each area up to the time of the analysis (by Rosenthal, 1976). The third col-

TABLE 2. EXPECTANCY EFFECTS IN EIGHT RESEARCH AREAS

RESEARCH AREA	NUMBER OF STUDIES	PROPORTION OF STUDIES REACHING $p<0.5$	ESTIMATED MEAN EFFECT SIZE (0)
Reaction Time	6	.33	0.23
Inkblot Tests	9	.44	0.84
Animal Learning	14	.64	1.78
Laboratory Interviews	22	.36	0.27
Psychophysical Judgments	23	.43	1.31
Learning and ability	33	.27	0.72
Person Perception	114	.27	0.51
Everyday Situations	96	.38	1.44
Median	22.5	.37[a]	0.78

[a]The value expected is .05 if there were no such process as interpersonal expectancy effects.

umn shows the proportion of studies reaching statistical significance for each area. Even for the least frequently significant research areas, the proportion of significant results was five times greater than would have been expected if there were really no such phenomenon as interpersonal expectancy effects. The last column of Table 2 shows for each area the estimated average size of the effect of the interpersonal expectation. The measure of effect size is a standard deviation unit. Thus, if we were dealing with commonly used IQ tests, the average size of the effect of interpersonal expectations would be on the order of 10 or more IQ points.

Future Research

A good deal is known about the phenomenon of interpersonal expectancy effects, but much more remains unknown. What are the factors increasing or decreasing the effects of interpersonal expectations, i.e., what are the moderating variables? What are the variables serving to mediate the effects of interpersonal self-fulfilling prophecies? Only some bare beginnings have been made to address these questions.

The role of moderating variables has been considered elsewhere and is being actively surveyed at the present time.[14] The variables serving to mediate the effects of interpersonal expectancies have also been considered elsewhere, and for the teacher-pupil interaction a four factor "theory" has been proposed.[15] This "theory" suggests that teachers, counselors, and supervisors who have been led to expect superior performance from some of their pupils, clients, or trainees appear to treat these "special" persons differently than they treat the remaining not-so-special persons in roughly four ways:

Climate: Teachers appear to create a warmer socio-emotional climate for their "special" students.

Feedback: Teachers appear to give their "special" students more differentiated feedback as to how these students have been performing.

Input: Teachers appear to teach more material and more difficult material to their "special" students.

Output: Teachers appear to give their "special" students greater opportunities for responding.

Work on this four factor theory is currently in progress.

Much of the research on interpersonal expectancies has suggested that mediation of these expectancies depends to some important degree on various processes of nonverbal communication.[16] Moreover, there appear to be important differences among experimenters, teachers, and people generally in the clarity of their communication through different channels of nonverbal communication. In addition, there appear to be important differences among research subjects, pupils, and people generally in their sensitivity to nonverbal communications transmitted through different nonverbal channels. If we knew a great deal more about differential sending and receiving abilities, we might be in a much better position to address the general question of what kind of person (in terms of sending abilities) can most effectively influence covertly what kind of other person (in terms of receiving abilities). Thus, for example, if those teachers who best communicate their expectations for children's intellectual performance in the auditory channel were assigned children whose best channels of reception were also auditory, we would predict greater effects of teacher expectation than we would if those same teachers were assigned children less sensitive to auditory channel nonverbal communication.

Ultimately, then, what we would want would be a series of accurate measurements for each person, describing his or her relative ability to send and to receive in each of a variety of channels of nonverbal communication. It seems reasonable to suppose that if we had this information for two or more people, we would be better able to predict the outcome of their interaction, regardless of whether the focus of the analysis were on the mediation of interpersonal expectations or on some other interpersonal transaction.

As a start toward the goal of more completely specifying accuracy of sending and receiving nonverbal cues in dyadic interaction, we have been developing an instrument designed to measure differential sensitivity to various channels of nonverbal communication: *The Profile of Nonverbal Sensitivity* or PONS.[17] It is our hope that research employing the PONS and related measures of skill at sending and receiving messages in various channels of nonverbal communication, along with related research, will help us to unravel the mystery of the mediation of interpersonal expectancy effects. That is the hope; but the work lies ahead.

NOTES AND REFERENCES

1. E.G. Boring, *A History of Experimental Psychology*, 2nd ed. New York: Appleton-Century-Crofts, 1950.
2. R. Rosenthal, *Experimenter Effects in Behavioral Research: Enlarged Edition*. New York: Irvington Publishers, Halsted Press Division of Wiley, 1976.
3. R. Rosenthal, "Interpersonal Expectations," in R. Rosenthal and R.L. Rosnow (Eds.), *Artifact in Behavioral Research*. New York: Academic Press, 1969, pp. 181-277.
4. J. Hixson, *The Patchwork Mouse*. Garden City, New York: Anchor Press/Doubleday, 1976.
5. A. Koestler, *The Case of the Midwife Toad*. New York: Random House, 1971.
6. N. Wade, "IQ and Heredity: Suspicion of Fraud Beclouds Classic Experiment," *Science*, 1976, *194*, 916-919.
7. O. Pfungst, *Clever Hans*. Translated by C.L. Rahn. New York: Holt, 1911; Holt, Rinehart and Winston, 1965.
8. R. Rosenthal and K.L. Fode, "The Effect of Experimenter Bias on the Performance of the Albino Rat," *Behavioral Science*, 1963, 8, 183-189.
9. R. Rosenthal and R. Lawson, "A Longitudinal Study of the Effects of Experimenter Bias on the Operant Learning of Laboratory Rats," *Journal of Psychiatric Research*, 1964, 2, 61-72.
10. R. Rosenthal and L. Jacobson, *Pygmalion in the Classroom*. New York: Holt, Rinehart and Winston, 1968.
11. F. Mosteller and J.W. Tukey, Data analysis, including statistics, in G. Lindzey and E. Aronson (Eds.), *The Handbook of Social Psychology*, 2nd ed., vol. 2. Reading, Mass.: Addison-Wesley, 1968, pp. 80-203.
12. R. Rosenthal, *On the Social Psychology of the Self-Fulfilling Prophecy: Further Evidence for Pygmalion Effects and their Mediating Mechanisms*. MSS Modular Publications, New York, New York, 1974, Module 53, pp. 1-28.
13. R. Rosenthal, "Combining Results of Independent Studies," *Psychological Bulletin*, in press.
14. See Note 3.
15. See Notes 3 and 12.

16. See Notes 3 and 12.
17. R. Rosenthal, D. Archer, M.R. DiMatteo, J. Hall, and P.L. Rogers, *Measuring Sensitivity to Nonverbal Communication: The PONS Test.* Unpublished manuscript, Harvard University, 1976.

From the Fall 1977 Et cetera.

DATE DUE